ON BEING A CLIENT

ON BEING A CLIENT

Understanding the Process of Counselling and Psychotherapy

David Howe

SAGE Publications

London • Thousand Oaks • New Delhi

SAGE Publications Ltd
6 Bonhill Street
London EC2A 4PU

SAGE Publications Inc
2455 Teller Road
Thousand Oaks, California 91320

SAGE Publications India Pvt Ltd
32, M-Block Market
Greater Kailash - I
New Delhi 110 048

British Library Cataloguing in Publication Data

Howe, David
  On Being a Client: Understanding the Process of
  Counselling and Psychotherapy
  I. Title
  616.89

  ISBN 0-8039-8888-5
  ISBN 0-8039-8889-3 (pbk)

Library of Congress catalog card number 93-084342

Typeset by Mayhew Typesetting, Rhayader, Powys
Printed in Great Britain by The Cromwell Press Ltd,
Broughton Gifford, Melksham, Wiltshire

CONTENTS

ACKNOWLEDGEMENTS

For patience well beyond the call of duty, first thanks must go to my friend and colleague Diana Hinings, who not only listened with kindness to me talking rather a lot about my several obsessions but also offered wise words and gentle counsel of her own.

The skilful and much appreciated work of Phillida Sawbridge and the counsellors at the Post-Adoption Centre, London, first set me thinking about the subject-matter of this book. I owe them a large debt of gratitude.

And finally I am pleased to have this opportunity to thank Brian Thorne, Director of Student Counselling at the University of East Anglia, Norwich, and Susan Worsey of Sage Publications for their timely advice and encouragement.

PERMISSIONS

The author and publisher would like to thank a number of publishers for their kind permission to reproduce extracts from the following: *A Secure Base: Clinical Applications of Attachment Theory* by John Bowlby (Routledge & Kegan Paul, 1988); *One to One: Experiences of Psychotherapy* by Rosemary Dinnage (Viking, 1988) copyright © Rosemary Dinnage 1988; *The Experience of Psychotherapy* by William H. Fitts (Van Nostrand Reinhold, 1965); *Consuming Psychotherapy* by Ann France (Free Association Books, 1988); *The Consumers' View of Family Therapy* by David Howe (Gower, 1989); *The Client Speaks* by John Mayer and Noel Timms (Routledge & Kegan Paul, 1970); *The Counselling Relationship* by Susan Oldfield (Routledge & Kegan Paul, 1983); 'The psychological interior of psychotherapy' by David Orlinsky and Kenneth Howard in *The Psychotherapeutic Process: A Research Handbook* edited by Leslie S. Greenberg and William M. Pinsof (Guilford Press, 1986); *Patients View Their Psychotherapy* by Hans Strupp, Ronald Fox and Ken Lessler (Johns Hopkins University Press, 1969); *Understanding Ourselves: The Uses of Therapy* by Joan Woodward (Macmillan Press, 1988).

Every effort has been made to trace all the copyright holders, but if any have been overlooked, the publishers will be pleased to make an acknowledgement at the first opportunity.

INTRODUCTION

1 Love and Work

Each year more and more people seek the help of a counsellor or psychotherapist. No one knows the exact number, but tens of thousands if not hundreds of thousands of individuals probably find their way to one or more of the many practitioners who specialize in offering 'interpersonal help' with personal worries and concerns. Many operate privately and independently. Some, such as student counsellors based in universities, work in institutional settings. And yet others practise in voluntary agencies, offering services to a wide variety of clients including, for example, women who have been sexually abused as children, mothers who have relinquished a child for adoption, and couples whose relationships are running into difficulties.

These practitioners work primarily as counsellors and psychotherapists. However, other professional groups also find themselves in a counselling relationship with their clients from time to time. Social workers and teachers, doctors and nurses, police personnel and priests regularly become involved with people who are upset, confused or distressed. The growth and explicit recognition of counselling and psychotherapy (I shall use the terms interchangeably) are a matter of considerable curiosity, both as a sociological phenomenon and as a psychological event. Why do people seek counselling and what do they want from it?

This book examines what the clients of counsellors have to say about their experiences of the psychotherapeutic process. For example, it seems interesting to note that clients consistently say similar kinds of things about their experiences of being helped (and not being helped), no matter which school of counselling they have attended, independent of the counsellor's theoretical leanings, and irrespective of the counsellor's preferred range of techniques. Why should this be so?

Although there has been a steady interest in the client's point of view, it is still unusual to begin an investigation into the nature of counselling and therapy by looking at the world from the perspective of the client. Traditionally, one starts by describing the theoretical position of the therapist, or one begins by outlining the basis on which the client and her or his difficulties can be explained and treated. In other words, books on counselling and therapy generally open with the practitioner's view.

For example, exponents of each of the various schools of counselling offer their preferred brands of theory and practice. These produce contrasting ideas about what makes people tick and do the things they do. The counsellor's view therefore gives us diversity, debate and a general busyness of ideas.

However, we soon discover that starting with the client's perspective provides us with a number of benefits and one or two surprises. The views of clients create a much simpler picture. They offer a single experiential view and a common account of their experiences whatever the psychotherapeutic orientation of their counsellor. Generally, findings which are regular and crop up in a variety of situations often hold the key to a deeper understanding of what is going on. I shall argue that the regularity and relative simplicity of the client's view provides us with powerful and telling evidence about the nature of psychotherapy and the human relationships that go with it.

In following the client's perspective we are valuing what people *say* rather than what they *do*. Behaviour reveals only so much of the other's inner experience and it is certainly not the only yardstick by which to measure counselling. By asking people to *say* what they feel about counselling, we tap the experience in its own terms as well as from the subject's point of view. We are likely to learn a good deal about the nature of counselling by entering the frame of reference of the client – a view from the inside.

Talking Cures and Making Sense

There has been a steady build-up of knowledge about what takes place in the psychotherapeutic process. We also have a modest number of accounts which describe clients' own experiences of counselling and therapy. The result is that we can now provide a useful *description* of what takes place in the therapeutic process. Perhaps the most important finding is the identification of a number of general processes and experiences that appear to cut across the different schools of treatment. These processes, therefore, are 'not specific' to any one type of counselling or brand of psychotherapy. Early workers in this field referred to them as the 'core conditions' (genuineness, empathy and warmth), factors which are necessary, and maybe even sufficient, if counselling is to be effective and satisfactory. More recent studies have refined and elaborated our understanding of these 'non-specific' factors and packaged them together into something called the 'therapeutic alliance' – an old concept given a new lease of life. In the alliance we meet old counselling favourites: the significance of the personal qualities displayed by the counsellor, the atmosphere of the encounter, the experience of the relationship.

We therefore have the curious and challenging idea that therapy and counselling, when they work, succeed *not* because of specific factors associated with particular theoretical schools and their preferred techniques, but because of the presence of general, non-specific factors that just happen to be present when therapists do whatever they do. If this is true, then school-bound therapists and counsellors practise under a considerable delusion. It is not the specific technique that is important but the manner in which it is done and the way it is experienced. So, for example, it is not the interpretation of the transference or the identification of reinforcers which are important, but rather the friendliness of the therapist and the empathy shown by the counsellor that matter. No longer can it be thought that the technique just happens to carry with it a variety of rather common, even mundane human qualities (warmth, a preparedness not to judge or criticize, a wish to understand how the other feels), but the reverse.

The common qualities that inform human relationships turn out to be the important elements, and these can be carried by a variety of conversational devices including structuring one's interaction with the other person using particular types of therapeutic technique. It does not matter which technique you use, so long as the 'non-specific' ingredients that characterize successful relationships are present.

I shall want to lend this line of thought considerable support, but with one major qualification, the effect of which is to produce an even more curious state of affairs: the traditional non-specific factors and the therapeutic alliance *themselves* are only a vehicle for promoting and carrying even more important activities – talk and dialogue.

All therapies and counselling styles involve people talking – talking to someone, talking at someone, talking with someone. In a way, language and talk are so obvious that we tend to forget about them when analysing the counselling experience. Surrounded by water, the fish may be oblivious of the pervasive and vital part that it plays in its life. Similarly, talk is the medium in which counselling takes place. It is the stuff of relationships. It is what we use when we interact. But why *do* we talk when we are worried, bothered, hurt, puzzled, distressed, excited? It is not at all obvious. And yet talking is what most of us do when our emotions are running high.

The argument will be that talk activates the language field in which the self was formed. We might wonder, therefore, whether it is in fact the act of talking itself (rather than talk acting as a vehicle for carry-ing the actions and content of a particular therapeutic technique or counselling style) that is potentially helpful. If this is the case, then it is talking which cures and not particular therapeutic schools and their preferred techniques.

Furthermore, and at first sight in apparent contradiction to much of what has been said so far, the conceptual frameworks and tech-niques specific to each therapeutic schools do matter, not because they have alighted on the truth, but simply because they offer *a* way (but not *the* way) of making sense. In other words, particular therapeutic frameworks and their associated techniques themselves constitute a set of 'non-specific factors'! The non-specificity which they have in common is the attempt they each make to *make sense* of the client's experience. No matter that each school of therapy seeks to make a different sense, a sense specific to that psycho-therapeutic technique. The important non-specific element, present in all techniques, is the attempt to make sense itself. The sense will be different in each theoretical case, and some ways of making sense might appeal more than others. However, the important common factor is the attempt to make personal experience meaningful and for the client to make some sense of what he or she does, thinks and feels. If the client is successful in his or her attempt to make sense, it hardly matters that her counsellor is a Rogerian or that his therapist is a Freudian.

The 'core conditions' and the 'therapeutic alliance' are important, and for clients who lack an emotionally integrated sense of self the presence of these factors may be the major thing of value in the rela-tionship. But for mainstream clients, the alliance and the core condi-tions are critical in so far as they allow and promote talk, dialogue and the need to make sense. In themselves alliances and relationships can be pleasant, comforting and reassuring, but their role is to act as a catalyst which promotes the processes that bring about change and new understandings. I may never learn to write well and enjoy the satisfaction of expressing my thoughts creatively without the friendly support and encouragement of a mentor. The quality of the relation-ship with my mentor may indeed be critical if I am to gain the con-fidence to put pen to paper. But it is writing that I must do if I am to create, discover and express.

From Description to Explanation

'The social formation of the self' is another concept that will be of great help as we seek to examine the nature of the psychotherapeutic experience. Defining this concept will require us to step outside the usual bounds of counselling and therapy. We shall have to grapple with some subtle, even slippery ideas that are having an exciting effect on a number of disciplines includes developmental psychology, sociology and neurobiology.

Each field is developing an interest in the relationship between the individual and the environment. Indeed, what is being revised is the notion that we can even think of the individual self and the social environment as discrete entities separated by firm boundaries. The individual human self, so it seems, is only able to form within the realm of social relationships. The self does not arrive preformed. Psychology and sociology, biology and culture relate to each other in ways which are much more dynamic than was once thought possible. Processes which are essentially hermeneutic in their character are required if we are to understand the generation of mind and consciousness, the emergence of the self, and the fundamental importance of social relationships in human affairs, particularly in times of distress.

It will be apparent that, in tackling clients' experiences of therapy and counselling in this way, we are moving from description to explanation. Using the burgeoning data on what takes place in the therapeutic process, including what clients have to say about their experiences, I shall shift the focus from analysis to interpretation, from *what* goes on in counselling to *why* it goes on. Once we have described what goes on in the therapeutic relationship, we should be in a good position to ask the question, Why? Why do the core conditions and the 'therapeutic alliance' emerge as general features of so many successful and satisfying treatments? Why do therapists think that therapeutic success is the result of their own technical skills and theoretical orientation, while clients point to the therapist's attitude and personality and the opportunity to talk with someone as much more important?

An Insider's View

Although accounts of the theory and practice of counselling are legion, descriptions of counselling by clients are relatively few. It is

only over the last 30 years or so that the consumers' view has been
regularly sought. Even so, the pursuit of these views has never become
a major component in the evaluation of counselling and therapeutic
practices. The belief that applied psychology is an applied science has
encouraged many therapists to examine their impact on people in a
science-like, linear, cause-and-effect fashion.

This is how traditional evaluations go: Identify the behaviour
allegedly at fault prior to treatment. Apply the treatment. And finally,
measure the patient after treatment to see if the unwanted behaviour
is still present. The evaluator is regarded as an objective observer.
Human beings, the model claims, are capable of disengaging themselves
from other people and society and objectifying them for the purposes
of study and causal explanation. The model requires that the behaviour
to be treated has to be available for observation and measurement.
Anything that is not visible and quantifiable is either denied or ignored.

The application of classical science to human action is just one small
part of the great shift that took place in the seventeenth century away
from a world that was to be understood as God-given and not
available for interrogation to one that could be explained in terms of
mechanisms that operated on principles which were rational and
discoverable – a clockwork world. This was the first step in reducing
the world, including people, to a construction of working parts, albeit
often arranged in vastly complex forms, but none the less available for
objective study, explanation and control. It was believed that the
modern human consciousness could disengage itself from the world of
other people and things. It could remain on the outside looking in.
And so the ground was laid for understanding the individual as meta-
physically independent of society – not of it, but *in* it and therefore
still liable to the causal forces that determine the actions and
behaviours of all objects in the world.

However, this way of proceeding assumes that the way to know how
people work is to look at them from the outside. But there are those
who believe that to model the study of men and women on the
classical natural sciences is totally implausible. Taylor (1985: 1)
believes that social sciences which model themselves on the natural
sciences lead to very bad science and are prey to three kinds of pitfall:
(1) they state the obvious in wordy and technical language, (2) they
fail altogether to address the interesting questions, and (3) they
attempt to show they really can capture the insights of ordinary life
in the reductive language of the natural sciences, expending more and
more energy defending themselves against the charge of irrelevancy.
Behaviourism offers the classic example.

Objective methods of enquiry have recorded and analysed those aspects of therapy and counselling that are externally visible, in the belief that this, somehow, produces raw but significant data on the therapeutic process. The psychotherapeutic process is examined 'as if it could be approached the way it actually is "in nature", distorted by the perceptions of the subjects', retort Orlinsky and Howard (1986: 498); and then, warming to their rebuke, they add: 'The fact that psychotherapy, like other human involvements, does not exist "in nature" seems not to have bothered these researchers . . . Participants' perspectives are necessary data for the study of social relationships. In psychotherapy, the patients' and therapists' construals of their reciprocal involvement are constitutive elements of the therapeutic process.'

The alternative method of enquiry, therefore, is to seek the client's perspective – to obtain a view from the inside. What do those who have been on the receiving end of counselling have to say? Did it help? In what ways? What was most helpful? What was least helpful? Were they satisfied? Consumers tell their own story in their own words. They say what was important for them.

This form of enquiry is not just a case of evening up the score, giving the consumer a chance to state his or her point of view, a tactic which may appeal to the researcher's sense of fair play. It also suggests that there is something fundamentally important in hearing what people in therapy have to say about their experience. Their point of view is peculiarly important in helping us gain a thorough understanding of the therapeutic relationship. Clients generate their own vocabulary to express what they want to say. They do not have to speak someone else's language. The conceptual abstractions of the researcher and the technical prose of the therapist are missing when the client speaks.

In listening to clients describe their experiences of counselling, we have something rather like the seismographic tracings made by geophysicists. When an earthquake takes place, waves of energy pass through the Earth and the ground shakes. This is literally what happens. We could simply use the seismographic trace to tell us when and where earthquakes take place, which is interesting enough. But geophysicists can also use the tracings to tell them even more fascinating things. The patterns and timings of a trace can tell the scientists about the structure of the planet Earth through which the shock waves travelled, the composition of the rocks and the movement of the continents.

Similarly, when the client speaks, we learn things about the psychotherapeutic experience itself as well as understanding some of the deeper structures that appear to influence the counselling relationship. The descriptions of the counselling experience tell us a good deal about what counselling is in terms of a social encounter; they give us clues about how it works and why it works and they reveal something of the characteristics of human beings in social relationships.

Studies which seek the views of clients tend to be one of three types. There are accounts written by researchers who have asked clients and patients to rate the quality and efficacy of their treatment. Clients give answers within the confines of the researcher's framework and choice of categories. Less structured studies simply ask clients about their experiences of counselling or therapy. The reports use the client's own words. The research style produces graphic accounts which often have an emotional impact on the reader. The third type of consumer view is offered by people who have been in counselling or therapy and have decided to write about their experiences. This produces accounts which are first-hand and unsolicited.

Reading these various accounts, it is not long before you begin to realize that they have a good deal in common – in content, in style, in vocabulary. The ideas and language transcend time and place, treatment regime and theoretical orientation. Clients speaking in the 1950s say the same things using the same words as clients speaking in the 1990s. Recipients of psychoanalytical-oriented practices sound remarkably like people who have been seen by person-centred counsellors. Whereas therapists and scientific measurers speak in a variety of theoretical tongues, clients speak a common language. The consistency of the messages really is quite remarkable. The words and language used by clients to describe their experiences are important. There are dangers in the use of a 'specialized psychotherapeutic language'. It can 'invade' and construct the client's experience. 'The nearer we stay to common speech,' believes Lomas (1981: 109) in his support for Freire, 'the less likely we are to destroy the meaning of those who seek our help.'

The regularity of the themes in the consumers' reports suggests there is a deep common structure to human relationships which is not readily apparent in each of the various schools of counselling practice. Many, though not all, therapeutic schools develop practices which either assert or imply a model of effective behaviour and appropriate functioning. However, such direct or indirect behavioural advice receives only passing support from clients. What is valued by clients is the act of communication and not the communication of acts. There is something about talking and the quality of the relationship between counsellor and client that tells us where we must look if we are to understand the experience of being helped.

Of course, there is little new in these observations. Good relationships, sympathetic ears and shoulders to cry on have been sought by all those of us who have at one time or another felt bothered and hurt. But although the observations are commonplace, it behoves us to be intensely curious about their near-universal occurrence. Why, when we are troubled or in pain, rejected or unloved, confused or afraid, do we find ourselves wanting to be with someone, to talk with someone? What kind of people do we seek? What is it about them that we appreciate at such times? It is not self-evident why we should want to talk when we are distressed. Why do we not work out our worries on our own, in silence, in our heads? What does talking aloud achieve? Answers to these questions suggest ways in which we might explain the universal messages contained in the views of clients, the similar 'success' rates recorded across different treatment schools, and why those in distress seek the company and conversation of other human beings.

Something Is Better than Nothing

In looking for answers to these questions, the first clues are to be found in studies which have tried to measure the effectiveness of counselling and therapy. These clues suggest that there might be a deeper order underpinning all treatment schools. As I have said, success rates have a remarkable consistency across different types of therapy. It was Eysenck who set the ball rolling in 1952 by claiming that the evidence seemed to suggest that counselling and psychotherapy were ineffective. The gauntlet was down. His challenge triggered a busy programme of research which has continued in full spate right up to the present day.

In behavioural terms the evidence remains inconclusive, but in market terms there can be little doubt about the success of counselling and therapy. More people than ever, in spite of the behavioural research, seek the services of counsellors and psychotherapists. Though sociologically interesting, this is a puzzle for clinical psychologists. However, the puzzle is a product of the epistemological assumptions made by applied behavioural scientists. Alter the mindset and the picture suddenly changes. So long as it is assumed that counselling and psychotherapy are simply about changing behaviour, the nature of the therapeutic encounter will continue to be misunderstood, inappropriately studied and wrongly judged. If psychotherapy is about understanding and meaning, then a different research approach might be required. Nevertheless, Eysenck's provocative conclusions helped the debate get under way. Subsequent investigations furnished the discussions with many new facts and findings as the researchers got busy refining and revising what we knew and did not know about the therapeutic process.

In 1961 Frank reported that about two-thirds of neurotic patients improved immediately after treatment regardless of the type of psychotherapy received. However, he also found that the same improvement rate was present in neurotic people who had received no treatment; they recovered 'spontaneously'. In the following decade a number of significant reviews of the research evidence

> concluded that (1) the therapeutic endeavour is, on the average, quite ineffective; (2) counseling or therapy itself is a nonunitary phenomenon; (3) some counselors and therapists are significantly helpful, while others are significantly harmful, with a resulting average helpfulness not demonstrably better than the average of no professional help; (4) through closer examination of existing theories and clinical writings, it is possible to identify therapeutic ingredients likely to lead to helpful and to harmful client outcomes, and, through research, to identify such ingredients. (Truax and Mitchel, 1971: 301)

And it was there, in the last of the authors' four conclusions, that the prospect arose of finding the formula that could turn ineffective therapists into successful practitioners, of turning counselling lead into psychotherapeutic gold.

Truax and Mitchel (1971) the proceeded to offer their famous 'core conditions'. It is possible to identify three core ingredients in the psychotherapeutic relationship which 'cut across the parochial theories of psychotherapy and appear to be common elements in a wide variety of psychoanalytic, client-centered, eclectic, or learning-theory approaches to psychotherapy' (1971: 302). Thus, an effective therapist is someone who is (1) authentic, non-phoney or genuine in his or her relationships with other people; (2) able to provide a safe, non-threatening, secure and trusting atmosphere through his or her own acceptance and feelings of warmth for the client; and (3) able to understand and have a high degree of empathy for the client on a moment-by-moment basis. However, it is not sufficient to have empathy and show understanding. The understanding achieved has to be *communicated* to the client.

Truax and Mitchel (1971: 340–1) conclude their review with some punchy remarks: (1) 'The odds are two out of three that [the therapist] is spending his energy, commitment, and care for mankind wastefully; he is either ineffective or harmful'; and (2) 'the personality of the therapist is more important than his techniques', and those who possess the core qualities of empathy, genuineness and warmth are likely to be more effective.

Research of this kind has poured into the journals over the years, with the basic message about the efficacy of psychotherapy undergoing only modest change. For example, in 1977 Smith and Glass, after reviewing nearly 400 controlled evaluations of counselling and therapy, concluded that on balance psychotherapy is effective but that there are negligible differences between the different schools of treatment, including both behavioural and non-behavioural (Rogerian, psychodynamic, transactional analysis, etc.) therapies (though five years later, Shapiro and Shapiro in 1982 sought to refine these claims slightly, favouring the behaviourists).

Again, this suggests that there are underlying common ingredients that are producing the positive effect. The technical differences associated with each type of therapy are superficial and have no real bearing on the client's experience, which is much more related to the personal qualities of the therapist than to the techniques he or she employs (also see Robinson et al., 1990). A decade or so later, Matt (1989) re-analysed the work of Smith and Glass using more stringent codings. They too found that psychotherapy was more effective than nothing, but on a more modest scale than that reported in the original review.

Experiences of Counselling and the Social Formation of Self

Although I shall develop the views of clients in more detail in later chapters, it will be helpful to introduce the main messages at this early stage. Not surprisingly they echo many of the findings of those who have studied the psychotherapeutic process (the things which take place when client and counsellor meet).

Observers of counselling, practitioners of psychotherapy and researchers of the helping process all have identified the same two or three basic elements in the therapeutic encounter.

The messages contains no surprises. They are a mild elaboration of other, more familiar aphorisms. In the words of Freud, therapy should provide clients with the opportunity to *love* and to *work*. Bowlby renders good therapy as 'feel *secure*, then *explore*'. Therapy is a *nurturing* relationship in which *development* can take place. The counsellor first *establishes a relationship* within which the client *learns to cope*. My own analysis of what clients say about the counselling experience identified three broad consumer messages: 'accept me, understand me, talk with me'. The essential ingredients appear to comprise a loving, understanding relationship in which clients can examine and analyse thoughts and feelings.

Our task is to elaborate and explore these simple messages. Like a good equation, once you start to explore the formula you find that a large number of phenomena can be linked together and explained within the basic framework of understanding. There is an economy of ideas. A little can explain a lot. The surface manifestations may appear many and varied, but they draw on a common source. In our case, we are most interested in the emergence of the self in a world of other people, language and relationships. 'Accept me, understand me and talk with me' return us to the social nature of self, particularly as it has been studied by neurobiologists, developmental psychologists and sociologists. And conversely, if we can begin to understand how the self forms as the individual grows in an environment of other people, we might appreciate *what* clients need from counselling relationships and *why* they need it. The clue lies in understanding the link between the formation of the self and the kind of experiences adults seek when they are distressed, hurt or confused.

There are distinct similarities between the developmental experiences of the child and the therapeutic experiences of the adult. This is not a coincidence. However, it must be emphasized that the troubled adult looking for a therapeutic experience is not necessarily seeking a return to or a wish to regress to the ways of childhood. What the adult client reveals as she talks of her experiences of counselling are the psychological and interpersonal procedures we employ when we want to make sense of what is happening and wish to move forward into a fresh emotional and intellectual order. This can only occur by the client returning to a relationship with another person. Immersion in a relationship is the method we must use if we are to understand the meaning of our experience and be helped in matters of the self. If we can make sense of what has happened, we may then wish to go on and construct new cognitive schemata out of which we develop more appropriate ways of coping.

If we acknowledge that our individuality arises in a social context, we may see ourselves in much more fluid terms. The individual self is not to be seen as a preformed, *a priori* construction which simply enters the world programmed to make sense of whatever it happens to meet. The self arises in relationship to others. Indeed there are strong versions of this argument which believe that the need to make relationships and *be* in relationship with others is a basic requirement for the generation of self and consciousness. Therefore the existence of self depends entirely on human beings being in relationship with other human beings.

Thus, if it can be argued that self, identity, personality and the basis of understanding are formed within a matrix of social relations, it will not be a surprise to learn that those who are experiencing personal and interpersonal problems seek a return to the kind of social relations in which the self originally formed. This is not regression in the sense that an individual is returning to immature ways of coping. The structures and processing characteristics of the brain, having formed in relationship with others, are then precisely equipped to make sense of those kind of relationships and the experiences that arise within them.

The Therapeutic Sequence

One of this book's aims is to develop a theory of counselling and therapy and to explain why people say the things they do about their experiences of being helped. However, it is the analysis and appreciation of the views of clients which provide the springboard for launching the theoretical speculations. Clients have a story to tell about their experiences of counselling and therapy. When the main points are abstracted and placed in narrative order, the following themes emerge, themes which have the potential to reveal some of the deeper rhythms of human interaction:

1 *Accept me*; accept you.
2 *Understand me*; understand you.
3 *Talk with me*; I want to make sense; I want to be in control; I want to feel worthwhile; I want to look forward.

'Accept me, understand me and talk with me' – the client's experiences of counselling and therapy – echo three major areas of psychological and social development in childhood: (1) attachment (the development of a secure emotional base); (2) understanding others (making sense of people and relationships); and (3) language (the communication of meaning and understanding). It is out of our experiences of attachment, understanding others and language that the self emerges.

In exploring the views of clients and linking them to the developmental perspectives, we might begin to understand both the helping process and the experience of being helped. This book is structured around the interplay between the views of clients and the dynamics that inform the social development of the child.

Part I records what clients have to say about the therapeutic alliance and considers the work of attachment theorists. Part II describes the client's need to be understood. This is followed by an examination of why human beings might need to be understood by others and the basis on which this might be achieved. Part III highlights the value clients give to the opportunity to talk with someone. Consideration is then given in Part IV to the role which other people and language play in the formation and re-formation of the self in social relationships.

PART I: ACCEPT ME

2 Warm and Friendly

Clients tell us that it is deeply comforting to be accepted by another human being. It gives confidence, it bolsters self-esteem, it helps people feel valued. In the warmth of a secure relationship, emotions recover their strength. For many people in distress, the experience of 'love' is not only necessary, it can be sufficient.

However, for others who are feeling profoundly helpless or in pain, disturbed or not coping, there is also the need to regain control as well as to feel comforted. Life has to return to some kind of order. Events have to be seen in proportion. In these cases, a loving relationship is necessary but it may not be sufficient. There is 'work' to be done.

Feeling Secure

The opportunity to describe one's feelings in an atmosphere of safety and acceptance is a powerful experience but one which is quite rare in everyday life. Only after we have been given the opportunity to describe our feelings can we reflect on them, subject them to examination and analysis and return them to our control. In the words of Susan Oldfield, the benign effects of counselling stem 'both from that part of the experience which derives from a warm, secure relationship, based on mutual respect, and from that part which offers and expects quite strenuous rethinking and exploring of experience' (1983: 27).

If love and work capture the main dimensions of the client's experience, this suggests that people value opportunities which encourage them to feel good and think well. Consumers tell us over and over again that they appreciate therapists who attend to their feelings and help them think about themselves. But first, we shall concentrate on 'love', two elements of which are acceptance and understanding – Winnicott's 'holding environment' redolent of the early relationship between a mother and her baby (Winnicott, 1965), a safe place to lower one's defences, be vulnerable and be held together while the rebuilding takes place.

Ultimately, our attention will be drawn to those elements in the therapeutic relationship which encourage clear and honest talk, but people do not talk to just anyone about anything, and this is where the quality of the relationship comes in.

Clients, in effect, appear to say to therapists, 'If you accept me, I might be able to accept you, and then we might have the basis of a relationship'. Piecing together the experiences which clients have of this opening phase of therapy, the following story, as told by the client emerges:

> First, I need to *feel secure* and I need to feel safe. My sense of security will be helped if I perceive you to be *warm and friendly*. And finally, you must *accept me* for what I am. You must *acknowledge* my thoughts and not deny my feelings, however bizarre or painful or perverse they might at first appear.

We shall now follow the story in more detail over this and the next chapter.

Talking to a Stranger

Clients say a good deal about the need to be accepted, the value of being understood and the desire to talk within the balm of a warm relationship. When these ingredients are missing and the therapist is experienced as a cold, detached observer who does not really seem to understand the client's distress, the urge to talk is upset. Therapies and therapists that frustrate the client's need to talk are viewed in a dim light. When we are in pain or despair, when we are upset or frightened, when we are confused and uncertain, the urge to talk can be strong. The urge inclines us towards other people. A pressure builds that only talk seems able to relieve. But with whom to talk?

Many people find that friends and family offer a willing and sympathetic ear. However, there are occasions when we feel that those to whom we are close are not the right people to listen to our worries. 'I have to feel that I can turn to somebody more than my family, because sometimes talking to a stranger can be a lot more helpful than talking to family' (Cantley, 1987: 28). Friends and relations might not be able to keep a confidence; there is always the fear that one's private concerns might become public property. 'With a friend,' thought Mrs Brent, 'you can confide in them, but you don't know who else they're going to tell. But with these people, you know it's in complete confidence' (Mayer and Timms, 1970: 45). And in a similar vein, a

Family Service Unit client said:

> Neighbours might sometimes start talking about you if you told them your problems, and even relations think, oh christ, she can't cope with nothing. But a social worker's got a kind of silence, they can't sort of go round and tell everybody about you. They're a bit like a doctor, and have got to keep it to themselves. (Phillimore, 1981: 71)

Other clients were less worried by a breach in confidentiality and more concerned about the confusion that might ensue if other family members became involved. Mrs Stone thought to herself:

> well how can I go to my mother-in-law and tell her and ask for her help when I'm leaving her son. And then I thought to myself, if I go to my own mother, she'll just put the blame on to my husband and that'll make it more difficult. Because I'm her daughter, it's natural. You're their own and you can't do no wrong. So that just makes matters worse. So I thought it was better to talk to a stranger. (Mayer and Timms, 1970: 42)

However, there is always a risk in talking to someone else, whether friend or stranger. Will she be interested? Will he understand? Potentially, the counsellor looks an attractive prospect. Announcing that she is available for those who want help, people who wish to talk are drawn towards her. However, arriving at the door of the therapist does not guarantee a sympathetic ear. The closer one gets to exposing one's thoughts and feelings to another, the more vulnerable one is likely to feel. Feeling vulnerable produces anxiety. And anxiety is something which people try to avoid. The effect of feeling anxious is to propel the client away from counselling.

In order to help the client break through this critical point – where attraction and repulsion are present in equal measure – the therapist needs to tip the balance of appeal her way. The client's feelings of anxiety have to be reduced. The prospective patient must begin to feel less vulnerable. The atmosphere created by the counsellor should convey feelings of safety and comfort if any worthwhile dialogue is to take place. 'The sequence of experiencing anxiety, searching for solutions, and failing to find them,' noted Strupp et al. (1969: 60) in their second study of 131 clients, 'may go on for quite a long time before a person seeks professional help. Over half of the patients in our study were aware of difficulties for more than a year before they took action, and many others delayed for more than two years.'

One of the first questions the client will ask herself is 'Do I really want to talk to *this* person?' soon followed by 'Is she someone with whom I *can* talk?' It is possible to consider the elements which either encourage or discourage dialogue. When clients describe their

experiences of counselling and therapy, three such elements loom
large in the reports: the physical setting in which counselling takes
place; the style, manner and personality of the counsellor; and the
characteristics of the therapeutic technique employed. The quality of
place, *person* and *practice* appears critical if dialogue is to be
established.

First Impressions

The first stage in the client's therapeutic career concerns whether or
not she is willing to become engaged in the process of help. Her first
impressions of place, person and practice often have critical bearing
on her willingness to proceed. The client's distress has driven her to
seek help but she has still not handed herself over to the treatment
enterprise. Feeling vulnerable, the would-be client is wary. She needs
to be reassured that it will be safe to reveal herself to this other
person. She has to be convinced that the risks in talking about
personally painful and difficult concerns are worth taking.

First impressions count for a lot at this stage and many an enquirer
is lost to counselling because he or she was put off by the initial
response. Telephone calls, receptionists and reception facilities can all
play a key role in the client's passage from caller to consumer. Laura
had attempted suicide and the hospital social worker had suggested
that she seek counselling. The Citizen's Advice Bureau gave her the
telephone number of a practice which employed counsellors and
psychotherapists and eventually Laura made an appointment. This is
how she describes the approach to her first visit:

> I felt incredibly nervous about this appointment. I arrived at the street
> twenty minutes early and walked around the block so many times that I
> thought I would be noticed. At last it was two minutes before the hour
> and I entered the building to be directed to a consulting room by a rather
> uninviting receptionist. I wish therapists and counsellors could just imagine
> what it feels like for a client to come to a stranger for help when you feel
> this is your last hope. (Allen, 1990: 21)

Four elements make up the client's first impressions: speed of
response; friendliness of response; understanding reaction; and a willingness to listen. The responses indicate whether the counsellor and
her agency are likely to understand and appreciate the client's
emotional condition.

Mrs Cain recalled that 'It's difficult to go to a stranger and talk to somebody, but she did everything in her power to relax us and she was very good at that' (Maluccio, 1979: 59). Angela, a young adopted woman, summed up her satisfaction with a specialist counselling agency saying that she received 'a prompt, caring and understanding response with an early interview which was much appreciated' (Howe and Hinings, 1989b). In contrast, Mr Hogg felt that the local duty social worker 'sounded totally disinterested as if I was a pain in the arse. You need something like the Samaritans, not bloody social workers. I mean, if you get a toothache you don't, you can't wait a week for some airy-fairy thing, can you now, be honest' (Howe, 1989a: 57). Many consumers steeled themselves to ask for help only to be told that they could have an appointment in four weeks' time. The delay seemed insensitive and uncaring:

> When you'd got to make appointments and everything, and you didn't have much choice if you wanted it in the near future, and, actually one disadvantage was I felt sometimes, it was ridiculous – especially after the first one we had to wait a whole week, and I didn't feel I wanted to wait a whole week – I wanted to go back in about two days. (Cantley, 1987: 15)

It is not just what you say, it seems that where you say it is also important. Places were assessed in the same terms in which people were talked about. Their character mattered. Some were soft and inviting, others were hard and aggressive. When rooms were experienced as warm and soothing, people felt secure and disposed to talk. Wanting to feel comfortable runs throughout the therapeutic experience and applies to rooms every bit as much as to relationships. If the setting is functional and office-like or looks like an interrogation room with unrelieved white walls and a tiled floor, it is not an environment in which people are likely to release fragile feelings or first thoughts. 'There was nothing else there,' said Mrs Spree, 'nothing comfortable. I personally felt . . . uhmm . . . we thought, you know, *family* therapy, like, it would be cosy' (Howe, 1989a: 52).

Sainsbury's interviews with families receiving help from a social work agency revealed an interesting aside on this theme. It seemed that some working-class men felt uncomfortable when the social worker visited their home. Home was a place where these men expected to be dominant and the social worker (often a female) appeared to usurp this jealously guarded status. Sainsbury (1975: 55) wondered whether another location might not have been preferable for these men.

Ann France (1988), describing her experiences with psychotherapists at various times, has interesting things to say about the setting for therapy. She believes that the comfort of the chairs and the way a room looks do matter. 'Having experienced all kinds of arrangement,' she concludes, 'my own feeling is that the more natural the surroundings, the more they are part of a normal house, the easier the relation is' (1988: 68). Of course, not everyone agrees about the details of the ideal therapeutic setting; but, not surprisingly, there is broad agreement about the value of environments which feel warm, safe and accepting. Not a few clients add that 'a nice cup of tea' or 'a good cup of coffee' would have been very welcome. The gesture seems to symbolize acceptance and understanding.

Some schools of therapy, particularly family therapy, use mechanical and electronic gadgets to aid treatment. In order to help the therapist, supervisors and observers not only witness the encounter through one-way screens or television cameras, they can also communicate with the therapist by telephone or earpiece. The use of such equipment clearly helps therapists, but the devices can have an intrusive quality which makes some clients feel exposed, invaded and vulnerable. Such experiences raise anxieties, and clients become preoccupied with the threatening nature of the machinery rather than the healing potential of an informed therapist:

> Mrs N.: The television was there to help them interrogate you; that's the only word I can use. They ask you questions and you try to answer them the best way you think.
> Kate: I felt they were spying on us.
> Mrs N.: You see, what they used it for was, like, if she [the therapist] wasn't asking the right sort of questions, they [the supervisors] would correct her and whisper in her ear through the microphone and get her to keep on at us. (Howe, 1989a: 52)

There is a clear message in these accounts which says that people cannot settle and concentrate on themselves if they experience their surroundings as unfriendly and threatening. If the environment is inhospitable, austere and demanding (technically and visually), the client's attention is directed outward rather than inward; she is intent on protecting herself rather than opening up, and she will talk defensively rather than creatively.

Warm and Friendly

First impressions matter. They encourage clients to step over the therapeutic threshold. However, this does not mean that the client is yet engaged in or committed to the counselling experience. The client needs to feel accepted by the counsellor; her feelings have to be allowed and acknowledged. Maluccio (1979: 61) discovered that when *counsellors* are asked to recall the first session, they tend to mention the problems and issues which were presented. But when *clients* are asked the *same* question, they remember the feelings they had and their reactions to the helper.

Perhaps the most basic therapeutic responses are warmth and friendliness. Clients mention it repeatedly as a major factor in their assessment of the help given. The 'warmth factor', as Strupp and his co-researchers describe it, 'permeated all ratings and assessments' (Strupp et al., 1969: 17). Giving help has to be more than simply 'doing a job'; counsellors, said a client, should be 'interested in people, not cases' (Sainsbury et al., 1982: 78). Being helped requires warmth and friendliness, interest and understanding. 'It's got to be done on a friendly basis with me,' announced Mrs Underwood. 'It's no good them coming and just sitting and listening to you, and not caring a damn, you *know* they don't. They don't feel for you' (Sainsbury, 1975: 89; see also Sainsbury et al., 1982).

It is hard to overestimate the importance of these simple but critical elements in the therapeutic encounter. Warmth and friendliness appear to be basic components of successful human relationships and the personal reconstructions that can and do take place within them. They suffuse much of what clients have to say in this chapter. Many others who have reflected on the therapeutic experience have reached a similar conclusion. Janet Sayers, during an interview about her book on Helene Deutsch, Karen Horney, Anna Freud and Melanie Klein, said that she was 'primarily concerned with the effectiveness of therapy, an effectiveness, she confides with a smile, that "is distinctly related to the degree to which the therapist is nice"' (*Guardian*, 1991a: 17).

It is possible to identify six themes in the client's recognition of a 'nice' therapist:

1 Comfort.
2 Good therapists are real people.
3 The relationship.
4 Liking and being liked.
5 Truth and honesty.
6 Support and being there.

Comfort

If you are upset and in a state of confusion, if you do not know which way to turn and you want help, the least you expect from the other person is a degree of friendly comfort. This is how Eileen, who was feeling troubled and very depressed, experienced her counsellor when she first walked into her room: 'Well, I was ushered into the room and Charlotte was standing waiting for me and I was immediately taken with her warmth and sincerity and her graciousness and she made me feel so comfortable' (Edmunds, 1992: 62). Jeffrey, an international tax consultant who felt in personal difficulty, said of his experiences of psychotherapy: 'It's a process I think that does require some warmth, some comfort. If I had found somebody who was totally blank, cold, I'm not sure I'd have ever got to first base' (Dinnage, 1989: 120). By the time Ann France was with her third therapist, she said she had a much clearer idea of the person she was looking for: 'I knew that I required flexibility and warmth, coupled with strength and detachment' (1988: 35). When warmth and friendliness are absent, the client's opinion is harsh:

> One day I had been very shocked and upset; after the session I felt very shaky about leaving. I was hurt, then, by the cold professional manner. I would have liked some warmth then – a cup of tea. I was very angry then – about the situation and with the counsellor. It was difficult to go off again and face it all. The professionalism seemed very unbending. (Oldfield, 1983: 77)

Elizabeth recalled that her therapist showed her 'no friendliness at any point. When I first came he would say, "Good morning" or "Good day", or something like that . . . I think ordinary, normal friendliness is part of making you feel like a person rather than something to be processed, a robot' (Dinnage, 1989: 106). Therapists who go in for long silences rarely fare well in the eyes of patients. Such silences are experienced as awkward, threatening or rejecting. 'Total silence rarely conveys warmth or friendliness,' observes France (1988: 183).

Good Therapists Are Real People

Although therapists who impose themselves and their ideas are not liked, nevertheless clients express a preference for therapists who come across as 'real' people. Such therapists are more than a 'technique-in-action'; they have their own personality and sense of humour and a recognizable character. 'In so far as the psychotherapist sets himself apart from his patient,' writes Lomas (1973: 17), 'giving the impression – even if only implicitly, by reticence – that he is a different order of being, his capacity to heal is reduced.' Person-centred counsellors refer to this quality as *congruence*, one of the 'core conditions', defined as the ability of the therapist to be himself or herself in the therapeutic relationship. What the counsellor does and says is consistent with what he or she thinks and feels. Clients describe this as 'being genuine', 'being straight' and 'knowing where you are with them'. Furthermore, 'The counsellor who is congruent conveys the message that it is not only permissible but desirable to be oneself' (Mearns and Thorne, 1988: 14).

Ann France, writing about being a consumer of psychotherapy, devotes a whole chapter of her book to 'the therapist as real person'. She insists that in order for therapy to be realistic, both the patient and the therapist have to present themselves as 'real people'. For example, one of her therapists 'brought himself into therapy sufficiently for me to be sure that he meant what he said, when expressing ideas or feelings, and this was an extremely therapeutic aspect of our encounter' (1988: 97). Later, France says that she does not want 'to be invaded by someone else's views. But this does not mean that I do not want to know them. On the contrary' (1988: 176).

When the therapist remains remote, coming across as no more than a textbook performer, there is no real person with whom to engage. 'He was a psychiatrist who didn't like to say anything,' remembered Hugh:

> he sat there in silence, and physically he turned me off and eventually the thing terminated when I identified him with a muskrat in one of my dreams. He was this enormous muskrat that came down to this pool I was in . . . and I climbed out of this thing and there he was, a great rat coming down on me! I realized it was him and I'd had enough of it. (Dinnage, 1989: 96)

In more extreme cases still, the personality of the therapist does emerge, but it is not liked and can be experienced as downright unpleasant. 'He was a horrible type, that doctor . . . sarcastic, mocking'; 'He'd put me down all the time for thinking I knew it all' (Dinnage, 1989: 182, 205).

However, some clients recognized that it was possibly the therapy and not the therapist that was at fault. They spotted the strange effect some techniques had on the therapist. The Pye family had experienced a course of family therapy. They had known the therapist as a field practitioner prior to and outside therapy:

Mr Pye: He [the therapist] was the middle-man, you see. They fed the
    questions through him. He was all right on his own, a very nice person
    in fact. Like, when he came round ours and he was very nice.
Mrs Pye: He even agreed with us on a lot of things.
Mr Pye: Well, in fact he agreed with us on three different things which
    them at the back in their meeting [supervisors watching the session live
    on video in another room], like, they didn't agree.
Mrs Pye: But of course he didn't have a leg to stand on.
Mr Pye: His hands were tied, you see. But, personally, you know, him
    hiself, he seemed very nice. A very reasonable person.
Mrs Pye: Very nice. There's good and there's bad but he was one of the
    good ones. He listened whereas the others thought it was a family
    problem. So you see, when he [as the therapist] was seeing us at this
    family therapy he couldn't be his self. (Howe, 1989a: 55)

Therapists enjoy intellectual stimulation every bit as much as
clients. However, there is the danger that counsellors and therapists
can be seduced by exciting ideas, new theories and daring skills. The
world of therapy has many prima donnas who seek rapturous
audiences for their virtuoso performances. The attraction becomes the
therapy and not its purpose. There are many fashions, too, in the
world of therapy. It is fun to try out new techniques; there is pleasure
in meeting other therapists at conferences and workshops. Technical
innovations are just as likely to meet the needs of the therapist as
those of the client. And clients who refuse to play the new game can
easily be dismissed as people who are resisting change, or their reactions can be explained as a further manifestation of their pathology
as defined by the theory. When the client meets a technical junky, she
is no longer being dealt with by a person but a technique. Mrs Pound
did not warm to the enthusiasms of her family therapists:

I thought I weren't getting anywhere with any of them so I stopped going.
I was upset, you know, I was actually angry to think I did ask for help and
got nothing that I did feel helped. I did feel that this meeting as a family
and everything was an interest of theirs, you know, something they liked
doing. I didn't feel they really took any notice of how I was feeling. (Howe,
1989a: 72)

And in similar mood, Mr and Mrs Spree found their experience of
therapy confusing and alienating:

Mr Spree: The panel [supervisors watching the session live in the next
    room] kept interrupting. It was very off-putting, very confusing. We
    never seemed to get anywhere.
Mrs Spree: He'd say something like . . . er . . . after he got a message from
    the panel, 'Oh, I've got to bring in Rachel now' and you were cut short.
    I felt like a guinea pig.

Mr Spree: I did, actually, too. We were like puppets and it was like they were experimenting with us, because they'd found this camera and things, and could try out certain techniques of interviewing. (Howe, 1989a, 53–4)

The Relationship

The quality of the relationship is of central concern to most clients. In the words of Lomas (1981: 2), 'the essence of what we call psychotherapy lies in the circumstances of this meeting [between counsellor and client] and the attitudes of the partners rather than in any theory of psychopathology'. France is in no doubt about the fundamental value of the relationship in therapy: 'The quality of the relationship seems to me unquestionably the most valuable part of the experience. It provides the security and motivation indispensable for the more cognitive work in the therapy, and for survival during the really testing moments' (1988: 242).

Oldfield was quite clear that the clients she interviewed 'were emphatic about the essential qualities of this relationship, and their need to trust it totally, while still grappling with feelings, both positive and negative, arising within it' (1983: 171). She quotes one of the counselling centre's users who said, 'I think the most valuable part of the series of sessions was the gradual formation of a relationship.'

Oldfield stresses that the healing agents 'are more likely to lie in the pervasive and not entirely conscious effects of the counselling *relationship* and less clearly in the cognitive work that is done' (1983: 104, emphasis in original). However, although Oldfield is right to give primacy of place to the emotional quality of the relationship, it does seem that, for many patients, the ideal relationship contains both love and work, empathy and analysis, security and exploration. Indeed, Halmos, in his examination of counselling, concluded that 'psychotherapy has to be an appropriate mixture of mothering (management) and analysis (giving insight)' (1965: 50).

However, there is always the danger that such a seductive mix of warmth, stimulation and undivided attention becomes an addiction. The problem of dependence is ever present as the attractions of the relationship take over from the purposes of therapy. Dinnage's interviews with clients of psychotherapy reveal this constant danger. Jill said:

I don't think you realize how strong the power of therapy is until you're in it. One can't sometimes grasp . . . it's very difficult to explain what it is, other than at some level it's a dependency. And now, you see, my therapist has had a baby, I haven't seen her for three weeks, and there are all those feelings again about being rejected. (1989: 157)

Patrick described how he had a great problem every time he had to have a break with his analyst, particularly over weekends: 'I found it very difficult because I was in a very needy and very childlike dependence on the analyst . . . I went into a depression every weekend' (Dinnage, 1989: 210).

A long quote from Fitts, who carried out a study on clients' experiences of therapy, upon which he reported in 1965, allows us to end this section on the importance of the relationship on a positive but demanding note:

> Do not try to change [the client] by taking away his defenses and do not try to build up or strengthen his defenses, but *provide the kind of relationship in which he no longer needs his old defenses, and they will gradually fade away* . . . it means that where other relationships have been fraught with fears of rejection, criticism, punishment, control, judgement, or ridicule, the therapy relationship is free of these characteristics. Where others have misunderstood and rejected, the therapist understands and accepts (not approves – or disapproves – but is willing for the client to be whatever he is). Where others have been inconsistent, the therapist is consistent . . . Thus we see that psychotherapy is above all a relationship. (Fitts, 1965: 10, emphasis in original)

Liking and Being Liked

The volume of research and anecdotal material that links the client's view of therapy with her perception of and feelings about the therapist is impressive. Sainsbury and his colleagues suggested that the services received by social work clients were equated with the personalities of the social workers: 'The service must be all right if *she* works there'; 'If they're all like him, it's OK'; 'The best thing he could do would be to resign' (1982: 136).

Equally important is whether or not the client thinks that the therapist likes her. Warm recognition not only is a comfort, it boosts a person's self-esteem, which, in the case of many clients, is in a poor condition. Only when other people begin to like you will you begin to like yourself. And if you like and love yourself, you will be able to love in return.

'My mother,' said Harriet, 'had somehow given me very deeply the idea that I was a non-loving person . . . But what I seemed to be getting out of the analysis . . . was that I *could* love people' (Dinnage, 1989: 137). 'I was surprised,' recalled Margaret, to find myself able to believe the therapist's positive thoughts about me. Apart from the family, by whom I do feel loved, it had never occurred to me that people would like me, or to think why they seek my company. I had a poor self-image. Now I think more about and of myself which I know makes me a better person. (Woodward, 1988: 86)

Strupp et al., who studied a total of 175 clients of psychotherapy in two consecutive investigations, were left in no doubt about the significance of the client's attitude:

It seems that the amount of improvement noted by a patient in psycho-therapy is highly correlated with his attitudes to the therapist. Indeed, psychotherapy was seen by our respondents as an intensely personal experience. More important, the therapist's warmth, his respect and interest . . . emerged as important ingredients in the amount of change reported . . . the more uncertain the patient felt about the therapist's attitude toward him, the less change he tended to experience. (1969: 77)

Helen, on a personal level, agrees:

I think from the moment I met him I felt an antipathy towards him. And I always had the feeling that he really did not like me. I know it's not necessary, I've read books where it says that it's not necessary for the patient and therapist to enjoy some sort of mutual liking, that, in fact, it could get in the way . . . But I don't know. Sometimes he used to go out of his way to say, 'Look, I'm sure you're a marvellous person' – I just never believed it. With Mrs Smith, in those few sessions, she never had to say anything like that but I felt – how can I describe it? – she liked me! (Dinnage, 1989: 24)

However, for some, the good therapeutic relationship had many of the features of a loving encounter: the therapist was interested in the client; he or she was sensitive and sympathetic; they talked at length about feelings and intimate concerns. Usually, when someone behaves like this, they are in the early stages of being in love. In Dinnage's (1989) interviews, a number of patients described how they fell in love with their therapist:

Well, immediately, within one week, I developed this strong feeling for my analyst [Carmel]. (1989: 43)

One thing right from the beginning that was very strange was that I had awful sexual feelings . . . I don't know whether they were about him, but I was just roused . . . It went on for several weeks [Margery]. (1989: 65)

I thought he was just wonderful from the start . . . I think I thought as soon as we'd got the tiresome business of analysis over we'd be sort of together in bliss for ever . . . [by the third year] The talking seemed to be irrelevant really; life was a question of whether I was *with* him or *without* him [Harriet]. (1989: 133–4)

Truth and Honesty

Knowing where you stand with another person is a basic requirement
if you want to establish truth. And you need to trust the other person
if you are to be open with him or her. Further, you need to be open
and frank if he or she is to understand you and be of help. Strupp
and his colleagues concluded that 'a sense of mutual trust was unquestionably a *sine qua non* for successful psychotherapy; in its absence,
little of positive value was accomplished' (1969: 17). Honesty, openness
and trust appear repeatedly in the accounts given by consumers.
'Fundamentally I find Mrs Smith to be absolutely rock steady,' said
Helen; 'I trust her, which I don't think I can say of any other human
being in my life' (Dinnage, 1989: 27).

In contrast, when honesty and openness are absent, clients become
wary and suspicious. 'They don't tell you what they think,' said Mrs
G. of her family therapists, while Mrs D. believed that 'They never
let you know the end result of their conversation or anything. I still
feel they knew something which wasn't actually said' (Merrington and
Corden, 1981: 254). Some clients vetted what they said, not trusting
the therapist and what he or she might do with what was said, doubting his or her motives, suspecting some hidden purpose. Mr and Mrs
Kegg did not trust their family therapist:

> Mrs Kegg: Half the answers we gave, we didn't exactly lie, but we were
> consciously . . . er . . . we watched what we say; we were extra careful
> because they could run them videos back every time to check on what
> you had said so you were extra careful . . .
> Mr Kegg: Really it meant that partly it was all a waste of time because all
> you said is what you thought they wanted you to say. (Howe, 1989a: 49)

Equally unsatisfactory are practitioners who, though not dishonest,
are perceived to be evasive, 'not straight':

> as it happened I felt the woman did a better job – not knocking him [the
> male worker], but the woman was a lot more – I find him very soft,
> whereas I needed to be told . . . he would beat about the bush a little bit,
> you know, very nice, very polite, whereas she would come straight out
> with it and you know – at least I know where I stand with her and that
> helped a lot more. (Cantley, 1987: 19)

Support and Being There

In a world inclined to be indifferent, arbitrary and careless in its
responses, someone who cares and is there when you need them is

rare and therefore likely to be well regarded. Warmth and reliability are a potent combination. Reliability is a close relative of trust. If the client meets with another who is consistent and regular and does not let her down, she will learn to trust and thus be enabled to tackle the world more openly, confidently and realistically. Elizabeth said that her second analyst, Mrs Weiss, 'was sort of lifting me up. [My first analyst] pushed me down all the time . . . by the time I'd been with her a few times, I felt I could walk straight' (Dinnage, 1989: 111). Counsellors and therapists who provide security and comfort offer a haven, a calm centre to which to run when the emotional turbulence becomes too great. The good therapist can contain feelings which threaten to spin out of control.

'Just being there' was a surprising source of comfort. Counsellors who were willing to be telephoned between appointments, or give people just a few minutes outside regular times, were highly valued. The comments of mothers who had given up a child for adoption and attended the Post-Adoption Centre in London illustrate the benefits of a straightforward willingness to be available: 'The main benefit for me is knowing that they are there when I need them'; 'Willingness to be available at times of crisis, and to give me plenty of time, made me feel valued and OK' (Howe, 1989b: 23). Three-quarters of clients who had received the services of a mental health crisis intervention team contacted a helper after 5.00 p.m. or on a weekend. It was clear from the comments of these clients 'that the fact that there was always "someone" available . . . was reassuring' (Davis et al., 1985). 'I think it's the fact that I know that they're open all the time,' answered one of Cantley's respondents (1987: 14):

> and I could go there and that at last when you're feeling really, really down and really, really, really on your own, you know that you're not . . . There's someone in the world who will wake, and let you in and talk to you, and that helps, and takes the edge off things.

Sainsbury and his co-researchers (1982: 20) believed that 'support and encouragement' were overwhelmingly the most helpful aspect of social work help over the long term, a finding which echoes Sainsbury's earlier work on families' perceptions of help in which 14 out of 26 (54 per cent) said that emotional support and reliability were 'the most helpful help' received (1975: 56).

3 Acceptance

When in a state of distress, we are awash with all kinds of difficult feelings. While some burst to the surface, others we suppress, uncertain about their legitimacy or reasonableness. Should I be angry and irritable with my ageing and demanding mother? Is it understandable that I should resent my wife's close and intimate relationship with our new-born son? The feelings are real; they are there, though they may be denied, ignored or simply wished away. In order to understand and handle such feelings, first we have to admit them before they can be scrutinized. However, this will only happen if the therapist allows us to feel safe and admit such feelings and if she facilitates their expression.

If the counsellor or therapist simply acknowledges the feelings of the client and does not judge them, this is the first step in a sequence of responses that leads to the client feeling better about himself. In full, this phase of the therapeutic sequence runs as follows:

1 The therapist *acknowledges* the client's feelings, recognizing that they are present, often with some force.
2 These feelings are not judged; they are simply *accepted*.
3 Indeed, the client is *entitled* to her feelings. 'What is needed,' believes France, 'is a friendly therapist, the creation of space where you are entitled to be just as you are, however defective' (1988: 111).
4 The effect of this is to *validate* and *affirm* the client's feelings; the feelings exist, they cannot and should not be denied. It is appropriate, indeed it is necessary, that they are expressed. The client's experiences are therefore valid; they should not be judged; they are taken seriously and indicate the client's condition.
5 By not undermining, devaluing or ignoring the other's feelings, the therapist helps the client feel more worthwhile and helps her level of *self-esteem* to rise.

Acknowledgement

Consumers of counselling and therapy say that acknowledgement and acceptance of what they are feeling are a major test of the helper's therapeutic ability. According to Strupp and his colleagues (1969: 101), a lack of acceptance of the client by the therapist was a fairly reliable predictor of a poor therapeutic outcome. Clients need to recognize their real feelings before they can examine them. 'It was hard for me to reveal these things to myself,' admitted one of Fitts's clients (Fitts, 1965: 125), 'and even harder to share them with the therapist. There were many times when I talked in circles only to find when I left that I had avoided the whole issue.' Thoughts and feelings have to be acknowledged before they can be worked upon. Another client of this same therapist reflected that

> The prime value of my session with you lies in the fact that here, with you, I can be more honest with myself than anywhere or with anyone else. In fact, it is difficult not to be honest in my thoughts and words . . . I could not lie to you without a great deal of difficulty and would not want to do so, for to do so would also mean deceiving myself. (Fitts, 1965: 65–6)

It is vital that the therapist creates a climate in which the release and identification of feelings are allowed. Not until clients recognize and face up to their feelings will they learn to understand and control them. 'The more you start owning things,' says one of Dinnage's interviewees, 'the more the emptiness and the sense of self fills up' (1989: 15). 'What a relief it was,' replied a counselling client, 'to be able to say to someone – no, it's not all right' (Oldfield, 1983: 73). France confirms the patient's need to feel safe and to be accepted: 'The more I felt secure in the feeling of being accepted as me, not necessarily liked, but responded to as an individual, the more I felt I was able to explore this self, and its more unsavoury aspects' (1988: 242).

Acceptance

The opportunity to express feelings, without fear, is highly prized. Margaret, talking about her psychotherapy, said:

> The crying was uncomfortable, but essential for me. I actually found myself starting on the way there, because there was something I desperately needed to cry about. It was a relief to know I could cry there, and to be able to say exactly what I was thinking and feeling . . . I had many memories of things that had gone wrong – all the 'bad bits', and recalled the anguish I felt as a child. Being able to go through those feelings again and to come out the other side still intact with the therapist to support me by listening and helping me, led me on to the next positive step. (Woodward, 1988: 85–6)

Many clients felt that they had not experienced much acceptance in their lives. To meet someone who listens and does not judge is both a surprise and a relief. Sue was in a highly distressed state during the first stages of her counselling:

> I felt that at least someone understands me and isn't telling me not to be silly. It was the first time in my life that someone hasn't said 'Don't be silly; it's not that bad; it will get better; you'll be all right' . . . She never criticized me. She was always there for me. She never said 'I don't want to hear about it'. She just accepted and said 'That's OK' and never told me off . . . I was allowed to cry and it was very helpful. (Edmunds, 1992: 68)

The Post-Adoption Centre is a counselling agency which specializes in helping those involved with adoption including adopters and adopted people. Those who used the Centre tended to hold very positive views about the service offered (Howe, 1990). As well as facilitating the expression of intense feelings, the counsellors, according to the users, readily understood and accepted such feelings. Many families also felt that there was an *egalitarian* quality to the proceedings in which parents were encouraged to define their own needs and understandings of the situation. Parents with adopted children exhibiting behaviour problems often approached the Centre not only with strong feelings of failure or guilt, but also with suppressed feelings of anger and disappointment. Mrs Keeling had adopted her son Jason when he was 14 months old. A year later she gave birth to James. She continues her story:

> I began to find looking after Jason more and more difficult. He was an irritable child and I was having problems with him. I visited my doctor about my feelings but he just smiled at me and obviously saw me as a neurotic mother. The adoption agency were not much better and didn't really listen to what I was trying to say. They were too busy trying to reassure me. It was not until I saw the counsellor at the Centre that I could admit, even to myself, that I couldn't love Jason – I didn't even like him. I hated dealing with him physically and I was so upset; I felt so guilty, so distraught. The counsellor gave me time and at last I could say out loud to her – and myself – that I couldn't stand Jason and I felt so, so bad about it but I couldn't make myself feel any different. She just listened and accepted that was just how I was really feeling. There was no point in denying it or giving me silly reassuring noises. It was such a relief to say 'I don't like Jason' and I cried; I couldn't stop crying but it felt better. I could start to face up to what was happening. Pretending was only making things worse. (Howe and Hinings, 1989a: 21)

When the client believes that her feelings are not accepted, there is despair, there is resentment:

But you know what I didn't like about tonight's session? I didn't like your suggesting things I could do about this situation ... I've been aware of these other possibilities, but right now such are impossible. Don't ask me why; they just are. Somehow I want to be accepted just as I am right now ... To me your suggestions were 'preachy' and violated something deep in me that wants to struggle through even such messes as I'm now in, to self-acceptance. I don't mean that I sadistically want to enjoy my present misery, but I desperately want to accept and love myself – *even in this.* (Fitts, 1965: 44)

A milder, but no less disappointing, experience of a therapist denying the client's feelings is described by Laura. She had attempted suicide and been advised to obtain counselling. Her first experience of psychotherapy had been a failure, but she fared little better with her second counsellor, Mary, who could not accept what she was trying to say. The example also illustrates that the virtue of offering one 'core condition' is not enough:

Mary was warm and soft – a very caring person. I imagine she would have been a lovely mother as long as the child did nothing wrong. It was certainly comforting for me to be with her and perhaps I needed that bit of warmth after the first cold experience of counselling. However, the honest assessment must be that this was also an experience of failure. I realized after only a few sessions that Mary was limited in what she could tolerate. When I got into my really desperate 'lost' crying she would try to take me out of it with some version of 'there, there, it will be alright'. That stopped me crying and helped to get me really stuck. Sometimes she looked anxious and embarked upon long stories about 'young people' she had known who had eventually 'found their way'. I tried to tell her that I did not need reassurance like this – I had survived much more desperate experiences. (Allen, 1990: 25)

Entitlement

'Entitlement' extends the notion of acceptance. Counsellors do not just accept the client's feelings; they also convey a message not only that it is all right to show such feelings, but also that the client is *entitled* to them. Working with older adopted people, counsellors recognized that for some clients it was all right to be angry about being given up for adoption. To be curious about one's biological mother was perfectly natural. Acceptance and reassurance about the reasonableness and normality of such feelings proved an important counselling skill. Here is a counsellor talking about her work with a young adopted woman:

Denise felt she was obsessed with being adopted. She wanted to come to terms with it. She felt that there was something wrong with her. Her friends couldn't understand and she got very frightened at her own feelings, fear that being adopted might mean that she is bad or mad, that there must be something the matter with her that she should be adopted. I told her that such feelings were common and quite reasonable under the circumstances. (Howe and Hinings, 1989b: 24–5)

Another counsellor at the Centre also describes how she allowed a client to feel entitled to her feelings of fear and confusion:

Sonia wanted to search for her birth mother but said she had lots of nerves about it, and wasn't sure if she was ready and yet couldn't stop thinking about it. I said it was perfectly normal to feel like that, that to think about searching for your birth mother was natural but also quite scary and I acknowledged that it was a really scary thing for her to do. (Howe and Hinings, 1989b: 25)

It is apparent in these examples that not only are feelings accepted but clients are also helped to see that they are entitled to have feelings which they may not think they should be holding. For example, people often experience guilt but they are less certain about whether they are entitled to feel anger. One of Oldfield's respondents said: 'Express what you feel and it will get better. Name feelings. You are entitled to feelings of anger and grief. This was the most important thing: entitlement' (1983: 70).

Feminist counsellors believe that it is extremely helpful for women to acknowledge their feelings, particularly those which involve guilt and anger. But more strongly, women should recognize that they are entitled to feel the way they do under the circumstances. Walker (1990) describes Suzanne's experience of counselling. When her first baby was born, Suzanne felt under pressure to be happy, joyous and celebratory. It revived old memories of similar demands on her to be happy as a child. 'Negative feelings were not acceptable, and if she expressed them that would make her unacceptable.' Her feelings about the glories of motherhood were compounded by her anxieties about becoming financially and emotionally dependent. 'In her own eyes it was as if she had become a child again. She could recognize, too, that when her first child was born, she had to repress all the rage inside her, since this rage made her feel guilty' (Walker, 1990: 16). In counselling, Suzanne was able to see how these patterns continued into adult life. This enabled her to cope better with her second baby, who was a far more demanding child:

I felt easier with her from the start, and much more in sympathy with her. I think, in a funny sort of way, she was expressing a lot of things I couldn't. She could be very demanding at the most inconvenient times. And I can remember not feeling resentful, but thinking 'good for you'. I wish I could have been like that. And, because she was difficult, people didn't expect me to be so happy and cheerful all the time. It was all right to be tired and grumpy. (Walker, 1990: 16–17)

Entitlement to feelings can also be eroded by kindness, and in some ways this is a more frustrating and difficult thing with which to deal:

At first I valued her reassurance and support a great deal. It was just what I had been wanting. After a time though I began to find this frustrating. Every time I began to feel depressed, ashamed, or frightened, she would rush in to rid me of these feelings. She could not seem to let me have my own feelings – to really feel them and find my way out of them. It was as if she felt no faith in me at all and thought that I was about to come apart. She made me feel like a little child. I guess we were trying to accomplish two different things. I was trying to grow a new personality and she was trying to patch up the old one; I was trying to let some of my real feelings out and she wanted to cover them up again. (Fitts, 1965: 29)

Validation

Once feelings are out in the open they can be examined, understood and confirmed. One of the favourite words that counsellors use to describe the recognition and confirmation of a feeling is 'validation'. Here is France talking about the merits of validation:

The most therapeutic aspect of the episode was her wish to be truthful, rather than protect herself. What most helped me was the open acknowledgement that my intuition, that had nagged at me for months, had in fact been correct. Namely, that she experienced my need as hateful and was to some extent rejecting me, despite her denials. My feelings were validated. Although I might have preferred to have been told to the contrary, truth was better than lies. (1988: 94)

There were times, however, when Ann France failed to have her feelings acknowledged or believed. She quotes David Smail, who said that 'the greatest comfort derives from having one's views, however despairing it may be, confirmed by someone else who is not afraid to share it'. She then tells of the time she was distinctly uncomforted when, in spite of her suicidal inclinations, her psychotherapist said: 'But you are not suicidal.' 'I was amazed,' writes France (1988: 153), 'at this refusal to validate my feelings.'

The step is but a short one, of course, from not validating feelings to judging feelings. There is almost universal agreement amongst clients that counsellors and therapists should not be judgemental. 'It was somewhere where I could go to talk about my problems without feeling I was judged in any way'; 'she . . . didn't judge; wouldn't criticize. I was free to say anything at all – I didn't have to censor or sift' (Oldfield, 1983: 72). But the examples are legion in which clients feel that they *have* been judged, and often judged severely:

> Then I was shunted along to the hospital to see the consultant psychiatrist there. He was the most inhuman person I ever encountered in the whole of my time. I just had the overwhelming impression that I was a silly little girl who'd reached a stage in her life where she didn't know what to do next, and if she'd just settle down and get married and have children she wouldn't have time for this self-indulgence. (Dinnage, 1989: 23)

Feminist counsellors are keen to encourage women to value their feelings. 'Encouraging women to trust themselves,' writes Walker (1990: 75), 'to become more assertive, and to be able to acknowledge and express anger are other central themes in feminist work.' Walker continues:

> Women's experience is heard; it is not invalidated or repressed. It is seen as an essential part of their being. It is recognized that their experience comes from an interaction of the internal and the external, but the first step in untangling this is allowing and encouraging the expression of that experience. Understanding cannot take place without providing an atmosphere conducive to trust, the freedom to say anything, and the belief that what is said will be accepted.

Self-Esteem

The result of all this acknowledging and accepting, validating and not judging, is to give people a belief in themselves, a belief in what they think and feel. They are not demeaned by their emotions, they are not diminished by what they think. In encouraging clients to describe their feelings, the therapist is also giving the message that the individual is worth listening to and worth understanding. The boost to self-esteem can be considerable.

> With regard to my sense of no worth, somehow she always ended the sessions leaving me feeling I had a lot of worth . . . being able to work together upon the problems of me, instead of being spoken *at* from the other side of the desk, was the most valuable part of it. (Oldfield, 1983: 64)

Being valued allows the client to feel more worthwhile. Orlinsky and Howard (1986: 496) believe that this enhances the client's courage to explore her concerns. The authors then describe the results of their own work analysing therapy sessions. They identify a therapeutic process through which they feel clients move in relationships which are judged to be successful:

> The therapists' affective message, 'I'm worthwhile and so are you' (Feeling Expansive) finds a response in the patients' affective message, 'I'm safe and OK when I'm with you' (Feeling Confident). With courage enhanced, and with the additional support of the therapists' message 'I care about you' (Feeling Intimate), patients can more readily tolerate and intelligently explore issues with which their experience has been 'I can't cope, I don't know what to do' (Feeling Anxious). In response to this, therapists say or do things that convey the message 'I understand and can handle what is bothering you' (Feeling Effective), and that leads their patients to sense 'It may not be so bad, I really can deal with it' (Feeling Relieved). (Orlinsky and Howard, 1986: 496)

Conclusions

Feeling Secure and Valued in a Good Relationship

Clients are constantly alert and sensitive to the interpersonal climate in which counselling takes place. The personality of the therapist, the manner of the encounter and the quality of the relationship create a climate which clients feel should be warm and consistent. In a study of the views of 63 patients of psychotherapy, Feifel and Eells (1963) found that the two most helpful aspects of treatment were 'those of talking over one's problems and the therapeutic relationship (therapist as a person)'. In short, the client is looking for a relationship which initially feels safe and secure.

'I needed to feel *warmth*,' recalls Laura (Allen, 1990: 27), 'and a sense of *commitment* . . . I also needed someone who would be prepared to *hold* me, not necessarily physically, though that would have helped. More than that . . . I needed someone who was so *secure* in themselves that they could reach out to *me*.' And in spite of putting words into the mouth of his client, Fitts captures similar feelings in the following interview:

> Client: I've noticed something very interesting lately about coming here. I used to go away following one of our sessions and on my way home I would realize that I was feeling different. Then I would realize that the tension was gone and that I didn't have that frightened feeling. It had faded away somewhere while we were talking. Well anyway, the interesting thing is that now I found myself beginning to relax in the same way as soon as I come in here.

Therapist: Maybe a kind of safe feeling?
Client: Yeah! That's it – safe – safe, like there's no real danger here . . .
   not here like everywhere else. (Fitts, 1965: 76)

A study by Heine (1953) of 24 people who had received psychotherapy identified the 'therapeutic atmosphere' as an important factor
in the clients' experiences of help. Favourable atmospheres were
created by feelings of trust and of being understood. Atmospheres
seen as counter to favourable changes included a feeling of distance
and a lack of interest on the part of the therapist. In addition, the
fear that the therapist might be judgemental produced a negative
atmosphere. This early paper shows that Heine is in no doubt about
the importance of the therapist's personality and the type of relationship he or she forms with clients:

> The medium through which theoretical material is utilized is the therapist–
> patient relationship. While the relationship may be circumscribed by
> theoretical and technical considerations . . . the personality of the therapist
> can never be more than partially obscured. It is not possible to be one
> personality outside one's office and a totally different personality when one
> is with a patient. It is a truism that a person whose interpersonal behaviour
> is broadly maladaptive cannot be consistently successful as a psycho-
> therapist, yet this simple observation is often diluted by token acceptance.
> (Heine, 1953: 21)

And 10 years later, concluding their study of 63 patients' views of
psychotherapy, Feifel and Eells (1963: 317) wrote: 'Of pertinence is not
only the personal feelings . . . of the therapist . . . but also the
patient's perception of them . . . Our findings, leastwise from the
patient's outlook, tend to bolster Rogers' view that attitudinal
elements in the therapy relationship are a consequential ingredient
accounting for change.' Along with Board (1959), the authors show
that patients value the opportunity to express feelings, the chance to
gain in self-understanding, and therapists who show interest in and
understanding of those who come seeking help. Strupp et al. (1969:
77) reported that clients described psychotherapy as an 'intensely
personal experience . . . the therapist's warmth, his respect and
interest, and his perceived competence and activity emerged as important ingredients in the amount of change reported by the patients.
The more uncertain the patient felt about the therapist's attitude
towards him, the less change he tended to experience.'
   Inspired by the finding that the patient's perceptions of the relationship between herself and the therapist was crucial, Llewelyn and
Hume (1979) decided to test two hypotheses: (1) that patients would
report 'relationship' and 'non-specific' factors to be more useful in

treatment than technical activities; and (2) that there would be no difference between patients who had received behaviour therapy and patients who had received psychotherapy with respect to the rated importance of the non-specific and relationship elements. The term 'non-specific' factors refers to factors in the therapeutic encounter which are not specific to a particular theoretical technique or school of practice. Such non-specific factors, therefore, might include things such as 'simply talking about the problem', 'encouragement', 'friendliness', 'warmth' and 'empathy'.

Analysis of 37 patients' experiences of therapy suggested that both the hypotheses could be accepted. The nurturing quality of the relationship, including such factors as the willingness of the therapist to listen to and respect the patient, seemed to matter more to most people than technical competence in the particular method of treatment. The authors find themselves in accord with Truax and Carkhuff (1967), who believed that it is the client's *perception* and personal experience of such qualities as warmth, empathy and genuineness which matter, and not the alleged or assumed presence of such qualities according to either outside observers or the therapist herself.

Kaschkak (1978) analysed the views of 15 psychotherapists and their 75 clients. Like her fellow researchers, she too found that clients, more than therapists, attributed change to such things as 'just having someone to talk to' and 'the therapist's nonjudgmental attitude'. In contrast, therapists were more likely to attribute change to their own techniques, supportiveness and the use of confrontation in treatment.

An exception to this rule is Peter Lomas, whose reflections on his own practice as a psychotherapist produced conclusions completely in tune with all that has been said so far by clients: 'the commonplace attitudes which are relevant to healing lie in the direction of warmth rather than coldness, trust rather than cynicism, closeness rather than distance, encouragement rather discouragement, spontaneity rather than calculation' (Lomas, 1981: 6). He believes that people are helped by 'wisdom and love' and not by 'technique' (Lomas, 1981: 7).

The Therapeutic Alliance

From time to time people working in the field of psychotherapeutic research review their findings and take stock. The papers collected by Greenberg and Pinsof (1986) provide impressive summaries of many of the topics so far considered. Each investigator contributing to the review was searching for the active ingredients in the therapeutic process. It is now recognized that the qualities of both the therapist and the client enter the dynamics of the therapeutic process. The interactions that take place between the main players are exceedingly complex and vary between the same therapist and different clients, different therapists and the same client, and the same therapist and the same client at different times (Suh et al., 1986).

The perennially intriguing finding that most psychotherapies are modestly successful no matter to which technical or theoretical school they belong has revived interest in the possibility of an underlying set of universal factors in successful human relationships. One such factor or concept is that of the 'therapeutic alliance', sometimes known as the 'helping alliance'. This is defined by Alexander and Luborsky (1986: 326) 'as the patient's experience of the treatment or relationship with the therapist as helpful or potentially helpful'.

The concept traces its origins back to Freud, who felt the alliance was established on two fronts: (1) the strength of attachment that the patient made with the therapist and the treatment process; and (2) the degree of friendliness, affection and sympathetic understanding shown by the therapist towards the patient. The client needs to see the therapist as someone who is capable of being helpful; feelings of rapport, warmth and confidence have to be generated. The client also needs to feel that she is an equal partner in the helping process. There must be the experience of a positive working relationship in which the client believes that she shares a common conceptual outlook with the therapist on her concerns, and they use the same tools for understanding (Alexander and Luborsky, 1986).

Indeed, Luborsky et al. (1985) have suggested that it is the personal qualities of the therapist that mainly influence his or her ability to form helping alliances. Included among these, according to Alexander and Luborsky (1986: 355), are the basic background similarities between clients and therapists. These include such things as age and religious activities. Kaschkak (1978) would also include the sex of the therapist in this list. In her study of 15 therapists and 75 clients, Kaschkak found that clients were more responsive to same-sex therapists. This was particularly true for women: female clients of female therapists rated the therapeutic outcome more highly than any other group. Further support for this view is given by Maluccio's study of 25 clients. 'In general,' he observes, 'clients felt more positively and were more satisfied with the service the closer they were to the workers in respect to characteristics such as age, sex, and family status' (Maluccio, 1979: 130). For example, one of his respondents said, 'As a woman, she understood me better', while another remarked, 'It would be better if the worker had been a woman.'

Moreover, there is now the belief that positive and productive treatment alliances do not occur by accident:

> They require the persistent, informed, and sensitive attention of the therapist. Technically, behaviorally, and affectively the therapist needs to be constantly attuned to the meanings of the dyadic communications that occur. Also, a mutually positive regard of the therapist and patient for each other, while a valuable component of the alliance, is in itself insufficient to achieve the aims of therapy. Only when the therapist and patient become collaborative partners in taking up the tasks of treatment (the working alliance) does therapy achieve its aims. (Marmar et al., 1986: 368)

In their own work on the therapeutic alliance, Marmar et al. (1986: 381–2) found that items which positively promoted the alliance included the following:

> (1) The therapist conveyed that he or she liked the patient, felt hopeful about therapy, was committed to help, encouraged and supported the patient, and conveyed a feeling of mutually working together; and (2) the patient felt helped, liked the therapist, and was willing to examine his or her behaviour and understand his or her problems.

Items which inhibited the formation of a therapeutic alliance included: '(1) The therapist was judgemental, criticized the patient, ignored the patient's wishes, and communicated annoyance about the patient's slow progress, and (2) the patient expressed anger, avoidance, resistance, and argued with the therapist.'

Clients appear to have no doubts from their own experience that warmth, friendliness and acceptance are necessary if the therapeutic relationship is to be established with the counsellor or therapist. We now need to consider why clients want to feel secure and wish to be accepted by their therapists.

4 A Secure Base

The feelings and attitudes of the counsellor as perceived by the client matter. They tell the client whether or not the counsellor is interested in her, accepts her, cares about her. She needs to feel safe and secure in the therapeutic relationship. This, of course, seems reasonable. But why? Although it feels instinctively right that the counsellor should be someone who cares about and accepts the client, it does not explain why those who seek help value certain qualities in those who offer it. We need to be curious about the client's view. We need to puzzle over it. Why *do* warm, interested and accepting counsellors have successful outcomes? Why *are* they experienced as helpful by clients? Ethological studies of the child give us some promising answers.

Infants and Adults

The similarities between early infant experiences and the ingredients of successful counselling have long been recognized by eminent psychotherapists. Adults who are faced with uncertainty or confusion, who are upset or anxious, display many of the characteristics of the young child who experiences anxiety or who is about to tackle a new and unknown situation. And like the infant, the troubled adult appears to need a secure base from which to explore the concerns which trouble him or her. For the child, a secure attachment is usually established with the mother or father. For the adult, it may be provided by a friend, a partner or a colleague, but often it is looked for in a professional helper.

The young child develops strong attachments to particular people in his or her environment. If the care offered by these people is consistent, sensitive, attentive and warm, this provides a secure base from which the child can explore his or her world. But if the care is inconsistent and the mother, for example, does not respond sensitively, accurately and with interest, the attachment formed is weaker and cannot be taken for granted. This undermines the child's confidence to explore and learn about the world of people and relationships.

These early interactions are influenced by our genetic programming and the quality of our social environment. The combined effect of our genes and interpersonal experience then helps generate particular neurological structures which enable us to handle social interactions. We are obliged, therefore, to use those same kinds of social interactions when, as adults, we find ourselves feeling anxious and uncertain and generally not coping. It was within our early relationships with others that we first learned (or failed to learn) to cope, and it is to those kind of relationships that we must return if we are to generate new or better ways of coping.

Therefore it is incumbent on counsellors and therapists to provide relationships with clients that are going to be experienced as warm, safe, responsive and accepting. Counsellors and therapists who fail to provide a secure base and a comfortable alliance make clients feel anxious and angry. In attachments which are insecure, the client's energy is spent on watching and monitoring the therapy with the therapist and not on exploring personal problems. Rather like the infant who experiences an anxious attachment to an inconsistent, unresponsive mother, the client works mostly on trying to understand, control and manage the unfulfilling 'therapeutic' relationship. On the face of it, this appears to be an ironic state of affairs.

The neurological structures laid down in infancy require the adult to use these selfsame structures (and the behavioural patterns they support) in situations which are akin to the infant learning to venture forth into difficult and untried areas of experience. Therefore, in order to understand why clients say that they should be 'accepted' by their therapists before they can explore experiences, we must examine in greater detail why infants need to feel accepted by their parent-figures before they can explore and cope with their environment.

Biology and Experience

Before we consider the work of various ethologists and the developmental psychologists, we need to recognize that a dynamic relationship exists between an individual's genetic orientation and the quality of her environmental experiences. There is subtle, creative interplay between nature and nurture, biology and culture, genes and the social environment. *Biology* and *experience* are not just two solid, unyielding givens that slug it out as the individual negotiates the world. They are sensitive structures that can influence as well as be influenced, respond as well as initiate, form as well as be formed. The character and structure of each are a product of their shared relationship.

The brain is programmed to handle experience, make sense of it, anticipate it, but the neurological structures it constructs in order to make sense of experience are themselves heavily influenced by, even totally dependent on, the quality of those experiences. For example, primates, including ourselves, are genetically programmed to develop the neurological capacity to process sense data received by the eyes into sight – we literally *learn to see* as our brains develop structures which can make sense of visual experiences. When finally introduced to light, chimpanzees raised in total darkness could not 'see' (Riesen, quoted by Klein, 1987: 33). Light entered their eyes and stimulated nerve impulses to the brain, but the brain had not developed the neurological structures to process and make sense of these new visual experiences. The visual world was not being conceptualized; it *meant* nothing. People born blind who later gain sight are very slow in learning how to see; triangles and circles are hard to distinguish visually, colours are confused, and a familiar object given a new orientation might not be recognized. The visual skills of the newly sighted are acquired only very slowly and rarely reach the levels of those who are born sighted (see Chapter 8).

In like manner, many cultural structures arise out of genetic requirements. The fact that we have to handle sexual relationships and ensure the development of our young requires us to develop suitable social arrangements. The actual details of those social arrangements are not genetically determined, though the requirement that we procreate and rear our young is.

Attachment Behaviour

A particularly useful theory for considering the ways in which clients experience counselling is that developed by Bowlby and his associates. Attachment theory, according to Bowlby, involves

> any form of behaviour that results in a person attaining or retaining proximity to some other differentiated and preferred individual, who is usually conceived of as stronger and/or wiser. While especially evident during early childhood, attachment behaviour is held to characterize human beings from the cradle to the grave. It includes crying and calling, which elicit care, following and clinging, and also strong protest should a child be left alone or with strangers. With age, the frequency and intensity with which such behaviour is exhibited diminish steadily. Nevertheless, all these forms of behaviour persist as an important part of man's behavioural equipment. In adults, they are especially evident when a person is distressed, ill, or afraid. (Bowlby, 1979: 129)

Attachment behaviour encourages the infant to maintain close contact with those who appear to be able to cope with the world. It is one of a number of programmed behavioural dispositions which include exploration, fear and wariness, sociability and the seeking of food. Not only does natural selection favour protective mothers, in terms of evolutionary survival there is also a contrary pressure to select mothers who promote their infant's independence and infants who seek independence. There is a complex interplay between these various systems, and how a child behaves in any one situation will depend on the current strength of and relationship between the various dispositions. For example, if the child is well fed and feels secure, novel and interesting situations will encourage him or her to explore his or her surroundings. Only if the situation is experienced as strange and worrying will attachment behaviour be activated.

Knowing that the attachment figure is available and responsive gives the child a 'strong and pervasive feeling of security' (Bowlby, 1988: 27). In effect, what is being claimed is that, from infancy on, human beings are *naturally* equipped to relate. To relate to others is a prerequisite for attachment, and attachment serves a vital function in the protection of the child as well as offering a secure base from which the child can develop a range of skills distinctive to human beings. So, relating with others is not an incidental feature of human life, nor is it simply learned. It is built into our biological make-up and saturates the way we do things, approach situations and experience events.

Ethologists, such as Bowlby and Ainsworth, suggest 'that infants are born with a biological propensity to behave in ways which promote proximity and contact with their mother-figure. According to their view, attachment then develops as a consequence of parental responsiveness to these innate behaviours during a sensitive period in the first years of life' (Rutter, 1980: 275). The child is programmed to be aware of and interested in, and to interact with, the behaviour of those who feature significantly in his or her life. But though programmed to interact, the *quality of interaction* has a profound bearing on how the child experiences self, others and the world beyond.

The Value of Attachment Behaviour

Attachment serves biological ends. There is an adaptive value in attachment behaviour. In the face of danger, security lies in being close to the mother. Anxiety can also be adaptive in evolutionary terms. In situations of danger and uncertainty, actual or threatened separation from the mother induces feelings of anxiety and a wish to be back with her. Attachment seeks to ensure that the infant has a secure base from which to explore the environment.

If the evolutionary success of human beings depends on our ability to co-operate and develop social skills, use language, model the environment and so learn to manipulate it, a long period of development is required. It is critical that the maturing infant remains safe and well protected during the many years in which he or she will be dependent on his or her parents. The biological make-up of the child and parents is so arranged that they become attached to one another, thus ensuring that during the vulnerable time of dependency there is a secure attachment: a safe, reliable and regular base from which the child can investigate the world and upon which he or she can develop physically and socially, conceptually and practically. It is of fundamental importance for the survival of the species that the infant is cared for during this long stage of early development. To some degree, therefore, it appears that attachment behaviours, so vital to the species, are pre-programmed. 'To leave their development solely to the caprices of individual learning,' writes Bowlby (1988: 5), 'would be the height of biological folly.'

Not only is the infant genetically disposed to stimulate interaction with his or her parents with the intention of promoting attachment, the child becomes increasingly skilled in reading whether or not the parent is offering behaviour that is consonant with attachment. 'Does my mother accept me?' asks the child. Thus, the quality of interaction affects the extent to which the child feels secure and so whether or not the world beyond can be safely explored. If attachment is weak, there is an immediate need on the child's part to concentrate on surviving, which leaves little energy over for the relaxed investigation of things, people and situations.

Thus, two elements characterize the success of human beings in terms of their ability to thrive as well as survive: (1) there must be behaviours which ensure safety in times of danger and uncertainty; and (2) there must be behaviours which encourage the exploration of the environment in order to understand it and exploit it.

The Origins of Attachment

Observations confirm that, by the end of their first year, most children have usually developed a strong attachment to their parents.

If they are separated from them, children become distressed. Attachment grows throughout the early months of the infant's life, but the ability to establish relationships and a closeness to other people is present from birth.

Responses of the Baby

The maturing infant becomes increasingly sophisticated in making perceptual discriminations. The ability to discriminate visually and auditorially is a critical pre-condition if selective attachments are to be established. Rutter (1980: 267–8), reviewing the research evidence, notes that visually babies favour more interesting and complex patterns, preferring moving to stationary objects, three-dimensional to flat objects and, after three months, the human face to other kinds of visual stimuli. It is not long, then, before an infant shows a definite preference for a moving human face. A similar story occurs with sound. Human speech becomes of particular interest to the baby and elicits vocalization in the child. In general, it seems that by three months of age a baby can differentiate her mother from other people. 'Obviously,' concludes Rutter, 'this constitutes an essential pre-requisite to the development of selective attachment.'

As the baby continues to mature, she begins to understand something of the mother's conceptual perspective, her thoughts, plans and feelings. The baby rapidly develops a 'working model' of the mother (Marvin, 1977), which now means that both mother and child have 'understandings' of each other that result in phased, co-ordinated and mutually satisfying communication.

Responses of the Parent

Equally important in securing attachment are the reactions of the infant's parents. Not only does the baby recognize and respond to what the mother and father do; they, in turn, respond to the social signals of their baby. Smiles, cries and babblings attract the interest and attention of adults. Mothers begin to recognize different types of crying in their baby. Rocking, picking up and talking all help reduce stress. Attention seems to soothe babies. Smiling plays a particularly important role in the development of social relationships (Rutter, 1980: 268). By three months, babies smile more often to mothers than to strangers. Bowlby (1988: 5) believed that parenting, too, has strong biological roots, which he felt accounted for the strong emotions associated with it. This does not necessarily mean that an adult will make a competent parent, for much depends upon their own experiences of being parented.

Interaction between Parent and Child

It is clear that what we see when mothers are with their babies is a two-way interaction. Infants influence the behaviour of their mothers every bit as much as mothers influence the behaviour of their infants. 'In a very real sense,' suggests Rutter (1980: 268), 'it is a dialogue in which babies and parents smile and vocalize to each other with the same type of flow (initiations, pauses and responses) characteristic of adult conversations.' Thus, warmth, friendliness and a general interest on the part of the mother in her baby help promote other developmental achievements.

Good relationships depend on the ability of people to be aware of each other's point of view, feelings and intentions. Behaviours are adjusted accordingly. Each partner should have a reasonably accurate model of the other's mental condition. There is much communication between securely attached infants and their mothers, which increases the level of sensitive understanding that takes place between them. A benign circle forms: security and enjoyment sponsor communication; good communication encourages accurate and sensitive mutual understanding, which brings feeling of security, confidence and self-esteem.

A Secure Base

The net result of the increasingly close and frequent interaction between parent and child is that usually between six and nine months the child develops a specific attachment to particular adults. The mother, or sometimes the father, is preferred to other people, particularly at times of distress, no matter what the reaction of that adult when the child approaches him or her. Rutter (1980: 269) identified four main features that characterize attachment: the effect of anxiety, the secure base effect; reduction of anxiety; and separation protest. A brief review of these features gives us further insights into the nature of human relationships and their deep-rooted origins in human biology and social development.

The Effects of Anxiety

Social behaviour is normally inhibited by anxiety, but attachment behaviour is *intensified* by anxiety. If a stranger enters the room, the child slows down her play and may well seek out her parent. Generally, when a child experiences stress or anxiety, she will either try to get close to her mother or father, or follow them about. Moreover, 'anxiety seems to increase attachment *regardless* of the responses of the attachment object' (Rutter, 1980: 269, emphasis in original).

A Secure Base

For our purposes, this is perhaps the most important feature of attachment behaviour. Children who feel securely attached to their parents are more able to explore the world about them. They know that when they return to their mother, for example, there is a welcome, there is comfort and reassurance. Novelty is a source of stimulation for children, and if they feel that there is a safe haven to which to return when the world beyond begins to seem frightening, new situations can be approached with greater confidence. Ainsworth (1967) found that children brought up in an affectionate, accepting home could, by the time they were two, venture into the world with increasing confidence. For example, a child whose mother is sitting on a park bench is able to leave her for some time and travel considerable distances (up to 80 metres). The child will return periodically, perhaps just for a brief rub against the knee or climb on the lap and chat before she is off again.

However, if the attachment is insecure, forays into the world become less attractive. If difficulties are met, there is no guarantee that they can be resolved and no certainty that there will be a secure base to which to return. A general wariness might develop.

But children who can begin to investigate the people and things around them start to learn many useful things that will serve them well in adult life. Exploration is an adaptive response. It helps produce competent people. It is good for the survival of the individual and therefore good for the survival of the species. Infants seem to play, chatter and move about more in their mother's presence than in her absence. Rutter notes a number of features associated with the secure base effect, including the observation that the presence of the person to whom the child is attached enables him or her 'to move away more readily' and that returns to base 'are not elicited by summonses' (Rutter, 1980: 270).

'This concept of a secure personal base,' wrote Bowlby (1988: 46), 'from which a child, an adolescent, or an adult goes out to explore and to which he returns from time to time, is one I have come to regard as crucial for an understanding of how an emotionally stable person develops and functions *all through his life*' (emphasis in original).

Reduction of Anxiety

This is probably the other side of the coin of the secure base effect, and in that sense it may well be an aspect of the same phenomenon. As we have seen, an infant is less distressed in a strange environment if her mother or father is present. This is now well recognized in hospitals where parents are encouraged to stay with their children.

Separation Protest

Normally attached children react in a particular way when temporarily separated from their parents. At first they *protest* – they cry, they are angry, and one way or another they demand the return of the parent. A second phase finds them more subdued and quietly miserable – they seem to *despair* of recovering the parent even though they remain watchful and preoccupied with the prospect of her return. Finally, after a prolonged separation, the infant appears emotionally *detached*, seeming not to care about the parent.

Secure and Anxious Attachments

In practice, Bowlby and Ainsworth (1982) recognize three principal patterns of attachment, ranging from the secure to the insecure, from the confident to the anxious. Again, the qualities that promote one type or another are of relevance to our concerns: on the one hand, there is a need to enter relationships; and on the other, there is the actual experience of that relationship. Here we are moving away from the in-built developmental propensities to relate and attach, towards a consideration of how these programmed inclinations are modified in the light of experience – in our case the responses of the mother.

Secure attachments find the infant confident that her parents will be 'available, responsive, and helpful' in times of stress, uncertainty and worry (Bowlby, 1988: 124). The mother is attentive and sensitive to the child's signals and is willing to respond with love and comfort, should the occasion demand. She is encouraging and helpful. With such assurances, the child can begin to explore the world with confidence.

Anxious resistant attachments are found in children who are uncertain about whether their mothers (or fathers) will be available to offer comfort and help in times of difficulty. The uncertainty makes the child prone to separation anxiety and she is liable to become clinging, and anxious about exploring the world. 'This pattern, in which conflict is evident, is promoted by a parent being available and helpful on some occasions but not on others, and by separations and . . . by threats of abandonment used as a means of control' (Bowlby, 1988: 124). Distress reflects insecurity in the relationship as well as the presence of attachment. Thus, the quality of the attachment needs to be recognized as well its strength.

Ambivalent or *anxious avoidant attachments* occur when the child cannot assume that she will receive love and comfort when she needs it. Often she will be rebuffed at the very time she seeks care and attention. The parent remains insensitive, unpredictable and inattentive. Insensitive mothers, rather like insensitive counsellors, can be insensitive in three ways: they may reject, they may interfere, or they may ignore. There is little sustained interest in the child's achievements or needs. And because their mothers are insensitive to their signals, these babies lack confidence in their mother's responsiveness and therefore their own worthwhileness. The child learns that seeking the love of another is a hurtful enterprise. Rejection and pain can only be avoided by becoming emotionally self-sufficient. Other people are not to be trusted; they let you down when you need them most; best to cope alone.

If you are genetically inclined to relate with those around you, but all your efforts lead to momentary arousals followed by disappointments, then you will experience pain and uncertainty. Feelings are expressed but not acknowledged. The other person does not appear to care. Clearly such a relationship is neither reliable nor safe. Fairbairn (1952) thought a child in such a relationship with her mother or caretaker would feel depreciated. The infant's own thoughts and feelings would appear to be without value in terms of other people's reactions, and a sense of worthlessness would follow. If love is given but not received, perhaps you are not lovable; perhaps you are bad and undeserving, which is why the world treats you the way it does. It seems that to want to love and be loved is wrong. To have feelings of love and to want to be in a close relationship with other people may become a source of shame and doubt; all they seem to bring is rejection and hurt, in which case the best thing to do is keep them well and truly suppressed. Attachments appear to be a source of pain, and so the only way to avoid further agonies and anxieties is to avoid such relationships. The natural desire for a close, trusting relationship, for care, comfort and love, is blocked (Bowlby, 1988: 55). The infant begins to disown her own feelings, and life becomes lived on an emotionally and intellectually flatter plain.

Bowlby (1988: 52) quotes a report by Clare Winnicott in which she describes a patient who was a professional woman, aged 41. She presented herself as emotionally self-sufficient but she had developed a number of psychosomatic symptoms. Her mother went out to work while she was still a baby and she was looked after by a German girl who left suddenly when the patient was two and a half years old. There followed six months of uncertainty. One day, she was taken by her mother to have tea with a friend; her mother disappeared, and she found herself in a strange bed in a strange house. Her mother's friend was a matron at a boarding school where the patient was taken as a pupil. She stayed there, including the holidays, until she was nine. Although in many respects her life turned out to be a success, her life remained emotionally dry.

Mothers or other caretakers who are not reliable and attentive need to be watched with a wary eye by the child. It matters to the infant whether or not the mother is listening, caring or responding. There is always an element of anxiety, for the child can never be certain that it will be loved or fed, comforted or stimulated, encouraged or played with. The mother is not in tune with her baby. Either signals are not received or they are read incorrectly. The child may be stimulated when she feels sleepy, given a bottle when he is not hungry. The infant has no feelings of being in charge. Unlike the securely attached child with an alert and sensitive parent, things happen to the insecurely attached child without anyone apparently taking any notice of the baby's feelings and wishes.

'An anxious infant,' reports Klein (1987: 240), 'has to stop "being", in order to deal with distress and in order to deal with the needs of the (m)other from whom help is needed.' The insecure child will feel more dependent on others and less confident in her own abilities to control and investigate the environment. Unlike the relaxed infant, who will explore the environment as a place of interest and excitement, the anxious child is more concerned with what it can snatch from it. The anxious child is intent on *doing* and less able to concentrate on the pleasures of just *being*. In Erikson's (1950) terms, there are issues of 'basic trust':

> [The infant] needs to feel confirmed as a secure, interesting, and interested self, in a secure relationship with the interested and interesting world of others. But the need to survive may make it fearful about the world, and interested mainly in seeing where distress and the alleviation of distress may come from. The question ceases to be 'Who am I?', 'Who are you?', and becomes 'What are you good for?', 'How do I have to behave to get what I need from you?' The environment becomes something to be exploited. The self and the other stand over against each other, and the primary relationship is not unified but exploitative. (Klein, 1987: 240)

However, other interpretations of these behaviours are possible (Kagan, 1989; Hinde, 1982). Kagan (1989), for example, invites us to consider two further possibilities. One concerns the child's innate temperamental tendency to become fearful or remain seemingly calm and relaxed in unfamiliar situations. The other considers how different cultures and parental practices view a child's ability to control his or her reactions in distressing circumstances. There is some evidence, according to Kagan, that German parents promote and value independence and self-control in their children. As a result many German children show less concern at the comings and goings of their parents. They may appear insecure according to Ainsworth's categories, but it might well be that they have loving and warm parents to whom they are securely attached. They have simply learned to control any feelings of upset when temporarily separated from their mother or father. Parents seek to create relationships with their children which they feel are desirable in their culture.

Moreover, believes Hinde (1982: 71), different circumstances may warrant different styles of mothering. Over-protective or restrictive mothers may help their babies survive in hostile environments, whereas permissive, *laissez-faire* mothers may encourage their children to be curious and exploratory, allowing them to learn much about their environment and enabling them to cope with new and challenging situations. 'On this view there is no best mothering style, for different styles are better in different circumstances, and natural selection would act to favour individuals with a range of potential styles from which they select appropriately' (1982: 71).

Clearly there are issues around the extent to which the strength of attachment to a parent alone determines a child's responses to strange situations and new opportunities. But it seems well demonstrated that children are biologically inclined to seek an attachment to an adult, though there can be no guarantees about the quality of the relationship with that adult. Furthermore, the child is able to read the signals sent out by her primary caregiver and she soon knows whether acceptance and concern are to be any part of the relationship.

The Quality of Interaction

Perhaps surprising at first glance, it seems that feeding and physical care do not in themselves promote attachment, nor does the amount of time spent with someone (Ainsworth, 1973; Bowlby, 1969). What does seem to be of critical importance is the *quality of interaction*. And a key element in this interaction is the sensitivity and accuracy with which a mother or father can read the infant's signals. Adults who are *interested* in the infant, *comfort* him or her and engage in *active* and *reciprocal* interaction are most likely to become that child's attachment figure. Fathers out at work all day may come home and play with their daughters in a way that the child finds exciting and stimulating. Mothers can spend time talking *with* their child and show a great interest in what he or she can do. In general, children become attached to those who are attentive, responsive and sensitive. Such parents can 'tune in' to the child's thoughts and feelings; they are able to discriminate between the baby's various physical needs and moods. The quality and strength of attachment are therefore a product of the infant's genetically laid-down predisposition to relate and the quality of relationships actually experienced. 'Human infants,' observes Bowlby (1988: 9), 'are preprogrammed to develop in a socially co-operative way; whether they do so or not turns in high degree on how they are treated.'

Rutter (1980: 272), in his review of babies' crying illustrates these points nicely. 'Probably,' he says, 'optimal responsiveness does not consist of an unthinking and undiscriminating rushing to the baby every time it cries. Babies' cries are of several quite different kinds . . . and it may be that it is the parents' ability to discriminate between these and to respond appropriately which is important.' Similarly, the way a mother responds to her baby's smiles and babbles is important. The reciprocal nature of their interaction generates a 'dialogue' of mutual interest and stimulation. Each responds to the other; each attempts to read the other's thoughts and feelings; and when mutual recognition and understanding take place, there is pleasure and comfort, an overall feeling of satisfaction and security.

Early Dialogue

The sensitive mother tends to regulate her behaviour so that it co-ordinates with that of her baby. Her movements are slightly slowed down; her voice is softer and in a higher pitch. So, although she lets her baby call the tune, her own responses are skilfully interwoven with those of the infant to create a dialogue. Indeed, claims Bowlby (1988: 7), 'The speed and efficiency with which these dialogues develop and the mutual enjoyment they give point clearly to each participant being preadapted to engage in them.' As the baby matures, not only is the mother adapting her responses to those of her child, but the child increasingly takes note of what the mother is saying and doing, thinking and feeling. Experiences become shared, feelings are validated, and the baby feels accepted. The world becomes a safe place in which needs are recognized, understood and met. There is a growing confidence in one's own self-esteem and ability to cope.

> One of the first things that is required in social communication is for you to be sure that your partner is actually attending to you and is involved in communication with you. Are you listening? Do you see what I see? Do you see what I mean? Clearly this degree of intersubjectivity is not present in the newborn and will take many months to develop. But within weeks of birth one can observe its beginnings. There are long sequences of interaction where the first fumbling links of intersubjectivity are made. The infant looks at the caretaker's face. The caretaker looks back into the eyes of the infant. A smiles moves on the infant's face. The adult responds with a vocal greeting and a smile. There is mutual social acknowledgement. The 'meaning' of this exchange does not simply depend on the action patterns employed by the two participants. Each must fit his sequence of actions with that of the other; if this is not done, the exchange may well become meaningless. An important means of knowing that a message is intended for you is that it follows an alternating sequence with yours. (Richards, 1974: 92)

The Quality of Experience and the Ability to Cope

In physiological terms, we are describing a brain which is programmed to establish attachments via the interactional stimulus of relating with other people. However, the actual construction of the neuronal struc-tures that secure satisfactory models of oneself in relationship to other

people only form as the infant actually experiences other people and
his or her relationship with them.

> In order to account for the tendency for patterns of attachment increas-
> ingly to become a property of the child himself, attachment theory invokes
> the concept of working models of self and of parents ... The working
> models a child builds of his mother and her ways of communicating and
> behaving towards him, and a comparable model of his father, together
> with the complementary models of himself in interaction with each, are
> being built by a child during the first few years of his life and, it is
> postulated, soon become established as influential cognitive structures.
> (Bowlby, 1988: 129)

These models might be modified and updated with further experience, but the early neuronal patterns that form to model the world
and handle future experience tend to shape the individual's perceptions and understanding. In other words, the individual begins to
make sense of people and things in terms of those structures of the
brain that have been fashioned in the face of previous experiences of
people and things.

The wider purpose lying behind the disposition to form attachments
is to encourage the child to explore the world so that he or she may
learn skills and understandings that will fit him or her to cope and
survive. Securely attached children have a safe base from which to
explore, but those whose attachments are less secure develop models
of themselves and their relationships with others which are less
coherent. New experiences are less easily accommodated and understood, and so exploration of the new remains a potentially distressing
experience and there is a reluctance to pursue strange, but possibly
stimulating, encounters. So, for example:

> In the case of the anxiously attached child ... this gradual up-dating of
> models is in some degree obstructed through defensive exclusion of discre-
> pant experience and information. This means that the patterns of inter-
> action to which models lead, having become habitual, generalized, and
> largely unconscious, persist in a more or less uncorrected and unchanged
> state even when the individual in later life is dealing with persons who
> treat him in ways entirely unlike those that his parents adopted when he
> was a child. (Bowlby, 1988: 130)

Josephine Klein (1987) offers an interesting line of thought in her
attempts to link the properties of the central nervous system, infant
experiences and the evolving structures of the maturing brain in the
field of human relationships.

She describes two kinds of changes which affect the neural pathways
of the brain (1987: 41-4). The first involves the environment

stimulating the senses of the individual. Light might enter the eye, sound the ear, touch the hand. The resulting nerve impulses travel from the eye, ear or hand and enter the brain where the experience is perceived. When the stimulus stops, so does the experience. In this way, the environment affects the processes of the brain and so may exert control over the individual.

The other kind of change takes place when certain nerve cells and the synapses between them are in constant communication with one another, busy processing perceptions, constantly trying to make sense of experiences. With increasing use, permanent neuronal structures become established in those busy bits of the brain. In this way, regularly experienced perceptions can be processed, modelled and ordered more efficiently – there is an increase in 'facilitation'. The brain makes sense of the familiar experience in terms of the conceptual models (stored in the biological hardware of the brain's nerve cells) it has already established in the light of past experiences:

> [The] difference, between fleeting and more enduring changes in the nervous system, make it possible for more central dominance to emerge. Central dominance, from this perspective, accounts for the relatively slight effect made by fleeting changes – particular messages being sent along at any moment of perception – on the more enduring structures which are slowly being built up in the course of facilitation, and confirmed by reverberation. This is how the organism controls its own behaviour, instead of being controlled by environmental stimuli only. Enduring changes in the pathways affect the reception and organization of subsequent messages, more than these later messages affect the existing organization. (Klein, 1987: 41)

Klein goes on to announce that central control represents a victory of the organism over the environment. Leslie (1991) suggests a distinction between what he calls 'primary representation' and 'meta-representation'. Primary representations are the direct experiences of the world which the brain stores. The information is literal; it helps the individual survive. For example, it is useful to know that lions are liable to eat you and that what you now face is a lion: better take evasive action.

Meta-representations operate differently. The brain is also capable of constructing conceptual models of the world; it is prone to hypothesize about events; it can make abstract descriptions of people and situations. As well as being modelled, the environment (including other people) can be *anticipated* and manipulated. Meta-representation is less a description of the world as actually experienced and more a device for *organizing experience* and representing possible situations.

Meta-representation is how we represent mental states. It is the basis on which we develop theories of other people's minds. Without a capacity for meta-representations, a child could not have a theory of other minds, although she would be able to cope with the world literally, behaviourally and concretely. The capacity to model and conceptually represent the world, particularly other people and their mental states, is thought by many to be part of our biological pre-programming.

> Here's what I would have done if I had been faced with this problem in designing *Homo sapiens*. I would have made a knowledge of commonsense *Homo sapiens* psychology *innate*; that way nobody would have to spend time learning it ... The empirical evidence that God did it the way I would have isn't, in fact, unimpressive ... Suffice it that (1) Acceptance of some form of intentional explanation appears to be a cultural universal. There is, so far as I know, no human group that doesn't explain behaviour by imputing beliefs and desires to the behaviour. (And if an anthropologist claimed to have found such a group, I wouldn't believe him.) (2) At least in our culture, much of the apparatus of mentalistic explanation is apparently operative quite early. (Fodor, 1987: 132–3)

Once the individual can begin to conceptualize the environment and gain central control, he or she can begin to use the environment for his or her own purpose. The brain is able to free itself from having to respond immediately afresh to new stimuli. Increasingly the young child can begin to model the environment (which includes other people) in its brain, analysing, anticipating and planning as it engages with the world. Action becomes increasingly thought out and planned in the light of past experience. And new experiences (meeting people, dealing with situations, sorting out things) are perceived using the structures already established through past experiences. Moreover, as our experience increases, our maps and models grow more clear, more structured, more defined. The corollary of this, though, is that each new experience has less impact on our increasingly established concep-tual (and neural) structures. The structures which formed as a result of past experiences then organize and shape present experiences.

> To sum up so far, structural changes produce enduring concepts, and perhaps quite elaborate structures of ideas and feelings which give meaning to much that happens. One consequence of such structures is to make it possible for us to expect events to happen which have not happened yet. Expectations can cause a message to get organized in a more powerful way than the message would warrant if the structures had not already become established, and in a more powerful way than other messages coming in at the same time. Expectations give meaning to current events. (Klein, 1987: 43)

Infants who have not had regular and assimilable experiences in particular areas of their life fail to develop coherent and integrated structures. In those particular areas, they are less robust. They do not have the neural or conceptual structures which allow them to cope with new situations in an enquiring, relaxed and eager fashion. There is no firm base from which to constructively explore fresh encounters, demanding events, promising opportunities.

Feel Secure, Then Explore

Experience tells us that loving relationships and deep attachments are important to most of us in adult life. We continue to seek out and value those who give us warm, close and supportive relationships. They offer a haven in times of stress and worry. They provide a safe place where we can take stock. They act as a sounding board when we need to think aloud and make new plans.

Now all this sounds very like the secure base sought by the infant when he or she wishes to explore the world beyond the mother or father. And indeed, this is exactly how a number of researchers and psychologists see it. 'The relationship that a child develops with his mother,' write Parkes and Stevenson-Hinde (1982: ix), 'is seen as a complex interweaving of reciprocal expectations and behaviours that forms a starting point for later relationships.' Adults who wish to examine their actions, their feelings and their experiences value a relationship in which they feel secure, warm and accepted. In such a relationship it feels safe to explore feelings and to think aloud. 'In short,' concludes Rutter (1980: 275), 'there is abundant evidence that social bonds continue to play an important role throughout the whole of life. In many respects these adult ties seem to share many of the properties of infantile attachments but systematic comparisons are lacking.'

In spite of the uncertainties of the evidence, Bowlby is in no doubt about the significance of the similarities between the nature and purpose of secure attachments in childhood and the value placed on warm, accepting and trusting relationships in adulthood in general and therapeutic relationships in particular. Unless a therapist can make the patient feel secure, therapy cannot even begin. The therapist must provide the patient with a secure base.

In providing his patient with a secure base from which to explore and express his thoughts and feelings the therapist's role is analogous to that of a mother who provides her child with a secure base from which to explore the world. The therapist strives to be reliable, attentive, and sympathetically responsive to his patient's explorations and, so far as he can, to see and feel the world through his patient's eyes, namely be empathetic. (Bowlby, 1988: 140)

The neurophysiological structures laid down in the early, sensitive and critical years of infancy are those which adults have to use when they need to tackle new situations or when they are faced with uncertainty. When the world is unknown or feels hostile, we too, as adults, need to establish a safe base from which to explore, a place to which we can return after making emotional and even intellectual forays. If the patient feels secure, not only will she have the courage to explore her own emotions and relationships, she will allow previously unacknowledged feelings to surface and become available for consideration. So before a step can be taken along the road of exploration, a strong sense of warmth and trust, interest and attention, care and concern, must be experienced in the counselling relationship.

Patients who have had insecure attachments in childhood may be very alert to any possible lack of interest on the part of the therapist. They will be apprehensive about criticism or possible rejection. In conversation, we need to have the other recognize, acknowledge and convey that he or she has understood what we have said before we feel able to move on. Failure to receive such recognition is upsetting; we feel devalued, our talk slows up, and we cease to explore. Unsatisfactory therapeutic relationships contain all the features of anxious and insecure attachments. Both the infant and the adult client find that their emotional energy is spent on watching and trying to manage the erratic and insensitive relationship, leaving little over for more constructive pursuits.

Analogies are hard to find, risky and rarely exact in this field, but counselling and therapy are rather like trying to modify a vehicle so that it can cope with more rugged country, perhaps run further and generally behave in a more versatile fashion. Such modifications are difficult to achieve out in the open country with only a limited set of tools on board. Indeed, it may be unwise and even scary to start tampering with the machinery when you are a long way from home and in a demanding environment. The safest thing to do is for the vehicle to return to the kind of setting in which it was originally constructed. There it can be taken apart, examined, redesigned, new bits added, old bits taken away. Reflection and experimentation can take place without any fear of being stranded or distressed. The setting has all the right materials both to take the design apart and to put it back together again. It is the environment in which the vehicle was created and it is the environment to which it must return if reforms are to be made.

If we are to examine and change the way we understand ourselves, we need to admit feelings, take off masks and let down defences. We are only likely to allow ourselves to become vulnerable in relationships which offer both protection and opportunities to learn. Counsellors and therapists who behave like inconsistent, uninterested, distant and unloving parents fail to provide a relationship in which the client feels safe. They promote anxiety and ambivalence. In such relationships, no work is done, no explorations are made, and no change occurs.

PART II: UNDERSTAND ME

5 Understanding People

The broad message from the consumers of therapy and counselling is that it is therapeutic and comforting to believe that another person understands what you are feeling and that he or she has an inkling of what you are going through. Much of what clients had to say in earlier chapters was suffused with the desire to be understood. In this chapter we tease out the experience in order to highlight its central importance in the therapeutic process.

Understanding, or empathy, is one of the original core conditions along with acceptance and congruence. Empathic understanding requires that the client is understood in his or her own terms. Patricia illustrates the effectiveness of being understood. She suffered vaginitis. However, in spite of some anxieties, Patricia felt that her ego received a boost when a young man became her boyfriend. But she did not feel able to sleep with him and eventually he walked out on her:

> I was heart-broken, and my vaginitis got ten times worse. It was at this point that my GP sent me to a therapist – thank goodness! For the first time, I felt that here was a person who really understood. She gave me a series of accounts written by women who have been through the research study into psychosomatic vaginitis. They described how they had felt and how their condition had improved. I read them the night I got them after a really depressed, painful day. In five minutes the fog in my head had lifted and the pain in my vagina had disappeared. It came back intermittently during the next few days, but I was so happy. I already felt a new person. (Woodward, 1988: 107–8)

The good therapist, as defined by users, attempts to enter the frame of reference of her client. In this way she might gain a sense of what it might feel like to be in that kind of pain, distress or muddle. One client said, 'I sort of felt, well, somebody understands and they're interested and they want to help and they don't think it's silly' (Mayer and Timms, 1970: 84). Another described how she found, to her surprise, that she couldn't stop talking once she recognized that her therapist had 'sort of lost' himself

> and climbed into my shoes with me to see how things looked to me . . .
> My main reaction to the first session was surprise . . . just plain surprise!

I was so utterly surprised to find that someone was really and truly *understanding* what I was trying to say. I always have such difficulty saying what I want to say. (Fitts, 1965: 26–7, emphasis in original)

What the counsellor must not do is impose her own ideas of what the experience should mean to the client. In summing up her experiences of therapy, Veronique said:

So it has been really a bit at a time, becoming in touch with these feelings, with someone who understood, was clear, took the time that I needed, was always active – and that is one of the things that I think is wonderful, he has not been one of those analysts who sit back and say nothing, but always full of intelligent, imaginative ways of understanding things. (Dinnage, 1989: 82)

Showing Interest

Many clients believe that understanding first requires the counsellor to be 'interested' in them and their worries. 'She'd sit down,' said Mrs Sanders, 'and she'd take the trouble to find out what was the matter with you. She was very – interested.' And then, speaking of her young daughter's death in a street accident outside her front door, she continued:

It was Carole who helped me – she *wanted* to be with me, and she was there at my command. She shared all our troubles with us. She felt it as much as I felt it. If she hadn't have been there, I don't know what would have happened – I think I'd have just gone mad. But she helped us carry on. She really pulled us through. (Sainsbury, 1975: 53–4)

Kline et al. (1974), after interviewing patients who had received therapy, learned that accurate insight and the perceived interest shown in them by the therapist were two of the three most important ingredients identified by the patients in the psychotherapeutic process.

Conversely, a lack of interest revealed a lack of understanding according to many clients. This often led to anger and resentment which eventually resulted in the termination of contact (Mayer and Timms, 1970: 75). This was the conclusion reached by Mrs Pound after a few sessions of family therapy:

I thought I weren't getting anywhere with any of them so I stopped going. I was upset, you know, I was actually angry to think I did ask for help and got nothing that I did feel helped. I did feel that this meeting as a family and everything was an interest of theirs, you know, something they liked doing. I didn't feel they really took any notice of how I was feeling . . . I feel they blamed me all the time. I know I'm not perfect. *I* know that, but they never got down to how any of us was . . . I felt misunderstood. Even now I feel upset about everything . . . I'm sorry . . . [Mrs Pound cried, and then after a few moments she recovered enough to continue] . . . In the past, there was one helpful one. He did make me feel as he understood. If you had a problem he would listen, you know, as if he was really interested, like he could follow exactly what it was you were thinking. (Howe, 1989a: 72)

Lietaer and Neirnick (cited in McLeod, 1990: 15) asked clients in client-centred therapy to write down what they thought might have hindered progress in the session just completed. Three types of hindering event were recognized, including the failure of the therapist to understand what the client was feeling. McLeod (1990: 15) reviews the findings in these words:

> First, clients felt that things went badly when they did not co-operate with the therapist by being silent, by talking superficially or by not daring to talk about some things. Secondly, problems in the relationship between therapist and client were seen as a hindrance (for example, the therapist not being warm enough, confronting too much or too little, not valuing or accepting the client enough). Thirdly, clients found it unhelpful when their therapists made interventions which took them off their own 'track', when the therapist said things that 'did not feel right'.

Some clients recognized that their counsellors were not only able to understand feelings but were also willing to carry on learning from clients. In this way the counsellors became even more effective in understanding people and their feelings. Mary had given up her baby for adoption 19 years before. The loss still pained her:

> I have always felt that the workers I know at the Centre have a greater understanding of the complex of emotions connected with being a birth mother than anyone else I have met, but they were still willing to learn from us. They never treated me as a client but have helped me feel more sure of myself and less degraded by what I have done. (Howe, 1989b: 23)

When the therapist fails to understand, does not even attempt to understand, or even imposes her own explanation on the meaning of the other's experience, the client's sense of isolation increases. There is no one with whom the feelings can be shared. They remain unspoken and locked away, unavailable for examination. 'No matter how I put it,' said Mrs East, whose husband evidenced symptoms of mental illness, 'I felt she didn't understand what it was like to live with a man like my husband' (Mayer and Timms, 1970: 73). Feelings have to be talked about; they should be described. Feeling that someone understands encourages you to talk more, and talking is the first step that the client has to take if she is to make sense of her own experience. As the therapist attempts to understand the client, so the client begins to understand herself. Conversely, therapists who do not attempt to understand the experience of the other frustrate that person's ability to understand herself.

Defining the Client's Experience

Imposing explanations rather than trying to see the world from the other's point of view strangles reflection and frustrates the struggle of the other to make sense of what is happening. In the following extract a counsellor honestly reflects on how theory got in the way of practice as she tried to impose her interpretation of how she thought the client ought to be feeling:

> I remember working with a recently 'separated' woman client. I kept waiting and expecting to see some element of sadness or loss or depression – but none came. I kept thinking that I saw hints of such emotions, but she denied these. So then I began to think that she must be blocking all these things, and I tried to help her to find ways through these blocks. I think I got pretty fed up with that. It was only after some weeks of distinctly inaccurate empathy that I realized that what was getting in the way was my personal theory on what recently separated people felt: that they would feel sad/lost/depressed. It had been extremely difficult for me to see this lively cheery woman who wanted a little bit of assistance with restructuring a new set of elements in her life. (Mearns and Thorne, 1988: 55)

The next quote reveals how desperate a client can feel when she is not understood:

> It had nearly come to blows between Dean and me. For me it was getting to be, you know, a really big problem. I couldn't stop thinking about it and it was getting all wound up . . . I was so distressed. But that family therapy never really got on to how I was really feeling, that I couldn't handle it no more. More than anything I just wanted to sit down and talk with someone 'cos that would have helped, you know, but it wasn't like that. You had to . . . er . . . like, listen to them. They never listened to you as such. I just felt lost; upset you know. It was hopeless really. (Howe, 1989a: 70)

Sarah had a similar wish to be understood, though she, too, was disappointed with her psychotherapist:

> it was all a question of being understood. I was trying to get across a lot about my mother, about how disturbed I was and that she had to do something about it, and also that I was longing for closeness, really, which she was afraid of. I mean, she was always telling me I was attacking the breast, and how destructive . . . But it didn't mean anything to me. Maybe I was attacking the breast, but it wasn't really the point . . . I feel sad about

her. You see, I think if you're understood, you don't need to act out in that violent way. If you're *really* understood, if someone is hearing your anger, then you don't need to. (Dinnage, 1989: 174–5)

Experiences in Common

However, there is one group of people who always seem to be able to understand – fellow sufferers, people who have undergone a similar experience. Self-help and support groups provide a ready and powerful source of understanding, and it is no surprise that such groups have had a long and significant tradition in the realms of counselling and therapy. Meeting other woman who had relinquished a child for adoption, one mother said, 'I no longer felt alone. I discovered that other people too have this monstrous pain to bear and they knew how I felt' (Howe et al., 1992: 120). And another woman who had been depressed recalled:

> They helped me get over the depression by bringing me together with other mums, who's got other problems, and you realize that you're not the only person in the world with a problem. We used to have small groups for talking about our problems. I think in a way the other mothers are more understanding, because probably most of the social workers haven't been through a lot of the things that they've been through. (Phillimore, 1981: 22)

Confidence, Control and Communication

With understanding comes confidence, and the burgeonings of a sense of being able to control one's own experience. Describing his experiences of psychotherapy, Mark said:

> The early sessions were characterized by my feelings of discomfort and embarrassment. What I found, however, was a person who was listening to what I was saying and seemed to understand some of the pain I was experiencing. A feeling of space began to emerge in the sessions; a sense that I was an important person in the relationship, and that I had some control both over the discussion and the pace of it. (Woodward, 1988: 92)

Empathy and understanding correlate highly with effective counselling. Researchers have put a great deal of effort into understanding clients' experiences of empathy, and much work has been carried out analysing the psychotherapeutic process and its empathic content.

Barrett-Lennard (1986: 446) has distinguished three phases in the empathic sequence. In phase one, there is 'empathic resonance' by the therapist to particular expressed and implied experiences of the client. In phase two, the therapist communicates his or her understanding to the client. And in phase three, the client senses the degree to which the therapist is actually attuned to his or her thoughts and feelings. Thus empathy, if it is to be helpful, appears to require both an accurate understanding of the client's experience *and* the communication of that understanding.

6 Knowing Other Minds

Those on the receiving end of therapy are quite clear that being understood by another is helpful. It is reassuring; it clears confusion and points the way forward. But *how* does one human being understand the thoughts and feelings of another? Indeed, *why* should we bother to understand the experiences of our fellows and why should it matter to us whether or not we in turn are understood? Why should being understood by another be something which is both sought and found to be helpful? On the face of it, what does it matter if you understand that I feel angry or confused? Of course, it might make a difference if you could then do something about it – perhaps suggest a way in which I might take revenge on the person who has made me angry or give me information that helps clear my confusion. But that is not what clients are saying. Simply to have one's feelings recognized and understood by another is something which is desired, valued and effective. Why should this be so?

Human beings spend a lot of time thinking and talking about what other people might be feeling, intending, planning, imagining. 'What do you think she's really up to?' 'I wonder how he is feeling now that she's left him.' Such wonderings can spiral into highly complex forms. 'What do they think I'm thinking?' 'I think that he thinks that I'm sulking, which is untrue, which makes me cross.' However, the intriguing thing is not just the knots into which people sometimes tie themselves, but to wonder why they bother worrying about what other people are thinking anyway.

We might, therefore, want to ask two questions about the universal practice in which human beings ponder the thoughts and feelings, intentions and beliefs of other human beings:

1 *Why* should we want to know what another person might be thinking and feeling? This question is rarely asked, but when posed it stimulates a burst of unexpected ideas.
2 *How* do we know (or think we know) the mental state of other people? This is the question asked most often. It is generally to be found in discussions about empathy and how to improve it.

Is it really possible, in fact, to understand another's experience, or is it just an illusion? Consider, for a moment, the behaviour of fish that swim together in large numbers. Shoals of fish dart and turn in split-second unison. Does each fish understand instantly the mood and intentions of all the others? Is there some form of telepathy occurring between them? Does the lead fish communicate its intentions very rapidly to the rest of the shoal? Or is the same external signal read by all fish at the same time in the same manner, producing the impression of rapid communication rather than a common response? It could be that, like the fish, the empathic other is simply reading the situation in exactly the same way as me, and she therefore 'knows' what I am feeling because she is programmed to feel the same way under similar circumstances. She is not understanding my experience in some direct, telepathic sense, but she is recognizing how she would feel in that situation.

Being understood by other people, and turning to others for sympathy and understanding, is such a universally recognized practice that it has attracted the attention of thinkers across the intellectual spectrum. Many disciplines have thought about how we might know other minds, how we might understand what someone else is thinking and feeling. Philosophers have contemplated the problem of knowing other minds for centuries. Psychologists have examined our perceptual skills in interpersonal behaviour. The social origins of self have impressed sociologists. Therapists know that tuning into the experiences of the client is a good thing but rarely go beyond recommending lots of it.

Over this and the next four chapters I want to outline a number of ideas which consider how one person might be able to understand the thoughts and feelings of another. Three broad methods of knowing other minds have been advanced:

One is metaphysical and believes that human beings have a deep-seated ability to commune directly with the experience of another. Biological or physical perceptions are not necessary. If we are able to allow ourselves to open up our being to the spirit and experience of another, we might know them directly.

The second is based on the quality of our physical perceptions of the world around us, particularly the world of people. Acute and sensitive observation of another provides strong evidence of their mental condition. The observer attends to and analyses the words and actions of the other.

The third is sociological. It recognizes that the 'self' emerges out of and develops within a shared social world. Our character and emotional make-up are constructed within a common matrix of social interaction.

In practice, these three methods can be mixed in a number of ways.

Some combinations emphasize the importance of alert physical observations; others are struck by the part that social experience plays in the formation of self and go on to examine the relationship between mind and society. I shall recognize four types of practitioner: the metaphysician, the social self, the resonator and the interpreter. As we move through the four practices, the shift is from direct to indirect ways of knowing other minds: from the perceptual and psychological to the social.

The Metaphysicians

When trying to explain how they understand the other person, most counsellors and therapists plump for the possession of a heightened set of perceptual skills. But there are exceptions. There is a tendency among the more mystically inclined to go for a less material explanation. Rather than alert observation, it is suggested that the most fundamental way to understand the mental state of another is to achieve some kind of metaphysical oneness with them. The other is experienced directly from the inside. In this position, I might 'know' you without recourse to physical observation and interpretation. If I can free myself of my own concerns, I can be open to your experience in some direct, non-material way. We might call those who adopt this position the metaphysicians.

Goldstein, for example, writes of 'knowing in internal ways the inner state of others at times without the benefit of specific clues' (1973: 69). There is a communing of spirits in which the other becomes known. This position has similarities with those who studied aesthetics at the turn of the twentieth century. Theodor Lipps, for example, in his investigations of the aesthetic experience believed that the observer of an object had to get on the 'inside' and fully identify with the object in order to appreciate its form and creative history from within. One projected oneself into the object, identified with it and then engaged in a process of inner imitation. In so doing one came to understand and appreciate the object in its own terms. Thus, in an act of empathy the observer could learn to know and understand the object of contemplation from within.

The Social Self

Early ideas about the relevance of the social nature of our selves to the understanding of other people were developed by the German philosopher Max Scheler. As part of his work on 'other minds', he took up the question of how we come to know other people. He rejected the theory of inference which said that we reason by analogy, that what the other person is doing is analogous to our own state of mind in that situation. However, Scheler believed that all the observer is doing in this case is imputing his own feelings to the other; it is a projection of what we in fact should feel in a similar circumstance. It presumes that you are feeling what I imagine I would feel if *I* were in your shoes. It tells us very little of the mental state of the other person, and at best merely encourages us to try to imagine what other people might be feeling in that situation.

Scheler's own account, originally published in 1913, demands that, instead of projecting our feelings on to the other, we 'entertain the experiences of other people as if they were our own' (Scheler, 1954: 246–7). The other's joy or misery, Scheler maintains, is experienced directly by us. Such feelings are given immediately, without recourse to our making interpretations of the other's gestures or words, in a sort of 'inner perception' or 'direct intuition'. We just know what the mood of the other is. And this is possible, Scheler explains, because conscious human beings are creatures who emerge out of a shared matrix.

Some of Scheler's ideas are based in the camp of the metaphysicians, but he does point us in the direction of the next group of theorists. He recognizes that we are social animals and that as self-conscious beings we emerge out of a common social pool. Scheler doubts whether knowledge of the self could ever precede knowledge of the other. The child lives immersed in a world of others. Only slowly does the infant begin to sense that she is the centre of this experience, that she is a separate person, a self:

> Even when we come to integrate our own self – to cut it out of the texture in which it had formed one indistinguishable strand alongside many others – we continue to see it against the background of a surviving, although progressively receding, common consciousness . . . It is this fundamental fact which, according to Scheler, explains our knowledge – our direct knowledge – of the psychic life of our fellow humans . . . *they* live in *us* because ego and non-ego have both emerged out of a common stream of life experience. (Stark, 1954: xxxix–xl)

Each self is formed in a similar social process. I know you because our psychological selves are formed in the same way. Our selves emerge and take on their form as our biology interacts with the surrounding social world. The broad character of our emotions and personality is shaped within the same dense web of shared social life.

Therefore the relationship between your mental states and your actions will, in broad outline, be similar to the relationship between my mental states and my actions. I know you by (1) *observing* your actions, and (2) *recognizing* the origin of their performance. Colloquially, we might say it takes one to know one.

Buber (1953: 249), a humanistic philosopher, said:

> the inmost growth of the self is not accomplished, as people like to suppose today, in man's relation to himself, but in the relations between the one and the other ... in the making present of another self and in the knowledge that one is made present in his own self by the other.

In this sense society is in all of us and it is this which allows us to know other people. Only because of the social formation of self am I able to produce anything of my own that is intelligible to others or, indeed, meaningful even to myself. Meaning is not something that is bestowed on the world by the individual independent of society. What we say means nothing until it means something to other people. This is a cue to introduce the work of Mead.

Mind, Self and Society

The essential features of the social origins of self were mapped out by the social psychologist George Herbert Mead in the 1920s at the University of Chicago. Mead anticipated many of the ideas that now inform this subject. I shall use his insights to consider how one person (one self) might understand another. Mead added a cognitive component in the form of 'an ability to understand' to the already established notion that empathy had an affective element (Goldstein and Michaels, 1985: 4). In the hands of Mead, 'empathy was no longer viewed as purely a perceptual awareness of an individual's affect or sharing of feeling, but rather an ability to understand a person's emotional reactions in consort with the context' (Deutsch and Madle, 1975: 270).

How do we become aware of ourselves? How do we become self-conscious? How does mind arise? Answers to questions such as these start us on the road towards explaining our apparent ability to achieve some understanding of the other's experience. In Mead's view, it was insufficient to say that a discrete individual, simply by virtue of being, became self-conscious. It was felt that language and the responses of other people are fundamental and critical if the individual is to develop self-awareness. Mead outlined how the entire self emerges out of social processes. The individual, of course, needs to be physiologically disposed towards the actions and conduct of others. It is in relation to other people that the growing individual's awareness of self is achieved. So, although the self needs a biological base which inclines the individual towards investigating the outside world, it is only by adapting itself to the environment and learning to control key aspects of this external world that the human organism begins to identify itself as subject.

The self becomes aware of itself *as it is* constituted in the flow of human intercourse. Human beings are creatures who constantly shape their actions in adjustment to others. Central to this process of mutual adjustment is social communication. The individual, who is also a member of the social group, constantly monitors the actions of others in the group as well as the group itself, and uses this information to get a picture of her own behaviour and what it is currently 'meaning' in the social group. The next action therefore depends on how both the group and the self have been understood by the individual.

As it receives sensory inputs from the external world, the individual organism becomes aware of its existence and what it means in the social schemes of things. As the individual is acted upon and in turn acts upon others, he or she becomes increasingly aware of himself or herself as a centre of experience. *The self emerges in its reflexive relationship with society.* Consciousness and action are closely linked; in engaging with the world of others we gain an understanding of ourselves. As the individual reflects on the possible meanings of the actions and communications of the other in order to produce an appropriate response of his or her own, the individual begins to consider himself or herself as the other would. The individual begins to respond to the self as a social object and thus takes the attitude of others towards that self.

> He becomes a self in so far as he can take the attitude of another and act toward himself as others act . . . It is the social process of influencing others in a social act and then taking the attitude of the others aroused by the stimulus, and then reacting in turn to this response, which constitutes a self. (Mead, 1934: 171)

Self-consciousness emerges out of this social process. The individual becomes self-aware, first by understanding the rules of the situation, secondly by seeking to make sense of other people's actions, and finally by attempting to fit her own responses within the overall context as she has interpreted it. The child begins to take the generalized attitude of the group towards her own self and so becomes able to treat her own self as an object. In responding to herself as others would, the individual becomes self-aware:

> We are conscious of our attitudes because they are responsible for the changes in the conduct of other individuals. A man's reaction towards weather conditions has no influence upon the weather itself . . . Successful social conduct brings one into a field within which a consciousness of one's own attitudes helps towards the control of the conduct of others (Mead, 1910: 131)

> The individual experiences himself as such, not directly, but only indirectly, from the standpoint of other individual members of the same social group, or from the generalized standpoint of the social group as a whole to which he belongs. For he enters his own experience as a self or individual, not directly or immediately, not by becoming a subject to himself, but only in so far as he first becomes an object to himself as other individuals are objects to him or in his experience; and he becomes an object to himself only by taking the attitudes of other individuals toward himself within a social environment or context of experience and behaviour in which both he and they are involved. (Mead, 1934: 138)

It is impossible to conceive of a self arising outside of social experience, says Mead, although once it has formed, a self can be solitary. 'The biography of the individual,' proclaim Peter and Brigitte Berger (1981: 57), 'from the moment of birth, is the story of his relations with others.'

The sum of the experiences which the individual acquires as she assumes the attitudes of others, both specifically and generally, form the social self – 'me' in Mead's terms. However, Mead believes that the individual is more than a passive reflection of society. As the self emerges, it can also recognize itself and behave independently, even though its origins and character lie within the structure of social interactions. This is the 'I', the self that is aware of who it is and where it wants to go, the self which can act on society in an independent fashion and thus change the social structure as well as be formed by it. Thus, the self is both a subject and an object. The 'I' is the subject which thinks and acts. The 'me' is the individual's awareness of self as an object in the world. The 'me' is the self which exists for others and the thing with which others act and interact (Swingewood, 1984: 268). 'Me' is what is known; 'I' is the knower (Cashmore and Mullen, 1983: 78).

It will be apparent, then, that as the self is constructed out of the activity of social life, all selves, at a given time and in a given place, are formed within a similar social matrix. As we develop, we take the role of others. We emerge as we see ourselves from the perspective of others; we form our awareness of self as we develop a dialogue with everyday social life. We are not born with a sense of self and an independent frame of mind, as many have argued; rather we gain mind and self as we interact with other people.

> What goes to make up the organized self is the organization of the attitudes which are common to the group. A person is a personality because he belongs to a community, because he takes over the institutions of that community into his own conduct. He takes its language as a medium by which he gets his personality, and through a process of taking the different roles that all the others furnish he comes to get the attitude of the members of the community. Such, in a certain sense, is the structure of a man's personality. There are certain common responses which each individual has toward certain common things, and in so far as those common responses are awakened in the individual when he is affecting other persons he arouses his own self. The structure, then, on which the self is built is this response which is common to all, for one has to be a member of a community to be a self. (Mead, 1934: 162)

A community of meaning establishes itself as people go about the business of social life. We understand each other because our selves arise out of the same community of others.

The Resonators

Much of the early thinking about the theory and practice of empathy in counselling was pioneered by Carl Rogers. The basic notion that we understand other people by understanding our selves was outlined and developed in a number of ground-breaking studies in the 1950s and 1960s. For example, Mearns and Thorne, modern exponents of person-centred counselling, describe empathy as the ability to step into another person's shoes and see the world through his or her eyes but without ever losing touch with one's own reality. They go on to say:

> Such a capacity is likely to be fostered by making the deliberate effort to move outside the confines of one's own normal social environment or subgroup. The counsellor does well to encounter those of whom she has little knowledge or those by whom she feels threatened or intimidated . . . Parochialism is the enemy of empathy but is as much a matter of attitude as of geography. Essentially it is the imagination which needs to be stimulated and enriched if the counsellor's empathic ability is to be improved. (Mearns and Thorne, 1988: 27)

Person-centred counsellors, including Rogers, define empathy as the ability not only to sensitively understand the experience of the other but also to communicate that understanding: 'detecting and describing', in the words of Danish and Kagan (1971); 'accurate reception . . . complemented by accurate feedback', according to Keefe (1976: 12–13). However, the full flowering of the definition is to be found in the writings of a number of authors, the earliest of which is *Listening with the Third Ear*, written by Theodor Reik in 1949. Like Mead, he believes that the concept of 'self' develops out of our infant relationships with other people. This may account for our capacity to know other people and it explains 'how one mind speaks to another beyond words and in silence' (Reik, 1964: 144). Indeed, anticipating advances in the neurophysiological sciences described in Chapter 8, Reik believes that the 'gift for psychological observation' is 'as inborn as a musical sense. . . Where it is not present, nothing will produce it' (Reik, quoted by Hannon, 1968: 159). A number of people have picked up these ideas and refined them (for example, Keefe, 1976; Goldstein and Michaels, 1985).

Four stages are identified as we attempt to 'comprehend the inner processes of others':

1 *Observation and identification.* The patient's gestures, expressions and speech 'communicate to us the vital expression of what he is feeling and thinking' (Reik, 1964: 132). There is accurate perception of the other's behaviour and an 'accurate understanding of the meanings of the other person's messages' (Keefe, 1979: 30).

2 *Incorporation.* Having gained a picture of the other, much of it at a preconscious level, we can absorb and assimilate the details into our own ego. This is 'the act of taking the experience of the other into ourselves' (Katz, 1963: 42).

3 *Reverberation.* Once in the unconscious, the counsellor 'resonates with the other's experience and feels an experience of his own, that is real for him, but which has arisen in reverberation to the condition of the other' (Reik, 1964: 353). We 'vibrate unconsciously in the rhythm of the other person.' Our mind acts like a tuning fork which begins to resonate to the observed condition of the other. Or, in the words of Katz: 'What we have taken into ourselves now echoes upon some part of our own experience and awakens a new appreciation' (1963: 44). Having perceived and absorbed information about the other, there is an unconscious sharing of emotions and the counsellor allows 'direct feeling responses to arise' (Keefe, 1976: 12).

4 *Detachment.* In this last stage, the professional observer withdraws, and regains the psychic distance necessary for objective analysis.

He reviews what he has experienced as he has taken up the thoughts and feelings of the other. And finally the other person is given 'accurate feedback'; the understanding reached is sensitively communicated.

In short, this means that the counsellor must experience *what* the client is feeling (identification), feel the client's experience *as if it* were his own (incorporation), evoke those life experiences of his own that may aid in understanding his client's experiences (reverberation), and engage in objective analysis using methods of reason (detachment) (Lide, 1966: 148).

There is still a strong suspicion that in some direct way the other person's mental state is knowable. It is assumed that, in Reik's phrase, the other's words and deeds 'communicate to us the vital expression of what he is feeling and thinking'. The empathizer is advised that she should be 'adept at reading nonverbal communication and interpreting the feelings underlying it' (Macarov, 1978: 88).

Mearns and Thorne (1988: 40) explain that, in empathizing with a client, the counsellor leaves aside her own frame of reference and for a time adopts the frame of reference of her client. 'She can then appreciate how the client experiences the events in his world; indeed she can even sense how he feels about events *as if* these feelings were her own' (emphasis in original). So, although the other's actions have to trigger our own thoughts and feelings, it is assumed that the actions which produce the resonance are in some way accurate clues about the condition of the other. It is the other's experience which is truly affecting our understanding and not some presumed interpretation on our part. A mystery remains. It is assumed that somehow the other's true mental condition is transferred to our minds which we can then contemplate *as if* it were our own. This assumption is not made by the group of theorists that we shall consider next.

The Interpreters

Although Alfred Schutz trod similar ground to that covered in the writings of Mead and Scheler, in many respects he has more in common with those who see interpersonal understanding arising out of our ability to contemplate our own experience. If we know the basis on which our own experiences are understood and gain meaning, we can understand, or at least interpret, the experiences of someone else. Alfred Schutz was not convinced of the ability of one human being to directly understand the experiences of another simply because their conscious selves emerged out of a common social process. Schutz remained fascinated with the uncertainty of human social understanding; he recognized that people seek to interpret other people and their meanings and that we do not necessarily have an intuitive grasp of the mental states of our fellows. As we shall see, this sociological insight, voiced in 1932, presages some of the more recent psychological and neurophysiological theories about the developing child and his or her ability to know other minds. Schutz provides an early, albeit provisional, bridge between mind, self and society.

Schutz categorically rejects the postulate that we can observe the subjective experience of another person precisely as he or she does – he describes it as 'absurd' (1972: 99). It presupposes, he argues, that we must have lived through all the conscious states and intentional acts that help constitute the other's experience. The only way I could truly understand the other's experience is to be that other person. But Schutz is quick to point out that this does not mean that we are forever denied the chance to understand another's experience. 'We are asserting,' continues Schutz (1972: 99), 'neither that your lived experiences remain in principle inaccessible to me nor that they are meaningless to me. Rather, the point is that the meaning I give to your experiences cannot be precisely the same as the meaning you give to them when you proceed to interpret them.' We apprehend the experiences of the other in her words or his actions – their 'field of expression'. I interpret your 'expressions' within my own meaning context. I am always interpreting your lived experience from my own standpoint, and indeed, *'everything I know about your conscious life is really based on my knowledge of my own lived experiences'* (Schutz, 1972: 106, emphasis in original). I can only interpret your lived experience in terms of my lived experience.

Throughout this argument, there is an implied injunction placed on the therapist to 'know thyself' if he or she is to know the other, a requirement familiar to person-centred counsellors as well as analytically trained psychotherapists. There is the presumption that what we see in the other can be compared with what we know of our own actions and behaviour. If we understand the reasons behind our own words and deeds, we might hazard an intelligent guess at what lies behind the actions of another. The intelligent guess at least gives us a starting-point for checking out the other's thoughts and feelings. The idea is that the more aware we are of the relationship between our own feelings, thoughts and actions, the greater will be our ability to *interpret* accurately the emotional and cognitive condition of the other.

What the other person does and says is seen as merely an indication of what might lie behind the deed and the word. It indicates the other's experience. We do not make sense of their experience by putting ourselves and our experience into their situation and imagining how we would feel. Rather we put ourselves in their position *and try to appreciate how they would feel in that situation knowing what we do of the other person and their history.* We still only have the experience of our own mental states to draw upon and guide us, but we use the other's situation and history to imagine how they might feel under those circumstances:

> the observer can draw more reliable conclusions about his subject if he knows something about his past and something about the over-all plan into which the action fits. To come back to Max Weber's example, it would be important for the observer to know whether the woodcutter was at his regular job or just chopping wood for physical exercise. An adequate model of the observed person's subjective experiences calls for just this wider context. (Schutz, 1972: 115–16)

In practice, conversation and social intercourse are even more complicated than this. The other person has her intentions. She may wish me to understand her or she may wish to mislead me, or indeed herself. She will be attempting to read me as I attempt to read her. We may help each other pursue a 'true' understanding of our respective experiences or we may dance around each other's utterances in some convoluted fashion.

However, the point being made is that, though we strive to understand the other person's mind, we can only attempt to know it with reference to our own. We *interpret* the other person's indications of their experience according to our own stock of knowledge. Thus, I can only know you by (1) *observing* your actions, (2) *comparing* them with what I know about the relationship between my own mental states and my actions and behaviour and (3) *interpreting*, on that comparative basis, your observed behaviour and what I know about you in the light of my own experience.

7 Natural Psychologists

Nicholas Humphrey (1986) is not only impressed by the ability of human beings to understand each other's states of mind, but he is also curious about why they should even bother about what other people are thinking and feeling. As he unravels the strands that comprise social behaviour, he finds himself wondering why human beings have minds and self-consciousness. What are they for?

Being a biologist, Humphrey was quite prepared to have his ideas stimulated by any member of the animal kingdom. Gorillas started him thinking. It was while he was studying these apes in their native African jungle that he began to wonder why they had such large brains. Food was plentiful, requiring little effort to collect. The animals did not move around much. Life seemed pleasant and undemanding. Indeed, the only thing that appeared to tax the average gorilla was the behaviour and actions of other average gorillas. The gorillas spent most of their time in the company of other gorillas, eating, grooming, mating, caring. This gave Humphrey his first insight. If the actions and intentions of each gorilla were of concern to other gorillas, then it was in the interests of each ape to develop the capacity to note, anticipate and make sense of the actions of his or her fellow apes. The only problems for gorillas were, therefore, social.

On the whole, these great apes are extremely accomplished at social living. 'They know each other intimately, they know their place. None the less there *are* endless small disputes about social dominance, about who grooms who, about who should have first access to a favourite food, or sleep in the best site' (Humphrey, 1986: 37). These primates are 'social tacticians'. They have sophisticated knowledge of the characteristics of others in the group, 'a flexible capacity to form co-operative alliances with some, so outmanoeuvring others in competition for resources', and a repertoire of tactics for social manipulation (Whiten and Perner, 1991: 3).

Attempting to read the thoughts and intentions of others requires a lot of brain power. Speculating, hypothesizing and reasoning demand complex cognitive procedures, hence the large brains. In evolutionary terms, there must be some advantage in being able to recognize and handle the behaviour of others. And if this is true for gorillas, how much more true for human beings. Humphrey was led to this observation as he reflected on his own personal situation:

I tried to put myself in the gorillas' place, and to imagine what – if anything – might really tax their minds. As I did so I found myself thinking equally about myself. Where did *my* real problems lie? The fact was that I had come to Africa not primarily for scientific reasons, but to escape an impossible human situation back at home. My marriage had broken down; I was deeply involved in an on–off way with another woman . . . My head (when not thinking about gorillas) was full of unresolved problems concerning my own social relationships. That was what I thought about by day and night, what filled my brain and presented me with a host of truly baffling questions. If I do this, what will *she* do? But suppose I did *that*, or if she did something else . . . ? Suddenly I saw the animals with new eyes. I realized that, for them too, their problems were primarily *social* ones. (Humphrey, 1986: 36–7)

As a species, our success has come from the advantages of living and acting co-operatively. Social interdependence allowed us to control our environment. But in order for this to work at an ever more elaborate level, human beings had to become increasingly interested in and concerned with each other's intentions and reactions. Social intelligence, believes Humphrey, is the key to the success of the great apes, chimpanzees and human beings. In order to survive and thrive as a social group, we need to be extremely alert to and adept at managing our relationships with others. There is an evolutionary advantage in being able to understand others and developing skills in social relationships. Therefore, we are psychologists by nature; we are natural psychologists.

We have large brains because we need to understand other people, and we need to understand other people if the evolutionary advantages of living in social groups are to be sustained. By attributing mental states to others we achieve a powerful ability to predict their behaviour. This allows us to work and live together co-operatively. But how are we able to understand other people? This is where Humphrey links together consciousness, social living and reading other minds in his concept of the 'inner eye'.

The Inner Eye

As human beings we do not merely observe and note the behaviour of others, we interpret what people say and do. In their actions and words we see people planning, hoping and seeking. We have ideas about what they are doing and what they are up to. Understanding other people is something we feel we are able to do. Indeed, without the ability, or presumption, to have ideas about other people's intentions and feelings, social life would be almost impossible. This ability is possible, according to Humphrey, because first of all we can observe and monitor our own thought processes. We are aware of ourselves in action. We have a self-consciousness. 'It is as if I, like every other human being, possess a kind of "inner eye", which looks in on my own brain and tells me why and how I'm acting in the way that I am' (Humphrey, 1986: 68). The explanation we have of our own behaviour can then form the basis of explaining other people's behaviour. 'We could, in effect, imagine what it's like to be them, because we know what it's like to be ourselves' (Humphrey, 1986: 71). I presume to make sense of other people's behaviour by knowing what informs my own. I understand you by understanding me.

In common with other biological models, the self, consciousness and mutual understanding are genetically programmed abilities. They are directed outward from the individual and facilitate social life. Indeed, it can be argued that consciousness provides the individual with a more powerful model of others' behaviour (we put ourselves in their shoes) than can be constructed by simply observing their behaviour (Whiten and Perner, 1991: 10).

It is not that we actually ever really know what someone else is thinking or feeling. 'Strictly speaking we have no hard evidence that any of our guesses about the inner life of other people are correct' (Humphrey, 1986: 73). But the biologist in Humphrey cannot really accept that nature is playing some dreadful trick. We all share a similar biology; we all value the presumed ability to understand other minds; the ability seems to confer distinct evolutionary advantages on our species. So, it seems reasonable to assume that for all practical purposes, and for much of the time, we are reading other people sufficiently accurately to make social life work to our collective benefit. The model we have of our own thought processes and feelings is the one we use to attempt to understand what other people might be thinking and feeling. 'Imagine,' says Humphrey,

> the biological benefits to the first of our ancestors that developed the ability to make realistic guesses about the inner life of his rivals; to be able to picture what another was thinking about, and planning to do next, to be able to read the minds of others by reading our own. (1986: 76)

Following the logic of this thesis, Humphrey believes that accumulated experiences increase our self-awareness and therefore improve our ability to understand others. Throughout our lives, especially during childhood, we have to learn for ourselves 'what it feels like from the inside to be a human being', to have a mind.

Around the second year, the child becomes aware of her own thoughts and feelings. She can start to develop a model of how her own mind works, and it is not long before she uses it to make sense of other people, their actions and their words. As her experiences amass, the model of other people's minds becomes more sophisticated and socially useful. The child stocks up on experiences and so comes to know herself and other people better. In the course of human evolution those with the widest possible experience are best prepared to handle social situations. 'In fact, if psychology means survival, and experience means psychology, then experience means survival' (Humphrey, 1986: 102).

The very long childhood of human beings provides the opportunity to develop a stronger and clearer self-consciousness, through experience, so that we can conduct our social relationships with greater skill, sensitivity and effect, which is to the collective advantage. The corollary of this, of course, is that those who have limited or distorted experiences in childhood will be less adept at knowing themselves and therefore knowing other people. They fail to understand the intentions of others; they read situations badly; social life can seem a bit of a puzzle. In terms of social relationships, they will be less competent.

Biology, Self and Society

Together, Humphrey and Mead provide us with the basic formula for answering why we need to understand and be understood. They also give us clear explanations about how we are able to do these things. Between them, they tell us that we can understand other people (we are psychologists by nature), that our social behaviour is a biological and evolutionary asset, and that in order to be good at social relationships we need to understand the minds of other people, which we can do by observing our own thoughts and feelings (self-consciousness).

It is Mead, however, who reminds us of the value of adding a social perspective when considering the problem of understanding other minds. His reminder points the way to a more subtle, and potentially more sophisticated, way of thinking about the problem and practice of understanding other people. The generation of a sense of self (of which to be aware) becomes possible only within a social context. The experience of self can never be prior to society. We emerge out of the social flux and form a self of which to become aware as we interact with others. We are therefore a product of social life in so far as we are made up of the same kinds of experiences that have helped form other minds. The same social 'outside' gets 'inside' the head of each individual. And because we are aware of our own thoughts and feelings, we believe that we can understand those of other people as we interpret their behaviour in light of our own.

8 Biology and Experience

We have learned to ask two questions about the wish to understand and the need to be understood. The first is: *How* does one person understand the thoughts and feelings of another? And the second is: *Why* should human beings be interested in the mental states of their fellow men and women? It seems that the best company to keep if we persist in asking questions of this kind is certain types of developmental psychologist and a number of very thought-provoking neurobiologists. Between them, they throw much light on our concerns.

In recent years, a number of exhilarating attempts have been made to link mind and consciousness with the development of the individual, as both a biological and a social entity. 'Humanity has evolved in culture, not outside it,' observes Neisser (quoted in Rieber, 1983: 126); 'people are not genetically adapted to growing up alone.' Such observations will help unravel the idea that, in order to understand ourselves, we need to understand others; and conversely, in order to understand others, we need understand ourselves.

Two things have been noted so far. First, there is an evolutionary advantage in knowing other minds. Second, we can know other minds because we emerge out of and are shaped by the same social environment. Neurobiologists and developmental psychologists have tackled the second part of this story with gusto and imagination. They introduce us to the brain and its development. But as well as examining this development as a biological event, they also consider the interaction between the maturing brain and its physical and social environment. In these models, there is a dynamic relationship between the developing brain and the external world of other people and things.

For our purposes, the striking thing is that, in order to develop a sense of self, a mind and language, other people play a critical role. Without the social environment, itself a creation of other minds communicating, the individual would develop neither a sense of self nor the use of language. Because we are formed in a common process, it is reasonable to assume that in broad terms other people's experiences can be recognized by and be intelligible to each one of us. There is no direct way of knowing the other person's experience from the inside. But by seeing what they do and hearing what they say, we can understand their experience, because if we did and said the same things it would mean something similar to us, because our selves have also been constructed out of the same social processes.

This is the particularly clever thing about such developments. To be human we have to co-operate with others. This we do by word and deed. In order to co-operate, speak and act in a meaningful way we also have to know that other people have mental states and that these states are informed by a person's subjective desires, beliefs and intentions. The formation of the self that needs to understand other people arises out of the brain's need to make sense of social experience. In its dynamic dealings with social experience, the brain develops structures and conceptual models that arise out of its relationship with the social environment. Thus, the social 'outside' in fact constructs the mental 'inside' which is then able to make sense of the 'outside' in precisely the right terms. This allows the individual to have a good working understanding of other people and the social environment. As a result he or she can cope with the social world. The individual becomes socially competent.

The Maturing Brain and Critical Periods of Sensitivity

The human infant is dependent on his or her parents for a long time. Throughout much of this period, the brain continues to grow and develop. The acquisition of many of our abilities, including those of sight, language and ultimately the recognition of self, depend on two things – (1) the right kind of nervous system and brain organization (biology), and (2) a certain type and amount of physical and social experience (the material and cultural environment). Many of the brain's physical structures – the layout and pattern of neurones – are formed as the individual experiences the world and interacts with it. The formation of these structures actually requires engagement with the external world. And in turn, these neuronal structures allow the external world to be perceived and conceived.

Blakemore (1988: 37) cites the case of the mouse with no whiskers. Before mice gain experience of the world, the region of their brain which is connected to their whiskers is undifferentiated and without apparent structure. However, as the mouse gains experience of the world with its whiskers, eight barrel-like structures form in the brain which correspond to the eight whiskers on the opposite side of the mouse's face. Cells clustered in the walls of a single barrel receive information from just one of the whiskers:

> How is this extraordinary correspondence between the structure of the brain and the structure of the sense organs produced? Both anatomical structures – the whiskers and the barrels – could, of course, be predetermined by instructions in the genetic code. But, alternatively, the nerve fibres growing into the cortex, carrying signals from the whiskers, might somehow *induce* the formation of barrels in the cortex. When Van der Loos looked at the brain of a newborn mouse he could see no barrels; they first appear a few days after birth. In a crucial experiment, he removed a single row of whiskers on one side of the face in a newborn mouse and then waited until the cortex had gone through the phase of barrel formation. When he looked subsequently at microscope sections through the cortex, he saw that one row of barrels, corresponding to the plucked whiskers, had totally failed to develop. (Blakemore, 1988: 37)

Nerve cells which carry activity from each whisker somehow cause the cerebral cortex to rearrange its cells to make a barrel structure to process the incoming messages. The outside world, via the sense organs, influences the physical organization of the developing brain.

Thus, we see that there are critical periods of sensitivity when the brain is ready to engage with an aspect of the social and material world in order to develop a particular neurophysiological structure and function. The brain is programmed to develop an *interpretative relationship* with its environment, but it needs the environment in order to develop the actual neurological structures of perception, appreciation and interpretation.

If crucial aspects of the environment are missing or deficient, distorted or confused at times of critical developmental sensitivity, the brain literally fails to develop adequate physical neuronal structures, networks and pathways which allow it to appreciate and handle specific types of information and experience. Thus, the notion of critical periods suggests that the appropriate experience *must* occur when the brain is most open or 'plastic' to that particular experience. A critical period is that time before the brain becomes permanently 'hard-wired', a time when the axons of nerve cells become covered in a thin sheaf of fatty tissue, or myelin, which facilitates more rapid transmission of impulses. As areas become myelinated they mature and lose much of their plasticity and the ability to change their fundamental functioning (Anastasiow, 1990: 198). The relationship between the brain's development and the quality of the environment has profound implications for all aspects of human development, including psychological development and social performance.

If we understand how the brain matures in its social and physical environment, we might begin to understand why it is that certain psychotherapeutic experiences are found to be helpful and why some people can practise psychotherapy better than others. Our excursion into neurobiology and consideration of the brain's hermeneutical development in relation to its social and physical environment suggests ways in which we might understand (1) why therapeutic alliances, core conditions and 'just someone to talk to' crop up again and again in client accounts of counselling and therapy, and (2) why different psychotherapies produce similar results and consumer evaluations.

The existence of critical periods is well observed in the development of sight and hearing, language and self-awareness. 'Again and again,' observes Blakemore (1988: 37–8), 'the growing developing brain passes through brief episodes of sensitivity during which it must be exposed to the correct chemical signals or the appropriate experience if the programme of maturation is to unfold normally.'

For example, if a cat or a monkey has one eye covered during its first few weeks of life, the neural fibres from that eye to the brain fail to form normal bands of termination. The actual activity of the seeing eye helps the brain form refined processing structures which gradually establish the brain's ability to produce good sight. The brain has the capacity to see but it must be exposed to the rain of sight in order for it to organize itself both to see and to make sense of what it sees. Blakemore continues, this time taking the human infant as his example:

> It is very likely that much of the same kind of process takes place in the visual cortex of the human baby during the first few months of life. If a child suffers some imbalance between the two eyes at this early stage, for instance because of a cloudy cataract in the lens of one eye or a drooping eyelid on one side, the child will subsequently have very poor vision through that eye, even if the initial problem is entirely cured. A baby's individual visual experiences, early in its postnatal life, influence the formation of nerve connections in its brain, which in turn affect the way that its brain can process visual information. The ability of the brain to modify itself, on the basis of its own experiences, liberates the individual from the chains of its own DNA; the minds of different people might otherwise be as similar as their muscles or their stomachs. (1988: 38)

Neurons, or nerve cells, are connected to other neurons through cell structures called axons and dendrites (Anastasiow's excellent review of this topic, 1990, forms the basis of this section). The connection point is known as a synapse. It is across the synaptic gap that each neuron communicates with other neurons. In the human brain there are billions of such connections. Early synaptic connections are genetically programmed. *Seventy-five* per cent of the brain's total development occurs during the postnatal period. When the baby is two or three months old there is a rapid proliferation of synapses. These are called *experience-expectant* synapses (Greenough and Juraska, 1986). This means that these synapses are expecting certain kinds of experience to trigger their permanent establishment. Should the relevant experience fail to materialize, the synaptic gaps that would be capable of processing that experience fail to form.

'The proliferation of neural connections proceed rapidly from 2 to 3 months to the second year of life in all areas of the brain. The synapses are programmed to be ready to receive experiences that are related to the species and that aid in adaptation' (Anastasiow, 1990: 200). Experience-expectant synapses are developed in all sensory systems, including the visual area which is ready to respond to light. A good deal of work has been done on sight and the way we learn to see, and these serve as a useful paradigm for other functions of the brain. The experience of light causes the appropriate neurons to be activated. It is neural activity that helps stabilize and make persistent synaptic connections. Following their stabilization, the unused, over-produced synapses die.

> Synapse stabilization is most vulnerable to environmental experiences during critical periods of development . . . These synapses store experience from the environment or become involved in structures that develop into functioning brain structures such as the visual system. The retention of the synapses is directly related to the evolutionary adaptational function that the extrinsic experience adds to the organism's survival. As Greenough and Juraska (1986) point out, the information the organism receives must be correct. Incorrect information can be learned as well as correct information, which may irreversibly damage the expected or normal range of behaviour of the organism. (Anastasiow, 1990: 200)

A nice example of how we literally have to learn to see is to be found in a delightful book by Shiela Hocken (1977). Shiela, though born not quite blind, gradually lost the use of what little sight she had throughout the first few years of her childhood. When she was in her late twenties she had an eye operation and regained her sight. Although presumably her brain had had some early, blurred experience of sight, it was much better equipped to process sounds, touch and smell. When her sight returned, Shiela recounts how difficult it was for her to interpret what she saw. After the operation there was nothing wrong with her sight, but she had to learn to see. This is how Shiela describes some of her experiences:

> Apart from mirrors, I had never thought very much about the existence

of pictures on the wall, either. I had known they were there, but the objects that blind people do not come into contact with constantly by touch are not retained in the forefront of the mind . . . Don [her husband] used to paint in his spare time, and there were some of his canvasses on the wall . . . To the left, I recalled there was a seascape. When I went to look at this, I encountered for the first time the difficulty which used to crop up quite frequently in those first few days out of hospital. This was the problem of relating reality to the image transmitted through the eyes to the brain, to a previous reality which was conditioned by touch or verbal description. Some objects that I saw for the first time I could identify immediately, although I do not know why. But others I had not the least notion of what they might be, until I felt them. The seascape I could make no sense of whatsoever. (Hocken, 1977: 172)

At first, Shiela was too frightened to go out walking on her own, so she took her guide dog, Emma, even though her sight was now perfect. Her brain could not meaningfully interpret the relative motions of all the objects that swept across her line of vision:

as soon as we were on our way, I suddenly saw the pavement rushing under me. It was so unexpected and frightening, that I had to tell Emma to stop. In a moment I recovered and we went on again. But then I saw the fence coming at us at a headlong rate, and the trees seemed to fly towards us as if they were going to knock us down. Looking down again I saw the pavement and even the shadows of the lamp posts were sweeping along towards me like solid black bars, making me think I would trip. (Hocken, 1977: 174)

As maturing organisms, human beings continue to pass through special periods of cognitive sensitivity when the brain is ready to establish new mental abilities. In order for these abilities to become established in the physical structuring of the brain, the maturing individual must be exposed to the appropriate sensations in the external world. The child must see colour, contrast, movement, shape and depth if the brain is to develop neuronal structures capable of processing the various dimensions of sight and assembling them into some integrated visual experience.

Language

The self, which is to be understood, arises in the interaction between the developing brain and other established selves. Language is the medium in which all this understanding takes place. It plays a critical role in the formation of thought. And many think that language helps define our world and the way we experience it. Human language exists for making ourselves understood. By using language we seek to convey inner mental states. When I want you to understand me, I use language to tell you about myself and my experiences. I know whether or not you have understood me by what you say.

To understand how we acquire language, once again we consider our genetic capacity, on the one hand, and the fact that we develop in a language environment, on the other. It is not simply the case that either (1) we have the innate capacity to develop language at any stage in our lives or (2) the language environment simply impresses its content, form and structure on the developing, passive brain as it is subjected to language experiences. Rather, there appears to be a dynamic relationship between the two, and both are necessary if the individual is to develop language.

Noam Chomsky set the pace with his challenging ideas about the universal presence in all human languages of a deep common structure and grammar. This suggested to him that our brains have a fundamental capacity to provide us with the basic rules and structures of language. His initial views on language development suggested that the brain has a built-in programme which provides it with the basic rules for acquiring language. 'Chomsky contended that the capacity for language is uniquely human and is *not learned through experience* . . . but is innate' (Blakemore, 1988: 179). Language growth is determined by intrinsic, genetic factors:

> in the case of language, it is natural to expect a close relation between innate properties of the mind and features of linguistic structure; for language, after all, has no existence apart from its mental representation. Whatever properties it has must be those that are given to it by the innate mental processes of the organism that has invented it. (Chomsky, 1972: 75)

Chomsky uses the term 'universal grammar' to characterize the general capacity of human beings to establish language. 'What initial structures,' poses Chomsky (1972: 79), 'must be attributed to the mind that enables it to construct such a grammar from the data of sense?' Environmental factors trigger and shape language growth as the biologically given capacity grows and matures during the first few years of life.

Blakemore (1988: 180–1) quotes the work of the anthropological linguist Derek Bickerton, who worked in countries where people from many language backgrounds were brought together. In Hawaii, for example, indentured labourers from China, the Philippines, Puerto Rico and Portugal were brought together to work on the sugar planta-tions. The first wave of adults had no common tongue and improvised a makeshift language, called pidgin speech, which had a limited vocabulary and no true grammar. Although the adults created pidgin speech, they were unable to provide it with any structure. They were past the critical age at which syntax develops. But not so for the next generation. The children of these immigrants found themselves in the midst of this pidgin English, but they imposed grammar and syntax and created a creole language. Blakemore quotes Bickerton, who believes that syntax develops in the children naturally. 'It's instinctive, and you can't stop them from doing it. I think the only explanation you can have for the way syntax works is that, somehow, it is built into the hardwiring of the brain.' It appears, according to Blakemore, that people have in their brains the inherent machinery to make language (1988: 181).

However, since Chomsky's pioneering work, an even more dynamic relationship had been recognized between the brain and the language environment in which it finds itself. The child needs to be exposed to language. However, language is acquired by use, not by listening and learning. Simply being exposed to a language is not sufficient; the child needs – indeed wants – to do something with it. Bruner quotes John Austen's celebrated phrase that learning a language is learning 'how to do things with words' (1990: 70–1). The child needs to understand the context in which the language is being learned and to recognize the significance and purpose of what is taking place. Language is therefore learned within the meanings that inform that context. Bruner believes that the human infant has a 'readiness for meaning'; there are certain classes of meaning to which we are 'innately tuned' and for which we 'actively search' (Bruner, 1990: 72).

Thus, the brain is not simply a passive organ waiting to be stimulated and instructed by information received by the senses. It actively seeks and stimulates and prompts its environment in order that it may acquire experiences which 'hard-wire' its structures in such a way that they are able to read and respond to the environment in just the way that most suits the properties of the environment which it has to cope with and respond to.

Although our brains are programmed to develop language, they need to be exposed to people talking, communicating and gesturing for language to be accomplished. As it is immersed in a language environment, the brain develops and strengthens those neural networks that have the potential to structure themselves to handle language and speech. As with other capacities, it seems that there is a time – a critical period – when the developing brain is particularly sensitive to language. Between the ages of one or two and seven years of age, the child's brain is programmed to develop its ability to handle language.

Without hearing others speak (or see them sign in the case of deaf children), the brain will not establish those neurological structures that are associated with language. And to prove the point, there are a number of bizarre examples in which for a variety of strange and horrific reasons children have been completely deprived of an environment in which language or communication of any kind is taking place (see Blakemore, 1988: 192; Frith, 1989: 16–35). Whether abandoned to live in the forest or left chained and isolated in a filthy attic, such children do not hear language when the brain is in its critical and sensitive phase. When rescued and introduced to normal language, they fail to develop full and fluent speech. The sensitive period lasts until the child is around seven or eight years old and it is during this period that a child must be regularly exposed to a language environment if true language is to be learned.

This leads us to the heart of the argument. If language carries meaning and culture and language also constitutes thought, then the meaning and culture that are present in the language we share enter my head as well as yours. Therefore those born into the same language and culture share a common world of meaning. To this extent they have the basis of a common understanding. No longer do we need to see the individual as in some way unbridgeably separated from others, an island of thought and sentiment unconnected to other islands. However, there is an important corollary to this thesis. If I do not have language or I have a different language, then I may not be able to share your particular meanings. Therefore, we may find it difficult to understand one another and easy to misunderstand one another, and a gulf will exist between us.

The Quality of Experience

Eccles (1989: 215) proposes that many of the higher-order functions of the brain develop their extreme diversity and subtlety in relation to the experiential world which interacts with relevant parts of the brain by a process of 'self-creation and self-organization'. Much of what we are able to do as human beings (see, speak, co-operate, understand) does not arrive pre-programmed into the hard-wiring of the brain. Rather, according to Stebbins (1982: 394), genetic templates transmit *potentialities* or *capacities* rather than adult behavioural traits. Furthermore, not only are our genes unique, but so is our experience. There is no way in which we can disentangle the impact of our genetic uniqueness from our experiential uniqueness (Eccles, 1989: 237). This highlights the critical part that the quality of experience plays in the physical and operational development of the brain.

Three kinds of environmental experience can influence the brain during its critical and sensitive periods of development: normal experience, lack of experience and abnormal experience. It seems that the more optimal environments are associated with the development of more complex, better-defined neuronal structures which arise in the brain as a result of the richness of experience, and once formed these structures allow the individual to experience that aspect of the environment in a fuller, more skilful and competent fashion.

Individuals who have suffered a lack of experience (for example, a lack of light, language or social relationships) are less able to handle and process the experiences which they have lacked. Once the brain has passed its period of critical sensitivity for that particular experience (and this can vary a lot depending on the experience), it loses a good deal of its 'plasticity' and so is less able to develop the appropriate neuronal structures which could handle the experience in question. Although much of this work has concentrated on perceptual abilities such as sight, there are strong and compelling suggestions that many of our social and interpersonal skills are established during critical periods during the early years of childhood. Trevarthen (1983: 181) reminds us that much of the infant's perceptual ability in the first year of life is tuned to observation and interpretation of the behaviour and actions of other people.

Anastasiow (1990: 204) notes that optimal environments do not imply the deliberate training of the infant. It is the child or the young animal that acts on the environment through its own species-determined, self-directed exploratory activity. In other words, given a normal genetic potential, the infant will 'drive experience. Genes are components in a system that organizes the organism to experience its world' (Scarr and McCartney, 1983: 425). Development is not pre-coded in the genes merely to emerge with maturation. Suitable environments have to be experienced to stimulate the brain to develop the neuronal structures capable of perceiving and interpreting the environment's various aspects. Lack of suitable environments and deficiencies in the quality of experience upset the development of appropriate processing structures and reduce the individual's ability to cope with those environments and experiences.

The Maturing Brain and Social Experience

For our purposes, these discoveries open a rich seam of enquiry and speculation. To become self-aware we need to meet awareness in others. To develop language we need to be introduced to a language environment. To understand people we need people who understand. The curious thing about these mental capacities is that, although the brain is programmed to achieve them, the potential cannot be realized until the environment supplies examples and experiences of the potential state. Moreover, the quality of the examples and the experiences will uniquely shape the eventual realization of the potential. The environment is not simply a trigger which sets off the brain to produce language or sight or self-awareness. The quality and character of that environment affect the quality and character of the developing brain.

The environment triggers a dynamic relationship between itself and the developing brain, in which the brain responds to its experiences by developing structures and capacities which are capable of appreciating these experiences with increasing accuracy and effectiveness. The brain is programmed to organize itself to accomplish the particular ability, but in order for that ability to become established it must be encountered in the external world. Thus, the maturing brain must meet language and other selves in order to 'wire' itself for handling language and becoming self-aware.

However, what must also be noted is that, although the growing individual achieves the general capacity to handle language and self-awareness, the particular quality comes from the particular characteristics of the language or social environment with which the brain in interacting. The properties of the social environment with which the developing brain interacts in turn becomes a property of that brain. Unlike Mead's passive emergence of self out of society, this neurophysiological model recognizes that the brain is an active participant, programmed to develop certain capacities; but in order to fulfil the programme's potential, the brain needs to engage in particular experiences at critical times. There is a reciprocal relationship between the brain and the sensations it receives; each is shaped by the other.

So, although a mind cannot know another mind directly, each mind, each self, is programmed to construct itself out of the common experience of social life. Because of the social formation of self, we might know other minds. Awareness of our own experiences and thought processes gives us a way of understanding other people who have grown up at the same time in the same place. Although each individual's experience is unique, generic characteristics unite them.

Consider the artist and the products of her art. As she interacts with her paints, she produces a series of pictures. The properties of the paints open up possibilities as well as exert limitations on what can be done. The artist is both liberated and limited by her own eye on the world. Between the artist and her paints, a series of *different* pictures emerge, though each is recognizable as one of *her* works. In this sense, each painting is both like and unlike all the others. There is a common style and character which links them. There is an 'understanding' between them. Each one has arisen out of the interaction between a particular artist and a given range, type and quality of paints; and although no two paintings are the same, there is no doubting their common origin. Aesthetically and in terms of their construction, all the paintings are in sympathy.

Or consider what happens to particles of hot iron that cool in a magnetic field. As they cool, the particles of iron take on the direction of the magnetic field in which they find themselves. They, too, become magnetized. It is a property of iron that it is predisposed to become magnetic in a magnetic field. A particle of sulphur would not become magnetized. It is not in the nature of sulphur to become magnetized whether it finds itself in a magnetic field or not. Once formed, the particles of iron themselves exert their own local magnetic field, and should a future cooling particle find itself in their midst, it would become magnetic and also take on the direction of the local field. Each particle of iron has an 'understanding' of magnetism and this it holds in common with all other particles in that region. However, even though it has the potential to become magnetic, if a cooling particle is not exposed to a magnetic field, it will remain unmagnetized. The quality of the environment is therefore critical in the development of magnetism in cooling iron particles. The ability to generate its own local magnetic field will not have been realized.

In a similar way, the quality and character of the social environment affect the type of self which forms within social fields and the capacities which that self possesses.

9 The Development of Social Understanding

Studies of the way children learn to understand their social world explain both how and why we need to understand other minds. Human beings seem to have an inveterate interest in what other people are thinking, intending and feeling. Babies enter a complex social world in which they instantly become active participants (Dunn, 1988: 1). From the day they are born, infants have diverse and complex relationships with other members of that world. By their third year, children show a flourishing interest in other people's behaviour; they have a practical knowledge of the mental states of their fellows and they are curious about other minds.

Recognizing that other people have feelings, intentions and minds of their own is an important achievement in the process of becoming human and forming social relationships (Dunn, 1991: 51). Looking at family life and the complex emotional environment in which the baby finds herself, it becomes apparent why young children need to make sense of what is happening. 'It is clearly extremely adaptive to be able to "read" and anticipate the feelings and actions of the people who share your family world – especially those with whom you compete for parental love and affection' (Dunn, 1986: 103). We all need to make sense of social relationships and understand the rules that govern the behaviour and actions of those around us. People – whether in families, work groups or social gatherings – constantly discuss other people in terms of their intentions, feelings, beliefs, desires and motives.

If we are to succeed as human beings we need to be competent in social relationships. We must develop powers of recognizing and sharing emotional states, of interpreting and anticipating other people's reactions and of understanding the relationships between people (Dunn, 1988: 5). Knowing other people's intentions and sensing their point of view enable us to perform well in the community of others; this helps us negotiate social life as we work and trade, mate and exchange.

Social competence requires us to recognize the feelings, beliefs and intentions that lie behind other people's actions. In order to function well in social life, we need to understand, and often predict, the relationships between the outside world (of people and things) and internal states of mind (wants, beliefs, intentions). This ability has been termed 'mentalizing', and human beings seem addicted to it.

As she matures, the infant begins to recognize other people's mental states; she has a 'theory of other minds'. That is, in order to function socially, the infant needs to recognize that, like herself, other people also have mental states and that, in order to cope in the world, it is necessary to understand that other people have thoughts and feelings, beliefs and intentions and that these can be deduced from one's own experience. Theories are good things to have if you want to organize, distil and handle vast amounts of raw experience and undigested information.

The Infant's Interest in Other People

Human infants show an *active* and intense interest in other people, almost from the day they are born. They are alert to their intentions and responses. Young children show a great interest in the emotional state of others and what causes people to feel as they do. Psychological causality – the whys and wherefores of people's behaviour – appears to be of far more interest to young children than physical causality and the behaviour of things and objects (Hood and Bloom, 1979).

Babies learn quickly about things which appear to change as a result of their own actions. Many abilities appear inborn. For example, 'Infants appear to possess innately, or to develop quickly, remarkable abilities to perceive the actions and expressions of other people' (Spelke and Courtelyou, 1981). Reciprocal interactions are a source of great pleasure, interest and stimulation for infants. And in order to become more skilled at coping with other people, children need to become more proficient at reading other minds. This is helped by knowing one's own mind. In other words, the effect of being placed in a social environment is that we are programmed to respond to and interact with that environment so that we can get the measure of it for the purposes of social interaction.

However, in the process of getting the measure of it, that same social environment informs the way we learn to recognize, define and understand ourselves. 'The ability to make sense of other people is also the ability to make sense of oneself' (Frith, 1989: 169). Indeed, the theory which we apply to other minds is the same one we use to understand our own. We appeal to mental states to explain why we, and others, say what we say, or do what we do: 'I don't speak in groups because I don't want to make a fool of myself'; 'She's off sick today because really she doesn't want to meet that difficult client.' In all our dealings with others, we constantly employ a psychological interpretation of their behaviour. Carey guesses that infants are genetically endowed with brains which are disposed to conduct an intuitive psychology in interactions with others (Carey, 1985: 200). We are biologically oriented towards interacting with other people, and the results of that interaction allow us to develop a consciousness of self and a consciousness of others, an understanding of self and an understanding of others.

The child's interest in language is also stimulated, even prompted, by her wish to participate in the social life of those around. Even before speech, the child is busy pointing things out to others. The acquisitions of language, therefore, appears context-sensitive (Bruner, 1990: 71). If the child appreciates the nature and purpose of the context, she will grasp language more quickly. Dunn, in fact, argues that the emotional dimension in human affairs acts as a powerful factor in developing and guiding our psychological skills:

> Piaget is surely right to emphasize that the important developmental exchanges are not those in which social influence is impressed on children, but those in which they attempt to argue, justify, and negotiate. But my account stresses the significance of the affective dynamics of the relationships that motivate the child to engage in discourse about the social world, rather than solely to cognitive conflict of being faced with another person's point of view. It is the motivation to express himself within the relationship, to co-operate, to get his way or to share amusement, that, I suggest, in part leads the child to discover the ways of the family world. (Dunn, 1988: 186)

Having a model of how other minds work is crucial for successful interaction. Without it, our dealings with others become odd, even impossible, and it becomes very difficult to survive, socially and even physically. Young children are faced with many problems in their relationships: how to recognize another person's mood, how to gain their attention, how to know their intentions. In solving these problems and by beginning to manage their social world, children establish the beginnings of a self – a locus of feelings and the agent of actions.

It appears that human infants have an innate desire to communicate, particularly feelings and intentions. For example, normal 10-month-old babies, prior to having language, will often point to an object that is relevant not only to them but to the person with whom they are communicating (Frith, 1989: 146-7). The aim seems to be to share attention. In response, the baby's mother may say, 'Yes, that's the same colour as your rattle.' Mutual comprehension can be achieved, and this can be richly rewarding. It shows early evidence that the infant is aware of other minds and other mental states. It reveals that she is aware of her own comprehension, that she knows that other minds exist, and that these other minds have their own mental states which may be confirmed and learned about through acts of communication. By pointing to the rattle, the baby is establishing her own mental state and prompting confirmation both of the accuracy of the mental state and that the mother has a mental state too, which is both independent of the child's and yet comprehensible because it appears to share that understanding. The baby has signalled her own mental state and confirmed that this mental state is recognizable and of interest to the other person. *Thus, there are other minds and they are knowable.* The more the baby interacts with other people, the more elaborate and sophisticated will she become about the state of her own mind and the minds of other people.

> What matters in everyday communication is the point of the message rather than the message itself. In other words, as listeners we need to know *why* the speaker conveys *this* thought (rather than another), and as speakers we need to be sure we are understood in the way we *want* to be understood. (Frith, 1989: 132)

Most people in normal conversation pack all kinds of purposes and evaluations into their utterances. As we do, we intentionally, and unintentionally, both hide and reveal all sorts of mental states.

> We constantly pay attention to aspects of utterances that have to do not with their content, but with the intention of the speaker ... In fact, in ordinary conversations bare messages (where only content matter) are so rare that they tend to be interpreted in terms of some ulterior communicative purpose *even* if none is there. (Frith, 1989: 132–3)

Recognizing the Emotional States of Other People

A number of psychologists have explored the origins and the nature of the emotions in early childhood and they seem to tell us a good deal about the way we relate, emotionally and socially, to other people as adults. In particular, they not only throw light on how we manage our social relationships, but more importantly, they tell us why we have to be good at social relationships, good at natural psychology and good at understanding other people.

From birth, children show an increasing amount of emotional behaviour which seems to play a key role in developing the ability to understand other people, their thoughts and feelings. As they grow older, children not only react to other people's feelings, they also seem to provoke emotional reactions in other people. They can annoy as well as please. 'What is important here,' believes Dunn, 'is that children seem to anticipate their mothers' feeling state and get pleasure from the power to affect them in this way' (1988: 17). Dunn provides a number of fascinating examples from her own studies of young children at home with their parents and siblings. Children often confront their mother in ways which she can find exasperating.

Here is the example of Jay, aged 30 months (Dunn, 1988: 30). His mother and older brother Len discover a mark on the wall, and the following conversation takes places between mother and Jay:

Mother to Jay: Was it you?
Jay: Huh?
Mother: Was it you?
Jay: No. I think Len done it.

Although the denial is made, it is clear to all concerned that Jay made the mark. However, the denial seems to indicate that Jay could anticipate his mother's reaction, and such foresight allows him to take some, albeit not very sophisticated, evasive action. He has a conception of self, knows that there are standards of behaviour and understands that other people have emotional reactions when those standards are breached. A good deal of complex and subtle behaviour is going on in this little exchange which shows how elaborate and reflexive are Jay's cognitive, emotional and social skills, even at two and a half years old.

During their third year, children have a vexing habit of constantly asking the question, Why? In her Cambridge studies, Dunn observed that this question was often directed at the child's mother when she attempted to control behaviour. It seems that children begin to realize that other people have points of view and reasons which they need to know about. By confronting their mother, children can both enquire about her state of mind as well as provoke her in such a way that the postulated mental state is revealed. Here is Jay again, sitting in a closet, a place forbidden by his mother:

Mother: Come out now, please.
Jay: Why come out for?

Children have a mentalistic concept of emotion. Children, from a very early age, 'grasp that people's emotional reactions differ depending on the beliefs and desires that they have about a situation' (Harris, 1989: 2). Children have beliefs and desires of their own which they can recognize and talk about. They can also 'predict other people's reactions not by recourse to a set of generalizations linking beliefs, desires, emotions and actions, but by virtue of their imaginative capacity' (Harris, 1989: 3). Children can examine a situation in the light of the beliefs and desires that the other person brings to it and so simulate the intentions or emotions of that person. 'Their predictions about the other person will be increasingly accurate as their simulation improves' (Harris, 1989: 3). From early childhood onwards, we use working models in our head to make predictions about reality, including the behaviour and actions of other people. 'We each possess a working model of the other person (namely the psychological machinery that governs the relationships between beliefs, desires, actions and emotions in our mind); we observe its outputs, and base our predictions about the other person on those outputs' (Harris, 1989: 3).

As least as far as some of the basic emotions are concerned, it appears that from a very early age, and it might even be an innate ability, babies recognize the meaning of particular facial expressions. Babies adjust their social behaviour to the emotion being expressed. If the emotion is being expressed about a particular object, say a toy, the child's attitude to that toy will be influenced by the emotion – increased interest if the emotion was delight and decreased interest if the emotion was disgust. Thus, babies appear to approach or avoid an object in terms of the emotional message conveyed by the adult. By the age of one year the infant has the ability to attach meaning to particular emotional expressions.

Understanding the Emotional States of Other People

So far, we have simply recognized that infants can read and respond to some basic emotional states as expressed by other people. The next crucial achievement is to go beyond simple recognition and speculate about the person expressing that emotion: why is she happy or frightened or sad? This is the infant's second step in understanding other people and other minds.

One of the most important cognitive capacities of the human mind is the power to conceive of its own mental states and those of others. This occurs at very young ages. 'For example,' writes Leslie (1988: 19), '4-year-old children can understand how someone comes to have a mistaken *belief* about something. They can work out what that belief will be and what effect it will have on that person's behaviour. This remarkable feat needs a lot of explaining.'

Harris argues that children come to understand other people's mental states by relying on a distinctive type of imaginative understanding. Imagination and make-believe are functional. 'It allows the child to entertain possible realities and, what is especially important, to entertain the possible realities that other people entertain. It is a key that unlocks the minds of other people and allows the child temporarily to enter into their plans, hopes and fears' (Harris, 1989: 51–2).

Although we can experience empathy – crying when someone else is tearful, feeling angry as someone else's hackles rise – we generally do not employ this reaction to understand the emotions of another. We do not have to feel a particular emotion to know that someone else is experiencing that emotion. 'We may discern their feelings of anxiety or pride and feel no such emotion ourselves' (Harris, 1989: 52). All I need to do is imagine what you might feel in a given situation without having to actually feel that emotion: 'Briefly, I shall claim that children are aware of their mental states, and project them on to other people using a mechanism that depends crucially on the imagination' (Harris, 1989: 53).

There is plenty of evidence that even very young children can report their desires, beliefs and emotions. Around the age of two, children begin to describe themselves and other people as beings that can perceive, feel emotion and have desires. More particularly for his thesis, Harris observes that children comment on their own psychological states before they comment on those of other people. 'The general lag between statements about the self and about other people is important since it fits the claim that children are initially aware of their mental states, and subsequently interpret the behaviour of other people by projecting their own mental states on to other people' (Harris, 1989: 57).

Dunn (1988: 173) adds that, during the course of their third year, children begin to talk about knowing, remembering and forgetting; they consider mental states in themselves and in others. Indeed, questions about other people's thoughts and feelings increase throughout this third year of life. Children begin to recognize themselves and others as '"things which think," as things which *believe, doubt, wonder, imagine* and *pretend*' (Olson et al., 1988: 1).

In another paper, Dunn quotes the work of Zahn-Waxler, Yarrow, King and Chapman (Dunn, 1986: 101). Very young children are able to make fine discriminations in other people's needs, moods and mental states. Parental arguments cause distress – children will cry, hold their hands over their ears or try to comfort a distraught parent.

> By two years of age, children bring objects to the person who is suffering, make suggestions about what to do, verbalize sympathy . . . and attempt to evoke a change in affect in the distressed person. Such means–end behaviour implies that children can keep in mind the other's distress as a problem to be solved. (Zahn-Waxler et al., quoted in Dunn, 1986: 101–2)

Pretence, Imagination and Knowing Other Minds

Children also have a great capacity for pretence. On the face of it, pretending appears to be an odd ability (Leslie – see Harris, 1989: 57). In terms of evolution, it might seem that the individual would be best equipped if he or she could regard the world with a high degree of accuracy and objectivity. Imagining or pretending to be a lion does not seem to serve any biological or developmental purpose. Indeed, if anything, it seems to remove the individual from any sensible dealings with the world, unless, that is, there is functional value in developing capacities which give that individual information about possible mental states of significant objects in his or her world. This, of course, is the nub of the thesis.

Make-believe play is extensive from about 18 months onwards. Dolls, other objects and even pretend objects can be endowed with pretend properties: dolls may be mothers; wooden bricks can become chairs. However, 'Crucial for the case that I want to establish,' writes Harris,

> is the fact that children also start to endow dolls with mental states: desires and plans that may or may not come to fruition within that make-believe situation . . . The ability to pretend allows children to engage in imaginative understanding of other people's mental states . . . On the basis of such simple pretend premises, they can proceed to imagine the emotional reactions of another person who does have such a desire or belief. (Harris, 1989: 54–5)

As children mature, this imaginative understanding becomes

increasingly refined and subtle in its possibilities. As they project themselves into the mental world of other people by imagining what they want to feel, they can also recognize that different people may bring different desires and beliefs to the situation. These different mental states will variously affect how people feel and view the same situation. The presentation of a box of chocolates will create very different feelings in a fat man on a diet and a young wife on her wedding anniversary. Children soon begin to recognize that emotional reactions to situations depend not on the external properties of that situation but on the internal mental states that people bring to that situation. It is the mental states that have to be understood if people and their actions are to be anticipated and made sense of. This view no longer regards young children as egocentric, locked into their own views and needs, mindless of the thoughts and feelings of others as their inner states demand satisfaction. Rather, it sees the growing child as astutely aware and keenly interested in other people, what they are doing and what they might be thinking or feeling.

By the age of six, most children can begin to imagine the world from another's point of view. This allows them to predict the reactions of other people if they know the desires and beliefs of that person and the nature of the situation in which they find themselves. There is a similar logic underlying the ability to mentalize (that is, to understand that other people have thoughts, desires and beliefs) and to pretend. Pretence is the first step in the child developing a theory of other minds.

Analogy and Empathy

Although some psychologists have explained our ability to understand the other's mental state as evidence that we possess a 'theory of other minds', Harris prefers a modified version of such a notion. He argues as follows (Harris, 1989: 76).

Children have desires and beliefs of which they become aware and which they can describe to other people. They feel that there is nothing hidden or unobservable about their own mental states. Such mental states are not a postulate. They are experienced first hand. When children seek to explain someone else's actions, it is to these known mental states that they refer as they imagine the mental state of the other person. The psychological world of other people is constructed out of the child's own psychological experiences. Only in this more restricted sense can children be credited with a theory-like understanding of the mind. 'Their understanding of psychology is based upon their own experience, rather than on deduction from a set of theoretical postulates' (Harris, 1989: 77). There is no perceptual mechanism that taps directly into the other's mental state. These states are understood – we do psychology – by imagining and simulating the emotional state of the other person by analogy. Children can use their own conscious experience to understand the experience of others. We have a 'working model' of the other person (Harris, 1991: 299). 'In short, we can acknowledge that children, like scientists, rely on analogy, while at the same time denying that they proceed to the formulation of a theory of mind. Skilled mindreading . . . calls for the imaginative resonance of the biographer rather than the theoretical postulates of the scientist' (Harris, 1991: 302).

However, not all developmental psychologists see things this way round. Dunn (1988: 79), for example, argues that sensitivity to others is central to the development of self-awareness. As the infant has to deal with the actions of other people, he or she is required to become aware of their own thoughts and feelings and reflect on them as a factor in the dynamics of social life. But whichever way round one likes to see the emergence of self, the outstanding feature to appear in this landscape of thought is the child's recognition of and theories about other minds and that other people's actions can be explained as the combined result of their *desires and beliefs*. This marks the beginning of our interest in other people, their thoughts and their feelings.

Desires, Beliefs and Action

So far, we have considered those emotions which are not only univer-sal but also triggered by objective and usually observable conditions – happiness at the sight of a cold drink on a hot day, sadness at the departure of a lover. Four- and five-year-olds recognize and experience happiness or sadness depending on whether or not goals are realized. 'Older children, by contrast, gradually appreciate that people's emotional lives are not only regulated by the consequences of their actions, but also by an awareness of the emotions that other people will express towards those actions and their consequences' (Harris, 1989: 81). Children gradually learn to understand the nature of rela-tions between people and the factors which appear to govern those relations.

Approval and disapproval, responsible behaviour and irresponsible behaviour, and cultural expectations all play their part in generating emotional states. Pride, shame and guilt are emotions which are culturally inspired. Children begin to recognize which cultural expectations govern which behaviours in their society.

In a Meadian sense, notions of the 'self' and the experience of feelings are not the result of genetic programming but are a result of the individual's social experience in a world of meanings, expectations and cultural norms. There is a growing interest in how other people react emotionally to one's own behaviour. Knowing what these expectations are, we can begin to refine our understanding of other people's mental states in given situations. No longer is a person's feelings about his or her actions governed by the outcome. They are also affected by the cultural standards that surround the behaviour and its consequences. So, although fighting and aggressive behaviour may be approved in one society, bringing a sense of pride to the toughest and most pugilistic, in another culture the same behaviour may be condemned as a lack of self-control. The condemned individual would be expected to feel shame and a sense of failure. This new, culturally imposed layer of emotion is the product of how the child feels in relation to the emotional state of the adults present.

Thus, to know the mental state of the other requires the child to operate at two levels of understanding. First, the mental state of the observer must be known. Second, the child must know how the observed person will feel under the scrutiny of an observer holding those cultural views. As they mature, children

> cease to view people as agents pursuing their desires, and see them much more as social beings, whose actions are judged either by others or by the self. To explain this shift, I have argued that children become increasingly alert to the fact that the emotional state of one person is influenced by the emotional state of another. (Harris, 1989: 104)

Harris continues to refine the complexity and subtlety with which children and adults begin to understand their own and other people's emotions and mental states. We can try to hide our feelings from the ridicule of others. We might hold back our tears simply to save someone else from feeling distressed. We may attempt to control our emotions to stop ourselves feeling upset. The more we recognize the elaborate dynamics that may generate our own mental states, the more astute we become in recognizing and interpreting the mental states of other people. If we are sensitive to the emotional condition and intentions of other people, the more appropriate and effective will be our relationships with and social purposes towards other people.

Autism and the Consequences of Not Knowing Other Minds

The fundamental nature and far-reaching consequences of being able to understand other minds strike home when we consider what happens when such abilities are absent. Autism provides us with a dramatic, convincing and tragic demonstration of what happens to people who do not have a 'theory of other minds'. All our taken-for-granted social accomplishments suddenly disappear when we no longer have the capacity to understand what other people might be thinking and feeling.

Early investigators recognized that autistic children have difficulties in forming relationships – their ability to engage in reciprocal social interaction is impaired. Autism is now understood to be a type of mental disability due to abnormalities of brain development (Frith, 1989: 186). A specific neurological fault seems to affect the child's ability to make sense of other people's emotional and mental states. The effect of this on social relationships is devastating and in tragic form highlights the critical importance that we must give to the ability to have working notions of what other people are thinking and feeling. Without this constant interest in the mental states of other people, social life breaks down and with it the ability of human groups to maintain the complex social arrangements that sustain almost every facet of human existence, including sexual relationships and the ability to reproduce.

Autistic children and autistic adults often find that other people appear unpredictable and therefore frightening. Hobson reports an autistic man who said that 'other people talk to each other with their eyes', while another young man in a study by Rutter complained 'that he couldn't mind read. Other people seemed to have a special sense by which they could read other people's thoughts and feelings and could anticipate their responses and feelings.' He felt he could not do this; he was always saying the wrong thing and upsetting other people (reported in Frith, 1989: 144). One way of handling such fear is to reduce encounters with unknown others to a rather wooden, rigid, mechanical set of exchanges.

Autistic children are able to experience emotions themselves. However, they show little ability or wish to communicate their emotional states to other people. Nor do they appear interested in the mental states of those around them. Indeed, while most children begin to interpret emotional signals from a very early age, this behaviour is

not evident in autistic children. Autistic children are not only indifferent to other people's emotions but they also have difficulty in
grasping that other people have emotional lives at all (Harris, 1989:
197). So, if autistic people do not understand other people's expressions of emotion, they will find it difficult to form and sustain relationships.

Frith (1989), in her fascinating book on the enigma of autism,
describes a number of revealing experiments which throw light on the
nature of the poor mentalizing ability of the autistic child, a child who
does not properly appreciate the existence of mental states in other
people.

For example, when presented with picture stories in which one child
hides a sweet in a new location unknown to another child, compared
with normal children and Down's syndrome children, autistic
children failed to predict the actions of the deceived child, whereas
the other two groups were correct in their understanding of the
deceived child's actual behaviour (Baron-Cohen et al., 1986). The
experimental hypothesis was that autistic children fail to take account
of other people's *beliefs* when considering their behaviour. All three
groups of children had mental ages above three. In fact, the autistic
children had much higher mental ages than the others. They were
able to solve a great many logical problems of a literal nature.

In the experiment, two dolls were used: Sally and Anne. The following scenario was acted out:

> Sally has a basket and Anne has a box. Sally has a marble and she puts
> it into her basket. She then goes out. Anne takes out Sally's marble and
> puts it into her box while Sally is away. Now Sally comes back and wants
> to play with her marble. At this point we ask the critical question: 'Where
> will Sally look for her marble?' (Frith, 1989: 159)

The answer is, of course, 'in the basket'. Sally did not see Anne
move the marble to the box. She therefore *believes* the marble is still
in the basket, and so that is where she looks. In order to predict
action, we must understand that the actor's own beliefs have to be
taken into account. Most of the non-autistic children gave the correct
answer; indeed many found the game very funny and giggled when
'naughty Anne' transferred the marble. But few of the autistic
children gave the correct answer. They thought that Sally would look
in the box, the true location of the marble. They did not take Sally's
own belief into account.

Autistic children often describe events and actions in very literal,
causal and behavioural terms. They fail to generate a 'mentalistic'

perspective of the actions of other people. They do not read between the lines and they certainly do not recognize the practice of trying to read other people's thoughts. Motives, desires, beliefs, intentions – these psychological dimensions are absent in the autistic child's attempts to describe events or tell stories. Very often, therefore, they fail to understand what people might do or think when confronted with a psychologically inspired situation. Behaviour is viewed simply as it is. Notions such as deception or flattery, irony or persuasion are not considered in evaluating the character of the other person's words and deeds.

> Therefore, intentions that change the *meaning* of behaviour . . . present difficulties of interpretation. While the autistic individual interprets behaviour in a literal fashion, the opposite is true for the compulsive mentalizer; behaviour will be interpreted not in its own right but from the point of view of the intentions behind it. Such is the effect of a theory of mind. (Frith, 1989: 166)

In order to make sense of what other people are saying and doing, we constantly guess, monitor and evaluate what they might be thinking.

When we mentalize, when we have a theory of mind, we are looking for patterns and relationships, connections and explanations. We are seeking to *make sense* and *find meaning in* other people's words and actions. There is a constant wondering what lies behind what they say and do. Without such a search for underlying meanings, the world of other people would be a most unpredictable and puzzling place.

These observations are very similar to those made by Humphrey (1986) as he watched his gorillas and thought about the humans he knew (see Chapter 7). We make sense of other people because we are able to make sense of ourselves. We appeal to our own mental state to explain our actions; we seek to place a coherent framework around what we say and do rather than see them as random or unconnected happenings.

It is perhaps not surprising, therefore, to learn that for the autistic adult other people's actions are not only puzzling but often frightening. An inability to read between the lines produces endless misunderstandings. Desires and beliefs, pride and shame lie behind most of our actions. Failure to take these possible mental states into account would render our dealings with other people hopelessly inadequate. Frith (1989: 167) provides the following example. She first considers Lucy, a normal young woman, and her friends:

> With the way she says 'good morning', she conveys what mood she is in or, rather, what mood she would like to be considered to be in. (Thinks: 'I am not saying how awful I feel.') Peter reacts to what he thinks Lucy's

'real' mood is. (Thinks: 'Hmm, doesn't sound too good at all.') His reply, 'Shall I get you an aspirin?' would clearly seem mad, unless one assumed that a theory of mind was at work.

Frith provides two more examples before she then considers how the same remarks will be received by Lucy's autistic sister, Jennifer: 'Jennifer listens to Lucy's glum "good morning" and concludes that this morning is a "good" one. Lucy is not pleased at this reaction, but if she wants Jennifer to give her an aspirin, she has to say so.'

Alan Leslie (1987) believes that the autistic child's failure to understand other minds and the lack of pretend play, and in particular pretend play which requires the child to conjure up a mental state, are linked. 'The understanding of another person's mental state and pretence have important similarities' (Leslie, 1987: 414). They both require an ability to entertain statements that are in fact known to be false in order to explore, evaluate and explain other people's actions. If a child was 'congenitally incapable of this type of imaginative projection' he or she 'would observe the other person's behaviour and expression, but would not be able to imagine the beliefs and desires that guide that behaviour' (Harris, 1989: 208).

Not having a theory of mind means that other people are not understood in terms of what they really think or feel or want, but in terms of what they literally say or do. This produces problems in social relationships, and so other people are either mishandled or avoided. The inability to read other people's minds is a fundamental blow to a person's ability to function appropriately and effectively in social life. Other people's emotions, plans and intentions remain a puzzle. Almost all the skills that we employ in everyday social life, usually without much apparent thought, are a source of confusion for the autistic person.

10 The Origins of the Empathetic Counsellor

Awareness of and sensitivity to other people's mental states and points of view help us to develop, construct and recognize our own selves. Therefore, the self we develop is not only a cognitive achievement but is also a cultural construction. Thus, we might know other minds in two ways.

First, all human beings have a basic curiosity about their own and other people's mental states. Secondly, for those reared in a common culture, culturally inspired emotions will be understood by people from that culture. So, although there are a range of basic emotions which appear universal, many others are fashioned to appear under certain culturally defined social conditions. In other words, different cultures when faced with certain conditions promote the expression of different emotions. The particular emotion shown will not mean the same thing everywhere, and we each have to learn to recognize and express the emotional grammar of our own culture. Dunn sums it up in these words:

> The particulars vary, but what is common to all children growing up in families is the importance of understanding what is allowed or disapproved and how others will respond to their behaviour. Theories that focus on details of moral reasoning predict cultural differences; the argument presented here predicts common features in children's developing understanding across cultures, given the similarity in children's emotional interests in families everywhere. We would expect differences in children's behaviour related to differences in verbal articulation of rules, differences in the particular rules in question, differences in the individuals as outcomes – but commonalities in the concern of children for the feelings, goals, and behaviours of those who share their family world. (Dunn, 1988: 188)

It has been suggested that sensitivity to others is central to the development of an awareness of self. But here, we learn that the self of which one becomes aware is a product of culture as well as cognitive changes. In one culture the child may learn that a social self should be polite, well mannered and hospitable. In another, young boys may be encouraged to show bold, adventurous and boisterous behaviour. But in whichever culture the child finds himself or herself, 'a sense of self-efficacy comes from managing a particular cultural world; all gain pleasure from their own mastery of the difficulties – social and psychological – that face them, their own powers within that world' (Dunn, 1988: 80).

In this developmental perspective, the innate cognitive capacities of the growing child are no longer given priority over the social environment. It is not a case of a young mind imposing sense on the external world according to some in-built cognitive schema. Rather, the cognitive schemata that are created in the young mind arise as the child interacts with the world on a dynamic basis. The child's brain is programmed to build up an understanding of the physical and social environment, but it is the properties of that particular environment which give shape and structure to the child's developing cognitive apparatus. In the words of Light, 'the hegemony of the cognitive over the social has been challenged' (1986: 170). The social context in which the child finds himself or herself, an environment which has to be understood by the child if he or she is to cope, also helps constitute the child's cognitive perspectives.

Light (1986: 185) mentions the work of Walkerdine, who recognized the problems which arise if cognition is kept on the 'inside' while the context remains on the 'outside'. Walkerdine argues that the relationship between the inside and the outside, between cognition and social context, is 'a complex and dynamic one, in which meanings are created and negotiated. Social contexts, social practices and discourses are, within this account, granted a key role in the elaboration of the child's conceptual knowledge ... Intellectual development, viewed from this standpoint, is more a matter of recontextualization than of decontextualization' (Light, 1986: 185). In other words, the young mind does not approach the social world as a phenomenon which has to be analysed, conceptualized and thereby understood. The social world is understood as it is experienced. 'Mind' is situated in practical activity. Neither the mind nor the individual can be understood outside the social and historical contexts in which they find themselves (Ingleby, 1986: 298). The sense which the child has of the social context is in part the sense which the social context already possesses. In this way we are peculiarly well equipped to understand our social world, because, as we deal with that world, it actually helps shape the very concepts we generate in order to make sense of the people and situations that comprise it.

In similar vein, it is equally important to note that meaning – so fundamental to the business of social life – arises in the social use of language, and language is the medium which carries ideas, thoughts, attitudes and beliefs. In acquiring language we also acquire the text for the whole social system in which we find ourselves. Such a text becomes the medium in which all our knowledge, understandings and patterns of though are set. So, in learning language we share the medium in which meanings are held and trafficked. Once inside language we can both understand and be understood. And once language is inside us we have the mental apparatus to be aware of others and be aware of ourselves.

Why Two Out of Three Psychotherapists Are Wasting Their Energy

In Chapter 1 Truax and Mitchel (1971: 340–1) were quoted as saying that two out of three psychotherapists are wasting their energy and commitment. Although some therapists are undoubtedly effective, others are not, and may even be harmful. We might now be in a position to explain this claim.

If the dynamic relationship between genes and social experience results in the formation of individual selves, then strengths and weaknesses in either genes or social experience will have an impact on the extent to which the social 'outside' is able to articulate itself on the mental 'inside'. The more completely our brains have been able to explore and process social experience, the more we will be able to understand other people who have also been formed within that social experience. If the genes are at fault (as in autism), other people and social relationships will, to a degree, be misread and misunderstood. If social experience is deficient or incomplete, fragmented or incoherent (as in attachments which are insecure), other people and their mental states will not be fully recognized.

According to these arguments, good counsellors are both made and born . . . though probably made well before the age of 10. But the arguments also suggest that social experiences will differ across time and place. If the self is the result of the 'interiorization' of social experience (carried in language, meaning and relationships), and social experiences vary widely across time and place, then the ability of a self formed in one social environment to fully understand a self formed in another social environment will depend on the degree of similarity present in the meanings embedded in the respective cultures.

Different social 'outsides' get on the 'inside' of individuals located in different times and places. If two people come from different social times and places, they will occupy different universes of meaning. It cannot be assumed that they will perceive and conceive the world in quite the same way. Their experiences of ostensibly the 'same' event will be different. Therefore, communication and understanding between the two people will be that much more difficult. The language we use helps shape our thoughts and the way we see the world in which we live. And if thought is interior language, and language is socially saturated, thoughts and reason are properly social and communal. If we share a language, in many deep respects, we share a world – of meaning, of perception, of understanding. Different languages, therefore, shape different thoughts, different realities, different ways of experiencing the world. The aphorism 'another language, another soul' hints at the relationship between language, thought and reality. Therefore, every language carries a way of life (Midgely, 1979: 297).

This analysis has provocative implications for the level of understanding that is possible, say, between the sexes, between people of different cultures and between the old and the young (for example, see Maluccio, 1979: 130).

Natural Variations in Levels of Empathy

We have identified three variables which influence the effectiveness of the psychotherapist: (1) the genetically determined ability to model other people's mental states; (2) the quality of social relationships experienced during critically sensitive phases of psychological development; and (3) the particular linguistic, social and cultural environments in which the 'selves' of the psychotherapist and the client were formed. Psychotherapeutic effectiveness is adversely affected by genetic weaknesses in the individual's ability to model other people's minds (autism being an extreme example); by emotional and social privations and deprivations experienced during early childhood; and by marked social, linguistic and cultural differences between counsellor and client.

In exploring the biological and social basis of our ability to understand other minds, we can conclude that strengths and weaknesses in either of these two domains will affect that ability.

In the extreme case of autism, the neurological structures that allow the individual to consider other people's thoughts and feelings, and to relate them to their actions, are absent. Although other people's behaviour can be assessed in straightforward instrumental, behavioural and literal terms, the autistic person fails to consider other people's actions in terms of their hidden motives, beliefs and desires. It may be that all those who are not autistic have roughly equal potential to become adept at reading other people's minds. However, I am persuaded that there are a number of intermediate conditions between autism at one end of the spectrum and individuals who are naturally gifted in reading the minds of others at the other, individuals more able to generate models of the mental states of other people and so able to make sense of their actions in a more useful and accurate way, genetically endowed as they are with a general alertness in matters of interpersonal perception.

In fact, there is some curious evidence to support the claim that there is a natural distribution of empathic ability in the population. Asperger syndrome is recognized in people who have narrow and unusual interests, coupled with poor social skills and the inability to form close relationships; such people might, according to Frith (1991), be suffering a mild form of autism. People who have an extra-ordinarily detailed knowledge of railway timetables or who know all there is to know about 50 types of carrot, although often highly intelligent, remain inept at social relationships. 'They often talk with great skill and verbal fluency about their strange interest,' said Frith in a newspaper interview, 'but they do not understand that this is very boring for other people' (*Guardian*, 1991b). New challenges, sudden unpredictable demands and the subtle (and not so subtle) interplays of social relationships find those with Asperger syndrome unable to respond well or appropriately.

And what about early life experiences? The quality of the early social and language environment, it has been argued, determines many key abilities – language, the creation of the self, self-consciousness, psychological experience, psychological understanding. If these experiences are poor, damaged, deficient or distorted at times when the brain's capacity to develop processing structures are critically sensitive to the quality of the environment, the individual is less able to model the mental states of other people and is therefore less able to understand and conduct social relationships. Serious disturbances or distortions in the care given to a child in the first years of life may well impair his or her ability to form a fully coherent sense of self. And in the extreme case of children who have grown up with little or no contact with other human beings, weaknesses appear in their ability to gain a full command of language and the ability to establish a clearly integrated sense of self. A lack of a coherent sense of self and the inability to reflect on that self (be self-aware) might interfere with the process that allows us to develop a 'theory of other minds'.

Deficiency, deprivation and differences all have a bearing on the client's particular experience of psychotherapy. It may be no surprise, therefore, to learn that two-thirds of psychotherapists might be getting it wrong. This, of course, is a rather blunt assertion. In practice, some therapists will get it wrong with all clients all of the time. Some therapists will get it right with some clients some of the time. And some therapists will get it right with some clients all of the time. But only a very few will get anywhere near, given our three demanding variables, getting it right most of the time with most of their clients.

PART III: TALK WITH ME

11 The Chance to Talk

So far clients have emphasized the value of the nurturing qualities of the therapeutic relationship in which they are welcomed, accepted and understood. These qualities produce a powerful therapeutic environment which, for many, is sufficient and meets their needs. However, for others, although this warm and secure relationship is necessary, it is not sufficient. For this group there is a wish to give new meaning to experience. Feeling 'loved', they can begin to work, and work means talk – giving voice to thoughts, expressing feelings, describing, narrating, reflecting, puzzling, examining, analysing, debating, constructing. Margaret, a client of psychotherapy, vividly describes her feelings of exploring from a secure base: 'When I decided that I wanted to be "let out on a long life-line" I felt a sense of elation at striking out alone – yet knowing that I could go back to the therapist at any time' (Woodward, 1988: 89). And in similar evocative language, Fiona said of her counsellor:

> June [the counsellor] was a mother figure . . . she reminded me of a favourite aunty and she made me feel warm and I trusted her very much . . . I was crying all the time . . . She said that I was to imagine that I was a new born baby, and that she was going to help me stand on my feet and I was going to walk a few steps and fall down and walk a few more and fall down and then go home and walk on my own and then as children do I would have an accident and I would run back to mummy and she would make you better and then I would go back into the world again . . . and that was exactly how it happened. (Edmunds, 1992: 52)

In the following sequence, clients move from deconstructing the past to reconstructing the future. In recounting their experiences of counselling and therapy, clients describe six kinds of opportunity to 'work' and 'explore':

1 To talk.
2 To engage in dialogue.
3 To make sense of past and present experiences.
4 To control the meaning of experience.

5 To order and restructure thoughts and feelings – to make better
   sense in future.
6 To have hope and to look forward.

The Opportunity to Talk

It is a commonplace observation that when we are upset or disturbed,
worried or anxious, excited or confused, we want to talk, indeed we
need to talk. 'I need to get this off my chest'; 'I've got to talk to
someone'; 'I need to pour out my troubles.' 'Actually,' said Mrs
Mosca,

> I did more crying than talking . . . Once I got going I went through many
> feelings and emotions in that first meeting . . . I guess I had to get it off
> my chest . . . and then I felt good . . . as if I had taken a giant load off
> my shoulders . . . emotionally drained but good. (Maluccio, 1979: 60)

Feifel and Eells in their study of 63 clients of psychotherapy found
that 'the opportunity to talk' topped the list of what people found
most helpful (1963: 313). In their discussion of these findings, the
authors concluded that clients most value the opportunity 'to talk
with someone about their difficulties in an atmosphere of interest,
warmth, and tolerance'. However, they also remark that, in contrast,
'a goodly number of therapists conceive their aid as issuing strongly
from their professional mastery', a view which hardly recognizes and
certainly undervalues the part the client feels that she plays in the
exchange. 'The leitmotiv that sounds again and again in the patients'
replies,' continue Feifel and Eells, 'is the importance of sharing uncertainties and urgencies with an individual who will listen with respect
and treat with dignity their person' (1963: 317).

Although the demand for opportunities to talk is such a familiar
response, we hardly stop to think about it. Why don't we simply sit
down in a quiet corner and think about our distress and work
through it in silence? Or if we do sit down and ruminate, why does
it not seem to work, as Mr West ruefully discovered? 'When you have
a think and ponder all by yourself,' he said, 'you still don't know
what you are thinking after you finish' (Mayer and Timms, 1970: 86).
Giving voice to feelings seems an instinctive reaction, a natural thing
to do in times of high emotion. Mrs Good's marriage had been going
through a difficult time. When she discovered that her husband had
been unfaithful she felt 'at her wits' end':

> I was in a terrible state and walked the streets practically all night. It was raining and I was soaked to the skin. I remember that I came back to the flat, but I didn't go to bed. I just sat here and thought to myself, 'I must go somewhere and talk to somebody about this – I can't carry on like this.' (Mayer and Timms, 1970: 53)

If the emotional pressure is great, it may be that the sufferer is somewhat indiscriminate about whom he or she confides in. Friends are assailed and strangers buttonholed with the tale of woe. Most people, though, are more selective in their choice of confidant. Not anyone will do. Their listeners will possess certain qualities which make them attractive to those in distress. However, although particular friends, colleagues or partners may be willing and able to respond, it may be that the demands are too great or the needs too threatening. In these cases a more specialized ear is called for, though there is a gap of trust and anxiety to cross even when the need is great:

> I don't know why I'm writing to you but I just want to. I feel like crying on someone's shoulder, especially yours, why I don't know. Ever since I talked to you before, you're all I can think of. I felt like going through the floor today. I just couldn't sit there any longer. I can't explain how I feel. I want to sit down and pour my heart out to you but can't cut loose. I find it hard to talk to you and yet I want to very much. (Fitts, 1965: 27)

'I never used to tell nobody about my troubles,' recounted Mrs Watt, 'I just used to let it get me inside and then I couldn't stand it no more . . . Then all of a sudden it got on top of me. I went to the FWA [Family Welfare Association] and just broke down and told her everything' (Mayer and Timms, 1970: 50). Clients describe the simple need to talk. The opportunity to talk and the willingness of the counsellor to listen are of fundamental importance in the helping process.

For many, there is *relief* in just simply releasing feelings in a flurry of talk: 'pouring it all out'. Miss Bell described in these words the relief which she felt through unburdening: 'The first time I went, I was there two hours and I didn't stop talking once. It was marvellous and I felt very much better when I left. I was a completely different person' (Mayer and Timms, 1970: 82). The cathartic effects of releasing emotions have been observed by researchers in this field over many years (for example, see Lipkin, 1948: 143). 'He knows I talk to her,' said one defiant wife, 'and I've told him, "well, if *you* don't want to talk to them, they take a lot of *my* mind, and I feel better after"' (Phillimore, 1981: 46).

To vent feelings and to put into words all that we are thinking are among the first steps we take in trying to get a measure of what is happening in troubled times. Storr (1979: 24) observes that 'Putting things into words . . . clarifies both what one knows and what one does not know.' Certainly in the early stages of counselling, many people have so many thoughts and feelings that want to burst out, they may need several hours in which to talk: 'The worker we spoke to gave us time – about three hours – something we had never before felt entitled to. Our experiences were recognized and not denied or argued against . . . They never clock watched. They gave us time to talk through our worries' (Howe and Hinings, 1989b: 66–7). 'She was very good,' said Helen of her analyst, 'she sat and listened to me for about three hours on end' (Dinnage, 1989: 26). However for Miss Appel, the benefits came slowly but surely; there was no cathartic outpouring – more a steady flow:

> I had been so unhappy for so long that when my mother suggested I go to the agency I thought, *Wow! I'll be all fine and cured!* . . . So . . . when I first went in there, I went with this kind of illusion that there was this Good Fairy who was going to wave the magic wand . . . Well, it took me a couple of months to realize that the counselor wasn't a Good Fairy. Oh, she was just a nice lady to talk with . . . She gave me time to talk about myself and after a while I began to feel better . . . But it didn't happen overnight. (Maluccio, 1979: 55–6)

Although a good listener is something of a cliché in counselling circles, there is no denying her importance. Accounts of good therapy nearly always describe the therapist's preparedness and ability to listen. 'She doesn't need to *do* anything . . . she just needs to sit there and listen' (Phillimore, 1981: 20). Sue, in her early thirties, had felt rejected by her parents as a child and suspected she may have been sexually abused as a girl. She was bulimic, abused alcohol and drugs, and found herself in messy sexual relationships. She sought therapy:

> It was in a sort of office building but once you got in it was very cosy . . . and I walked in and burst into tears and cried for five minutes and then she began asking what the problem was and I came out with loads of stuff like my relationships and then to cope with what was going on, I was an alcoholic and an addict and bulimic . . . I felt just so relieved. I cried the whole way through and she was really sweet and understanding. It was the first person who didn't tell me to *do* anything. She just sort of listened. (Edmunds, 1992: 59)

Oldfield (1983: 71) says that the good listener is someone who is not shocked or judgemental. Michael's third therapist 'was wonderful . . . He was quiet, he listened very carefully' (1983: 153). The idea that someone is prepared to give you their undivided attention is both unusual and highly prized. Being worthy of someone else's interest does wonders for one's self-esteem.

'Time' and 'space' are two words found frequently in descriptions of satisfactory experiences of counselling and therapy: 'Space to talk'; 'Allowed us to talk for a long time about problems dealing with mental handicap'; 'She gave us as much time as we needed to talk about all our worries. It was a great relief to pour it all out' (Howe and Hinings, 1989a: 66–7). France, although the sessions with her analyst were restricted to one hour, nevertheless valued the luxury of having that amount of time devoted entirely to herself, allowing her to explore her own problems 'with the temporary setting aside of other people's claims on you, in a way that is not possible in the outside world' (1988: 122).

However, therapists who do not listen, who do not attend or who fail to give people enough time are viewed critically. Tales of terrible therapeutic experiences often tell of garrulous analysts and impatient counsellors. In the study of Sainsbury et al. (1982: 92) there were complaints by some families that interviews were too short or too infrequent, a finding which echoes the work of Feifel and Eells (1963: 314), who studied patients of psychotherapy. And a client of voluntary counselling said, 'I was always frustrated by the sense of fifty minutes not being enough. One had cried and cried, but not said lots of things' (Oldfield, 1983: 82). Elizabeth had nothing good to say about her analyst:

> I had a first impression of kindness, of concern and interest, which is pretty incredible . . . because it was bad. From the beginning. The first thing that comes to mind was that he did all the talking. I suppose it was him to me in the ratio of about ten to one. I thought I was going in there to discharge and to have someone listening and absorbing everything in a kindly way, instead of which the pattern throughout was that I would be allowed to say something and then it would be used to chastise me for the rest of the time. (Dinnage, 1989: 105)

Another way of not listening is to forbid the patient to talk, or at least not permit them to talk in a manner of their own choosing. Strongly directive therapies, and therapies which are high on technique and strategy, only allow the patient to speak and be understood in the language of the therapist. What takes place within therapy occurs inside the conceptual parameters laid down by the therapist, who defines what sort of things can be said and done. The therapeutic encounter is 'constructed' by whatever psychological theory underpins the therapeutic technique. All events take place within the construct which directs what takes place and interprets what happens within its own terms of reference. If clients and patients want to talk in a different language, their utterances will be either ignored or forbidden, interpreted or attacked. A mother of a difficult boy concluded:

> No one really understood what we lived through. They [the family therapists] never really did understand the situation. How badly it was upsetting us all. It was all too simple for our case. Just lots of questions. You answered one and boom! on to the next one. They never got to the bottom of anything. There was so much I wanted to say but I could never say it their way. (Howe, 1989a: 72)

The preference, then, is to talk about oneself and one's experiences in a way which allows feelings and thoughts to be explored in ways which are personally meaningful. Oldfield's respondents provide many examples: 'the freedom to range so widely helped restore my confidence'; 'I was free to bring up anything for discussion. I was invited to be as freely open as I wished to be – to cry, to break down, or anything . . . I was encouraged to speak as I felt' (1983: 72).

Rennie (1985) discovered that a lot more was going on in narrating events than simply telling a story. In his research he found that clients used story-telling in three ways: to deal with feelings of residual tension associated with the situation they were describing; to re-engage with difficult and troublesome feelings; and to stimulate new thoughts and ideas as clients struggled to make sense of what had happened. Stories, it appears, cannot be taken at face value. They may be designed to impress the counsellor or they may provide the client with a vehicle for exploring difficult experiences.

Oldfield, in her study of 52 clients of counselling, was struck by the emphasis placed on the importance of feelings. Feelings were a dominant feature of the problems presented. They were an essential part of the counselling experience. They were also a significant item in judging the outcome of help. Oldfield is in no doubt that most clients were wanting help with understanding and managing their feelings so that they could solve problems themselves. A good counsellor, therefore, is someone who accurately hears feelings and facilitates their expression. He or she participates in disentangling emotional confusions and helps clarify their origins (Oldfield, 1983: 171).

Women who had lived with the pain, often secret pain, of giving up a baby for adoption welcomed the opportunity to talk and release feelings that had often been held back for 10, 20 and even 30 years (Howe, 1989b: 22). 'Time to listen. Just being able to talk to someone about my feelings was a great relief to me,' remembered Alice (Howe, 1989b: 22). 'For the first time in twenty years,' said Moira,

I talked freely which I found a great relief. Talking to the counsellor made me remember things that I hadn't thought about for a long time. I think I had pushed them to the back of my mind. It was upsetting at the time but I had felt as though a great weight was lifted from me, and the guilt I suffered for years did not seem so bad. (Howe, 1989b: 22)

Dialogue

So far, I have implied that the prime need is for the client to talk, but that the talk is all one way, a monologue. However, it appears that talk, in order to be helpful and constructive, ultimately has to be experienced as two way, a dialogue, a conversation. Although the therapist may appear passive in the early stages of therapy – listening and attending – he or she becomes more active as the relationship develops. There is an increasing reciprocity and mutuality. The dialogue may not be equally balanced, but the person who is seeking help needs to experience the other as an active participant, even if the client still does most of the talking.

The urgent need to talk and release pent-up feelings gradually subsides as therapy progresses. The early phase in which emotions are described gives way to the client's wish to begin to explore her situation, to find out where she is, where she wants to go and how she wants to get there. In many ways, work of this kind is much harder. It cannot be achieved simply by the client talking. She needs the therapist to react, to struggle and think with her. This is the stage of dialogue. The therapist becomes more obviously active in the conversation. In the survey carried out by Strupp et al. (1969: 81), clients said that they wanted the therapist to be 'actively' involved in the 'verbal exchange'; they wanted to be kept 'moving'.

However, as we have observed, the therapist must not control the manner and the content of what is said, nor must she impose her preferred way of seeing things. She may suggest, she may wonder, she may even challenge. But she is not the sole arbiter of what is correct or what is true. France says of her psychotherapists that they 'did not lose sight of the fact that ours was also a dialogue between adults, who reacted to each other as real people in the present' (1988: 101). Many patients value an 'egalitarian' relationship. 'My own feeling . . . is that there is a need to meet on equal terms,' writes France, and a couple of pages later she argues that the dialogue should take place 'in a relatively normal interchange, in which the person feels free to explore their misconceptions with an equal, instead of exposing them to the scrutiny of a sphinx with a superior grasp of reality' (1988: 79, 81).

Mark had begun to develop symptoms of panic and anxiety in confined or crowded places. His family and friends did not seem able to understand, and after a number of unsuccessful treatments by psychologists and psychiatrists, he finally visited a psychotherapist:

> I was free to talk about anything under the sun. It meant that I began to trust someone, and in turn began to trust myself again. The anxiety and panic were seen as manifestations of conflict within my life, and the therapy sessions gave me a pressure-free opportunity to roam these troubled waters of my life. The therapist focused my various meanderings and utterances onto three key areas: family life, work life, and sexual relationships. With suggestion, prompting and discussion, I began to understand more clearly the marital relations of my parents and my consequent family role. The emotional, sexual and power relations of the family group had repercussions upon my own sexual and social life which began to make sense of the way I felt and acted towards others, and also how others felt and acted towards me. (Woodward, 1988: 93)

Sounding rather like a Hollywood 'B'-movie, one of Lipkin's 37 respondents clearly liked the direct, challenging style of his psychotherapist:

> If I was to get any sympathy here it was to be of a booting, two-fisted variety. This man not only called a spade a spade – he called it a 'dirt-shovel'. This struck deep. This man was awake, had an encouraging immediacy and a fine toughness in his approach. He was naming in plain man-to-man language what I had tried to explain in fancy terms, fake terms I had been trying to live my life in and had cluttered up because of them. This seemed to have touched a tender nerve, to be apropos of the over-all phony reserve in my unconscious refusal to admit, and call by name, the simple facts of life. (Lipkin, 1948: 143)

In cases where there was no dialogue and no equality in the relationship, therapy was viewed as a dull thing or an oppressive experience. There was a desire for 'feedback' from the therapist, so that the client would know what was being thought and what was going on in the relationship. Feifel and Eells noted that one of the most persistent suggestions made by clients was for more 'active participation' by therapists who were inclined to be 'too passive' and permissive (1963: 315–16).

June had had three years of therapy: 'There was no two-way stuff, you get no feedback . . . if we don't get feedback and we don't actually get led, which doesn't happen with that kind of therapy, then we just don't know where the hell we are' (Dinnage, 1989: 51, 53). Not only can an unwillingness to react be frustrating, it can also feel quite cold and hostile, as Laura recounts:

I was feeling vulnerable . . . and he gave me absolutely nothing. I think just one smile and cuddle would have melted me – it would have brought such peace. Instead, the way he treated me was just a more subtle version of the abuse I had already had in my life. My father had been cruel to me in a physical way . . . but this man did not even have to touch me to bully me. He did not respond to anything I said, so I gradually shut up . . . Certainly transference was happening . . . but it was also *real*. (Allen, 1990: 22)

Counsellors and therapists who did not demand work of the client, particularly in the later stages of help, were less well regarded. Their passivity became an increasing source of irritation. 'Sometimes I felt the counsellor should have been more active, asked more penetrating questions, revealed more opinions about my feelings or actions'; 'I think she was being what is technically called non-directive' (France, 1988: 76). France said her second therapist was a pleasant person who created a friendly climate, 'but it didn't help me get anywhere fast in therapy. We agreed with each other too easily and so I was not impelled to re-examine my views' (1988: 37). Although just being able to talk was helpful, some clients began to demand constructive responses from their counsellor.

Initially, it was really nice, just to come along and talk to somebody . . . Then I realized it was going to be up to me to decide and find out what I wanted from the sessions. This probably angered and confused me, but may have done me some good. I felt increasing annoyance that things seemed so one-sided. (Oldfield, 1983: 61)

Dialogue is the method by which the client explores. The therapist reacts to what the patient says; ideas are thrown into the discussion; feelings are aired and thoughts are discussed. Experiences which were previously overwhelming or chaotic are gradually understood and so tamed. The following example is given by a counsellor talking about her exploratory work with a young adopted black woman:

Emma still had this feeling that in order to be liked she had to please people, that she had to deny any needs that she might have in a relationship . . . I helped her explore memories of her past. There were lots of blanks. At first just a lot of feelings of hurt and pain. She remembered that she was hardly ever touched. It wasn't a family that went in much for touching or cuddling, but Emma felt it was particularly true for her as a young black child in a working class white family. 'Don't assert yourself. Sit quietly and put up with the affronts.' She felt she was expected to be grateful and that she had to please . . . I helped Emma recreate and sort of relive some of the critical childhood events that she recalled. For example, there was an occasion when she came home – still only a young girl – from a party in her tights in which there was a hole. 'You can't even be bothered to keep tidy,' her mother said, 'just look at the state of you.' The only way Emma learned to cope with this was to detach herself and, as it were, look down on the scene switching the sound off, she said, and distancing herself from what was taking place. It was clearly a survival strategy that she used as a child and that she was still using as an adult. But of course the price she paid for this as an adult was never to get too close to anybody and this was what she was missing and wanting and so it was useful to track this back to see its origins in childhood. (Howe and Hinings, 1989b: 25–6)

Making Sense and Finding Meaning

What happens when clients talk and therapists listen? What do clients feel is the result of dialogue? McLeod (1990: 12) identifies three elements in the middle phase of counselling: exploration, discovery and change. This is a time when the individual reflects on the self. Strupp et al. (1969: 14) 'forcefully call attention to the function of psychotherapy as an educational or re-educational process'. As a result of psychotherapy, many of the clients in their study were able to transform 'what seemed to be mysterious and mystifying symptoms into phenomena with explainable antecedents' (1969: 121).

The consumers of counselling and therapy report a number of benefits associated with talk and dialogue, but three in particular stand out. Good therapy and counselling:

1 Help make sense of experience.
2 Bring new meaning and order in life.
3 Improve self-esteem.

Uncertainty, anxiety, confusion and feelings of hopelessness are highly distressing. They dominate lives, interfere with work, destroy relationships. People have a desperate need to regain control over their thoughts and feelings and begin to live lives which are no longer consumed by runaway emotions. It is demeaning as well as debilitating to be constantly anxious and distressed. Putting things back into order calms the emotions, steadies the nerves and brings self-respect.

Feifel and Eells (1963: 317) in their research into the views of clients observed that, whereas therapists emphasized changes in behaviour and relief of symptoms as the main indicators of success, clients placed the accent on insight and understanding as the most appropriate measures of satisfaction.

Oldfield's clients hoped to do four things in counselling: (1) to change their feelings, gain relief from distressing emotional states and increase in self-esteem and confidence; (2) to gain greater understanding, both of self and of the problems to be dealt with; (3) to regain an ability to cope with life, and be able to work effectively again; and (4) to improve relationships (1983: 46). 'It is so hard for me to explain my feelings,' said one of Strupp et al.'s respondents (1969: 68), 'but I'm sure I'm a different person in attitude. I feel so much more relaxed – more confident, sure of myself, more attractive.' Ann France's recollections about why she thought psychotherapy worked also echo Oldfield's findings:

> I felt that problems had got out of perspective; that the degree of distress they caused me probably had less to do with their objective magnitude than with something inside me which found them intolerable. I wanted to understand my reactions and behaviour better, and felt that these were to some extent a repetitive pattern, so that understanding the mechanism might bring about change. (France, 1988: 21)

Although many of the benefits of therapy can be achieved through the simple release of feelings and the understanding shown by a caring therapist, making sense and finding meaning tend to come only after hard work and the deliberate examination and exploration of the self. It is within dialogue that the client can begin to understand the extent of her grief or measure the depth of her anger. In Oldfield's words, the counsellor begins to discover whether the client 'has, or can develop or recover, some degree of curiosity about his emotional experiences, which may itself lead to some shared work towards understanding them' (1983: 15).

Talking within the demands of a stimulating dialogue encourages clear thinking; it creates new thinking, and it helps clients to make sense. Talking about feelings, therefore, allows people to recognize the character of their various emotional states and subject them to examination: 'So it is we come *to know our own minds*,' observe Orlinsky and Howard (1986: 494). These two authors then suggest that the articulation of feeling not only allows the possibility of self-knowledge, it also gives the other person the opportunity to understand the client's mental state: 'So it is that we come *to know each other's minds*' (emphases added).

One of France's psychotherapists challenged everything she said. She made her look afresh at the tenets of her life: 'This often made it an uncomfortable experience, but it encouraged change. By systematically making me re-examine everything I said, or that had been said to me, it became possible to sort out true from false motives more clearly' (1988: 36). Veronique has equally strong memories of her analyst:

It was very reassuring from the first, though also a bit persecuting, a bit harsh. But I could tell I was with someone who knew what he was doing. There was a tremendous sense of relief and a real sort of clarity. Because when things get in such a muddle, there is a sense of fuzziness in the head, so that even proper intellectual thinking is hampered. I found my capacity to think things through clearly was coming back. (Dinnage, 1989: 79)

Clients who feel muddled, and therapists who are conversationally challenging, also cropped up in the replies received by Oldfield. One counsellor was described as 'someone who interjected with objective and penetrating things, that one isn't able to see when fighting through the fog of one's own warped ideas'; 'The therapist asked some very acute and penetrating questions. This was marvellous – like flashes of light' (Oldfield, 1983: 73).

The result of asking penetrating questions and dispelling fog was to put things into some kind of order. 'Many things seemed much straighter, after a few talks'; 'She always seemed to be able to pick out what was important in what I was saying' (Oldfield, 1983: 74). Good counsellors seemed able to recognize underlying themes: 'Things I was conscious of but hadn't related – all came together' (Oldfield, 1983: 74). 'As time went on,' reflected one of Lipkin's interviewees,

these problems which I could not comprehend myself were simplified and I discovered that they were not as great as they actually seemed at first. He helped me overcome a feeling of despair which made the problems seem harder to look at. He sort of helped me see myself as others saw me, and at the same time, helped me see other persons as they saw themselves. (Lipkin, 1948: 144)

Regaining control over one's thoughts and feelings is helped by finding some pattern in what otherwise appears to be a jumble of emotions. Identifying a feeling, examining a thought or finding a connection made the client feel less likely to be tossed along by strong emotions. The more the client talks within the rigours of dialogue, the more likely it is that she recovers a sense of order. No longer buffeted by disorganized thoughts and turbulent feelings, the client once more begins to feel in control.

Understanding and self-reliance are achieved through the experience of the relationship and the thinking that takes place within that relationship (Oldfield, 1983: 18). When emotions are in conflict, people feel distressed and muddled.

If this muddle can be patiently disentangled and the original conflict exposed, it can be re-experienced, re-evaluated and, perhaps, resolved in a more direct way . . . The counsellor, encumbered with less detail, may be able to see patterns and kinds of continuity which help the client to experience life in a meaningful way. (Oldfield, 1983: 18)

Simon, who was France's third psychotherapist, focused on the underlying meaning of what she said. He looked for

> the possible thread linking it with other communications in that session. In this way, he helped me reach the core of an experience and to see a pattern in apparently disconnected phenomena. This sometimes annoyed me because I felt he was imposing a pattern where there was none, reading a pre-existing text into my personal discourse; but this could be discussed openly, given the climate of mutual honesty and receptivity. (France, 1988: 38)

But without openness and mutuality, the experience is less satisfactory. Therapists who lay claim to all the expertise are rarely experienced as helpful. When she was 20, Olga experienced intense feelings of anxiety, distress and confusion. She saw a number of therapists over a period of time. The style of one particular therapist

> was considerably more structured than that of my very first psychiatrist, but the themes were much the same. There was something FUNDAMEN-TALLY WRONG with me; that tinkering and tailoring my ideas would create the 'right' combination of thoughts and I would then settle in to emotional stability. He was, however, the master tailor, and the tinkering went on within me. The connection between me, my emotional distress and the world of relationships and events outside of me was rarely discussed. There was, thus, no way I could understand the causes of my condition or the circumstances under which I would find health. (Woodward, 1988: 102–3, emphasis in original)

When Olga came to England, she found a new therapist:

> As therapy continued, the past was reintroduced. We jointly explored recurring themes and I began to make sense of a lifetime of methods – no longer appropriate – that I had devised for my psychic survival. I was addressed as an intelligent human being who got into trouble because of conflicting demands made by those whom I loved and needed. (Woodward, 1988: 104)

A powerful way of making connections and pulling threads together in order to make sense is to allow people to tell their story. Many feminist counsellors have recognized the value of the personal narrative. In describing work with Suzanne, Walker (1990: 1–21) illustrates the way clients can be helped to tell their story. Within the story lay patterns of living and ways of being which Suzanne needed to recognize and understand. As the weeks went by, an outline of her life began to emerge and more of the pieces began to fit together. 'Sometimes bits of the story have been told to different people, but because of this have never been joined together. The parts apparently do not belong to each other, and are not always related as aspects of the same experience' (Walker, 1990: 12). As feelings were expressed, 'Suzanne and her therapist began to make sense of the depression . . . they were able to make links to experiences in the past' (1990: 15).

A growing sense of order, an increasing ability to make connections, the recognition of patterns – all these lead to a better understanding of self and the meanings that clients give to their experience. Clients want to understand why they feel and react as they do. They want to make sense of their thoughts and emotions. 'I think I learned a lot about myself,' replied a counselling client, 'which has affected how I feel and how I behave (changed for the better I think)' (Oldfield, 1983: 96). And in a dramatic utterance, Margaret concluded, 'For the first time in my life I understand what I am doing' (Woodward, 1988: 87). 'Understanding what went wrong,' mused Jeffrey, 'understanding how it affected your behaviour – it makes a significant difference. But the bit I don't understand is that it has a healing effect. Why it heals I don't know' (Dinnage, 1989: 125).

Reflexivity

We might round off this section by considering what many people believe to be the core activity of counselling – reflexivity – in which the client monitors and evaluates his or her own thoughts and feelings and the understandings that might emerge out of such reflections. A number of people have explored the notion of reflexivity in therapy, but I shall concentrate on the research and writings of Rennie, who is particularly clear on this subject. He is also preferred because his ideas have been drawn out of interviews with clients on their experiences of counselling and therapy.

Therapy allows people to concentrate on themselves. In the therapeutic process, clients can explore, identify and examine important thoughts and feelings, some of which may have been known before therapy, and some of which arise out of the reflective process itself as difficult or stressful ('tension zones'). 'Once this process starts,' explains Rennie (1990: 160), 'clients increasingly have a sense of being on a path, or train of thought.' The client is in pursuit of meaning. But Rennie also reminds us that, although the client's prime interest is in chasing personal meaning, this is more or less sustained depending on the perceived quality of the relationship with the therapist. As we learned in earlier chapters, clients are supported, encouraged and strengthened by the various 'non-specific' factors in the relationship including acceptance, trust, warmth and understanding.

However, it is not always easy, even for very good therapists, to follow a client's 'path to meaning'. An inappropriate response by the therapist jolts the client out of her train of thought and obliges her instead to reflect on the relationship with the therapist. Like any other kind of interaction, a good deal of therapeutic time is spent trying to make sense of the therapeutic vehicle; the relationship itself now becomes the subject of reflection.

> Clients realize that they and the therapist are dealing with a highly ambiguous and complicated subject. Clients do not expect therapists to be highly accurate with every response and charitably write off 'dead time' in a session as something that is to be expected . . . Furthermore, clients appraise sessions as a whole and tend to be content if one or two highlights can be achieved. (Rennie, 1990: 163)

This tolerant attitude may be true if there is a good relationship between client and therapist, but an inaccurate response within the context of a poor client–therapist alliance simply adds further proof that the therapy and the therapist are not working. The client has to try to understand the frame of reference being used by the therapist in order to make sense of the discordant utterance: 'Now, why did he say that, I wonder?' 'To the extent that the thoughts and feelings generated by such responses continue to reverberate within clients, the relationship with the therapist can constitute the underlying theme of major portions of the entire therapy session' (Rennie, 1990: 164). This becomes particularly significant when the client perceives the relationship with the therapist to be poor. Energy is diverted from pursuing personal concerns to a preoccupation with the relationship with the therapist and how to manage it.

There is a final twist in Rennie's analysis. Not all interruptions by therapists are bad. Indeed, those made within the context of a good working alliance actually cement the alliance, allowing further opportunities to clarify what is going on, which, in turn, increases the control the client has over his or her experience. The interruption forces the client to evaluate the frame of reference which she is using as she follows a line of meaning, as well as the alternative frame suggested by the therapist. The therapist's response

> provides clients with a tool for objectifying their own processes so that they are in a better position to assume control over them; it clarifies the intentions beneath particular client and therapist responses and nullifies misunderstandings; it exposes each party's plans and strategies for the therapy and opens up the possibility of a negotiated and mutual set of

plans and strategies; and it gives the client a heightened sense of equality with the therapist which in turn increases the client's personal sense of power and self-esteem. (Rennie, 1990: 170)

Reflexivity, therefore, provides the client with an opportunity for changing direction as she follows various paths of personal meaning. Rennie is most careful to explain that (1) the client's reflections on the meaning she is giving to her personal concerns and (2) her monitoring of what is going on in the relationship between herself and the therapist in themselves do not bring about change. Too much reflexivity prevents the discovery of new meaning. Action is avoided. Too little reflexivity produces ill-considered, poorly conceived action. 'Hence,' concludes Rennie (1992: 21),

> reflexivity modulates action ... too much reflexivity leads to inaction, while too little reflexivity leads to action without direction ... It is through reflexivity that clients set the stage for change. It is through nonreflexivity that they undergo change. It is subsequently through reflexivity that they appraise the change that was experienced, and set the stage for yet further action.

Thus, new understandings have the potential to shift clients into new actions.

Controlling the Meaning of Experience

Making sense of experience and recognizing the patterns in our lives enable us to overcome our feelings of despair, hopelessness and confusion. Before we can take control we need to understand what is happening and why it is happening. But once we are able to make sense, we have the capacity to control our experiences. 'Once I got the understanding,' said Alice, 'the anger left. My understanding is actually teaching me a new way of living' (Edmunds, 1992: 40). John had experienced a difficult childhood. Like his parents, he too became an alcoholic:

> as I went through the process I understood how ineffective my mother had been and why she was like that because her childhood was lousy and so I realized that to blame her was not the issue. So the process allowed me to let go of the anger that I experienced about my mother and the damage that she did unwittingly. I can't change what happened but I can change me and how I perceive it. (Edmunds, 1992: 27)

Clients of counselling and therapy who have taken their therapeutic explorations this far observe that uncertainty and anxiety are much reduced and they are much less prey to the stresses and strains of poorly understood thoughts and feelings, particularly those generated in social relationships. To be in control is empowering; it feels good. To be in control bolsters confidence; self-esteem rises. This is how it felt for Margaret: 'Sometimes I got bits of it "right", and it felt marvellous – in control but gently so. If it didn't go "right", I knew I'd have another chance before long. It was my control – not somebody else's' (Woodward, 1988: 85).

After suffering deep depressions, Myra had sought counselling. Gradually she began to make sense of things, and this gave her confidence and the feeling that she had power and control over her own life:

> As each new shift was internalized I could sense a pattern developing. Feeling myself moving towards some unknown insight meant that I began to experience great faith in my ability to take power over my life and change my ways of relating. The most important fact was that it came from *within me* and I was free to choose how and when I used my change. (Grierson, 1990: 39)

Pamela, who as a child had been physically abused by her mother and sexually abused by a friend of the family, was beginning to make sense of how her early experiences had coloured her adult life, which had been very difficult:

> I started counselling when I was forty-one. My mother died when she was forty-one. I had actually lived my mother's life. Once I had reached forty-one I had nowhere else to go. I then had to find out who I was. Everything my mother did to me as a child I also did to my children. I took on her mannerisms, her makeup and her way of doing things . . . So, I was fifteen when she died at the age of forty-one. I didn't connect the two. So when I was forty-one I knew this was the time to go, but I didn't connect it. As soon as we did a family tree I saw the connection that she was forty-one when she died and I'm forty-one now. At the end of that session I felt ten feet tall. Absolutely brilliant because I knew then that my life was going to change and take on a new meaning . . . I knew I was going to get answers and those answers were going to be good enough to help me understand . . . I can change myself. I can't change others . . . and it's working. (Edmunds, 1992: 63)

An interesting aside on the subject of people's need to achieve control is found in a number of the client studies which considered the uncertainty engendered by some therapeutic techniques. These findings show distinct parallels with the work of Rennie on 'reflexivity' mentioned earlier. Broadly, if the client could not understand what the counsellor was trying to do, or make sense of how he or she was trying to do it, this produced feelings of confusion and uncertainty. The choices open to the client were to stay with treatment, but remain puzzled and not in control of the experience; alternatively, the client could terminate treatment, escape the uncertainty and thereby retain a certain kind of control of the experience.

After their fourth interview with a psychodynamic caseworker, Mr and Mrs Skinner finished their dealings with the agency. They had been concerned with the behaviour of their 16-year-old daughter:

> The social worker wanted to know all about our background when we were young and all that, and I said to my husband, 'Well, to my opinion, that's nothing to do with it' . . . When we came out of there the fourth time, my husband said, 'What do you think of it?' and I said, 'I don't know what to think of it.' Then my husband said, 'He just don't give you any idea what he's going to do or anything. He just keeps on saying come back and have some more talks and he says he's going to have more talks and more talks. Well, while he's doing that, we're not getting anywhere. Penny's the problem, not us.' (Mayer and Timms, 1970: 71)

Family therapy very often involves refined techniques which are outside of most people's everyday experience. In the case of Mr and Mrs Spree, the therapists worked in a team, with one member dealing directly with the family, leaving the others to supervise and observe proceedings through a television monitor connected to a camera in the treatment room. The observers could communicate with the therapist via a microphoned earpiece. Mr Spree was the stepfather of 14-year-old Rachel, but it was Mrs Spree who was most upset about her daughter's difficult behaviour. They recounted their first session:

> Mr S: Well first, what I felt was that it was them against us. There was no relationship at all. The panel in the next room could feedback to the person in the room with us, but we had nothing directly to do with them. They were like 'Big Brother' out there. I found it very disconcerting.
> Mrs S: We didn't even know who was in there.
> Mr S: It could have been anyone.
> Mrs S: I mean, if they'd given us a cup of tea first, that would have been helpful.
> Mr S: The panel kept interrupting. It was very off-putting, very confusing. We never seemed to get anywhere.
> Mrs S: He'd say something like . . . er . . . after he got a message from the panel, 'Oh, I've got to bring in Rachel now' and you were cut short. I felt like a guinea pig.
> Mr S: I did, actually, too. We were like puppets and it was like they were experimenting with us, because they'd found this new thing, this camera and things, and could try out certain techniques of interviewing. (Howe, 1989a: 53–4)

Mr and Mrs Spree could make little sense of the experience and never returned for the second session.

New Order, New Thinking

The therapeutic dialogue moves the client along a road which takes her from description to understanding, from making sense of the past to understanding the present. The calming effect of knowing what is happening and why it is happening is a major achievement. The final leg of the therapeutic experience sees the client creating a new order for herself as she restructures her mental outlook. This is a phase of reconstruction. Having looked at the past and reflected on the present, the client now looks forward and considers the future.

It is not possible to know what to build or how to build it, unless you know what materials you have to hand. You need to understand the properties of these materials, to know their strengths and limitations. When you know all these things, you can begin to construct a more robust and less fragile structure – a stronger self. New meanings can be given to old experiences. A fresh zest may return to the client's life as self-control is regained, and a sense of purpose is recovered.

A mother whose life had been beset by emotional problems reflected on the progress she had made as a result of psychotherapy:

> I am more or less working blindly, but still I do feel as I am going in the right direction. My relations with my family have improved a great deal from what they were two years ago. Also I have realized that my former hostile attitude toward other people was all wrong, and lately I have been trying to mix with other people, instead of avoiding them. For the first time I have discovered that delightful sensation of expressing my own real feelings and reactions (not without some trepidation) and along with this I have accepted the responsibility of my own self. (Fitts, 1965: 137)

Many feminist counsellors have developed the connection between understanding and control in ways which parallel the experiences of clients generally. Walker (1990: 75) writes that women should try to become responsible for aspects of their lives over which they do have some control. Understanding and making sense of how one's own experiences have been socially constructed are empowering.

> It is important that women are able to identify aspects of their world over which they have control, and, equally, understand those that arise from being in an essentially sexist society. This opens the door to controlling and changing some parts of their lives. But other parts may not be amenable to change. Knowing which is which, placing responsibility firmly where it belongs, taking charge of what is theirs, and saying 'no' to what is not, is a huge step forward for women. (Walker, 1990: 75)

France believes that psychotherapy should tend towards the organization of structure and meaning from 'inchoate experience'. She continues: 'Through bringing inspiration, insight and discipline to bear on the raw material something new comes into being. Psychotherapy is therefore creative rather than a question of following rules or a leader' (1988: 143). Strupp and his fellow authors summarize the basic steps of the 'work' phase in this fashion:

> One of the striking accomplishments of psychotherapy was ... the transformation of what seemed to be mysterious and mystifying symptoms into phenomena with explainable antecedents. The patient came to view his difficulties in the context of his interpersonal relations, and this new understanding was accompanied by the development of techniques for more adaptive, less conflictual and more satisfying ways of relating to others ... Feelings of confidence, assurance and mastery replaced helplessness, inadequacy and overwhelming despair. In psychoanalytic terms, the patient's natural tendencies towards synthesis, meaning, organization, competence and growth supplanted his sense of failure and helplessness. (Strupp et al., 1969: 121–2)

Successful therapy helps the client see her world anew, with a clarity and perspicacity that had been lacking. 'It is in a way a whole new life,' says Alexander. 'If I'm with acquaintances who haven't had analysis, I'm very much aware of feeling that there's an extra dimension to my perception of reality and relationships ... I'm not saying that I'm happier than these people, not necessarily; but there's no way back, you can't unscramble an omelette' (Dinnage, 1989: 40).

Feelings of Hope and Looking Forward

Concluding their views on the experience of counselling and therapy, clients whose opinions are positive often end by saying that they felt encouraged; they looked to the future with feelings of hope and optimism. 'I can now feel some hope for the future,' reported one of Fitts's (1965: 153) respondents, 'some reason for living, some purpose. I'm not just drifting any more or waiting for something to happen. Now I'm going to make some things happen.' A more modest, yet firm, sense of purpose was present in Margaret's life at the end of therapy: 'I know I'm pretty slow at re-shaping my life, but it's coming and I feel that I've got plenty of time. I just keep gently plodding on "unhooking" and being myself' (Woodward, 1988: 89).

Making sense of what has happened gives the client a feeling of control and so the future can be viewed with confidence. Pamela was in her mid-forties. She had been sexually abused as a child by a family friend as well as physically abused by her mother. Her father was an alcoholic:

the counselling gave me the tools to understand why my adult life had become such a complete mess ... If it hadn't have been for counselling I would have still been on that merry-go-round, although there was no piece in the jigsaw to connect. Now I understand that I am not a freak. I'm a normal natural young healthy woman and my life can take on a new meaning. It's allowed me to make choices ... I now have hope. I mean I know I'm in a good place today but I know the best is yet to come. (Edmunds, 1992: 37)

The Modest Ambitions of Clients

A regular note struck by clients when in this reflective mood is the satisfaction with *modest progress*. This accords with the observations made by Feifel and Eells (1963: 312) that, whereas therapists were looking for measurable changes in behaviour and symptoms, clients were content with gains in self-understanding. In the words of Lipkin in his early 1948 paper: 'A complete resolution of difficulties was often not necessary for clients to feel counseling had been of value'; and to this end he quotes 'Client No. 24': 'Truly I can't say that I've made as much progress as I'd like, but I'm going forward slowly that's to be sure. Seemingly the more I know of myself the more I want to learn about "me". I think to know myself thoroughly would help to know other people really better' (Lipkin, 1948: 145). A couple who had been having considerable problems with their 14-year-old adopted daughter summed up their experience in these words: 'In many ways she's still as bad. But we understand things better now. We don't get so wound up, and of course that helps us and it helps her. So we're optimistic. Knowing that other families had similar problems and survived also helped. They gave us hope' (Howe and Hinings, 1989a: 81).

And Mrs Bogdansky reached similar conclusions about the value of the counselling that she had received when she was experiencing difficulties with her daughter: 'There is no doubt that it helped. Counseling made me see what my daughter is like and what she is going through as a teenager ... Naturally I expected more ... You always do, but I was satisfied with what I got' (Maluccio, 1979: 108).

The Full Therapeutic Sequence

When we add together the three major client perspectives – accept me, understand me and talk with me – we define the full flow and character of counselling and therapy as experienced by clients. I make no apologies for ending this chapter with a long quote from Orlinsky and Howard. It sums up much of what has emerged from the present enquiry. After many years spent analysing what takes place in therapy, these two authors offer the following explanation of why therapy, when it works, works:

> Psychotherapy in all modalities typically provides an experience of relatedness with the therapist . . . that approximates what Winnicott has termed a 'holding environment'. This mode of relatedness facilitates an open, nondefensive frame of mind in which new learning (psychological, restructuring, growth) is most probable. While in such a state of self-relatedness, patients are encouraged by the affective messages they sense from their therapists to explore painful and problematic areas of experience that they would otherwise avoid because they have been unable to cope tolerably with them in the past. With the aid of effective therapist interventions (of one sort or another) patients bring a fuller range of their present psychological resources to bear on these painful issues, find relief from them, and emerge with enhanced confidence. It seems highly plausible that a knowledgable sense of the patient's Feeling Confident is the exportable product of experience in therapy sessions, remembering that this confidence has been tested and tempered by successful exposure to many of the patient's worst fears. That kind of confidence can be a stable, resilient foundation for one's self-esteem and morale, as it can also be a most favorable basis for engaging with others in the basic personal relationships out of which one builds one's life. (Orlinsky and Howard, 1986: 498)

12 Description

People like to get things off their chest; a trouble shared is a trouble halved. The clients of counselling are in no doubt that one of the most valued aspects of counselling is the chance to talk. It was one of Breur's patients, Anna O., who baptized this type of treatment 'the talking cure'. The simple act of giving voice to one's worries and concerns is in itself therapeutic. However, because it is such a common experience, the therapeutic effect of talking things through seems obvious; we take it for granted. But a second glance suggests that it is not at all obvious why talking to someone should make a person feel better. So why does talk cure?

A number of interesting answers have been given to these questions. Bowlby (1988: 130-1), for example, noticed that, in various studies, children who were securely attached, who felt loved and accepted, talked more openly and freely and with greater expression of feeling than children who were not securely attached. In the latter cases, conversation was fragmented, often impersonal, with much less reference to feelings. Bowlby then goes on to make the following point:

> These striking differences in the degree to which communication is either free or restricted are postulated to be of great relevance for understanding why one child develops healthily and another becomes disturbed. Moreover it will not have escaped notice that this same variable, the degree to which communication between two individuals is restricted or relatively free, has for long been recognized as one of central concern in the practice of analytic psychotherapy. (Bowlby, 1988: 130-1)

The curative value of talk has received three closely linked explanations. Each one has explored the way we make sense of ourselves and our situations *within social relationships*.

The *first* explanatory tack recognizes the creative nature of description in human affairs. Description organizes thought and shapes feeling. Talk and description help people to discover who they are – what is good and bad in them, what hurts or delights, and what is to be done (Klein, 1987: 382). In describing their experiences, people learn to understand themselves.

The *second* approach is struck by the story-telling quality that characterizes much of human discourse. This is particularly true of conversations which are felt to be therapeutic. The role of the narrative in human development and social understanding is given considerable import by some psychologists, and we shall look at this in Chapter 13.

The *third* explanation combines elements of the first two, but highlights the two-way nature of talk in the counselling relationship. Understanding forms within dialogue. This will be the subject of Chapter 14.

Description

When talking about her thoughts and feelings the client is doing more than simply reporting her mental state. In the act of giving voice to her inner condition, she is giving her experiences expression; she is allowing them to take shape.

Experience is lived but not necessarily understood. We may struggle with our emotions; we can be confused by our thoughts. By describing our experience – how we feel, what we think – we can begin to understand what it might mean. In giving our experience shape and form we are defining its boundaries and structure. Description therefore organizes the way we perceive and understand the world. So long as our emotional conditions lack either boundaries or structure, it is difficult to get a firm grasp or understanding of what is happening. The experience is present, but it is amorphous and poorly defined, it is hard to follow and difficult to understand. The experience feels unmanageable. Talking is the first step in providing an experience with form and structure, extent and scale.

The creative quality of description and talk has been powerfully argued by Raymond Williams (1965). The brain is inclined to organize its perceptions of the world so that sense is made of experience. 'Reality' is not received passively by the brain; 'reality' is organized and given meaning. In other words, human beings actively create the reality which they experience. The brain processes sense perceptions into a form which it finds intelligible, workable and manageable. As we grow and mature, our brains interact with the world. The brain is programmed to structure itself in the light of experience. In this way, we learn to see, read other minds and generally make sense of people and things. Human experience is no longer viewed as the subjective appreciation of objective phenomena. Human experience arises in a fluid relationship between the brain's innate desire to organize and find meaning, on the one hand, and the meaning and organization that are already present in the social world, on the other.

However, for human beings it is not just a single dynamic between the brain and the environment. Matters become even more subtle when we realize that one of the main ingredients of the environment is other people. Other people hold, offer and practice views about the way the world is and how it should be interpreted and understood. In our developmental progress, our understanding of the world is heavily informed by the way other people understand it. Thus, reality as we experience it is a human creation in two senses. Reality is a creation of the brain as it develops and learns to make sense of its perceptions. Reality is also a social creation made by people as they interpret the world around them. But these ways of 'seeing', according to Williams, are neither fixed nor constant. 'We can learn new rules and new interpretations, as a result of which we shall literally see in new ways' (Williams, 1965: 34).

The interplay between *inheritance* and *culture* influences the way the individual sees and experiences the world. Of course, different cultures have created different versions of reality, different ways of seeing. However, individuals within a particular culture may discover new ways of seeing things, new ways of experiencing reality. This is a 'creative' process. And if the individual can communicate this new understanding to other people, the community's experience and general outlook are also altered – the cultural context is shifted a fraction, and the world can never be experienced in quite the same way again.

This brings Williams to the heart of his thesis. We learn to see a thing by describing it, and we learn to describe it in terms of the meanings held about the world by our own culture. The description does two things. It gives form to our experience. And it locks us into the matrix of understanding that defines our cultural context. If we can adequately describe our experience we can both learn to make sense of our thoughts and feelings and confirm our social place.

Williams recognizes a clear link between seeing, describing and communicating. Our culture gives us the constructs by which to understand what various experiences mean. These are learned as we interact and communicate with other people. Such social interaction helps us recognize and understand our own thoughts and feelings and those of other people. The medium for both self-understanding and understanding other people is words, both received and sent. Acts of description are acts in which experience is thus defined, not just by the physical make-up of the brain but also in terms of the meaning constructs held by society and absorbed into the 'making-sense' structures of the brain. Not until an experience is described in some way is it actually realized. And as description has to be broadly rendered in the language and concepts of the host community, it will be capable of being understood by and communicated to others in that community.

Therefore, *describing experience* and communicating that description are a *creative* process which gives form and content to the thoughts and feelings that constitute experience.

> It is, in the first instance, to every man, a matter of urgent personal importance to 'describe' his experience, because this is literally a remaking of himself, a creative change in his personal organization, to include and control his experience. This struggle to remake ourselves – to change our personal organization so that we may live in a proper relation to our environment – is in fact often painful . . . the impulse to communicate is a learned human response to disturbance of any kind. For the individual, of course, the struggle is to communicate successfully by describing adequately . . . For unless the description is adequate, there can be no relevant communication. To think merely of making contact with others, rather than making contact with this precise experience, is irrelevant and distracting. Genuine communication depends on this absorbed attention to precise description, but of course it does not follow that the description is for its own sake; the attention, rather, is a condition of relevant communication. (Williams, 1965: 42–3)

The Organization of Experience and the Communication of Meaning

Like other people, artists need to describe and communicate the meaning of their experience, but they have a special capacity to find new ways of understanding, describing and communicating their experience. His command of this skill, according to Williams, is his art. Experiences are described in fresh, unexpected ways; the world is seen through different eyes, and the artist is someone able to transmit a description of this 'new' experience in words or paint, music or shape.

'There can be no separation, in this view, between "content" and "form", because finding the form is literally finding the content – this is what we mean by the activity we have called "describing"' (Williams, 1965: 42). Thus, the creative act is either a confirmation of established meanings or an extension of meanings. It is an organized set of experiences which are communicated to others.

Like the artist, we work on our experience, trying to find meaning as we capture it in description. We retell our thoughts and feelings, first this way then that, until it seems that we have got across, to ourselves as well as to others, the way we understand and feel about our experience. Only in describing the experience do we come to understand it. It begins to take shape and it starts to make sense.

In communicating the description, the experience is created, and the individual, as author of the description, is thereby changed. A new understanding enters her cognitive and emotional make-up. But it must be remembered that this is simply an individual subject working on a description of her experience, the better to understand it. As the experience is described and understood, so it changes the person's perception of the experience. In turn this demands yet more changes in the description: 'The man makes the shape, and the shape remakes the man' (Williams, 1965: 44). Art, therefore, is the organization of experience and the communication of meaning. The client, in attempting to generate new descriptions of her experience, is seeking to give such experience new meaning. Talking allows the individual to find new descriptions of difficult experiences.

The Community of Meaning

However, the analysis of creative endeavour does not stop there. The demand that we describe our experience links us back into the community of others. We understand our experience by describing it, but we describe it in the words and meaning structures of our particular culture. Thus, in offering a description we understand what our experience means in terms of our surrounding culture. 'The discovery of a means of communication is the discovery of a common meaning,' says Williams; and

> Since our way of seeing things is literally our way of living, the process of communication is in fact the process of community: the sharing of common meanings, and thence common activities and purposes; the offering, reception and comparison of new meanings, leading to the tensions and achievements of growth and change. (Williams, 1965: 47, 55)

Psychologists, in treading very similar terrain, have also recognized that meaning has to be reintroduced into psychology and that talk about meaning involves locating people and their minds in society, for that is where meanings are created and negotiated. When an individual infant enters the world she is immediately immersed in culture and language, both of which are saturated with symbols and meanings. The developing brain finds itself in a cultural world of meaning every bit as much as a world of solid things.

Culture is a product of history rather than nature, and it is to culture that we have to adapt. We no longer think of the biological brain simply acquiring language, nor do we see culture merely adding the refining touches to our biological needs:

> As Clifford Geertz puts it, without the *constituting* role of culture we are 'unworkable monstrosities . . . incomplete or unfinished animals who complete or finish ourselves through culture' . . . It is man's participation *in* culture and the realization of his mental powers *through* culture that make it impossible to construct a human psychology on the basis of the individual alone . . . to quote Geertz again, 'there is no such thing as human nature independent of culture.' (Bruner, 1990: 12)

The human brain and its associated psychology, therefore, are organized around the processes which generate meaning and so link the individual to culture.

Meanings are of value only if they are shared, and so it is in the interests of the individual and others to construct a shared world, a socially constructed reality. Adopting the words of Williams (1965: 50), 'since the meaning and the means cannot be separated', the counsellor must thoroughly understand the experience of the other and make it a part of himself so 'that his whole energy is available to describe it and transmit it to others'. England, who has made a thorough study of Williams's arguments and adapted them to work with clients, sums up matters in this way:

> The process of communication is the process of finding common meaning, and thus the process of finding community, and so society . . . Williams's account shows that people *make* their understanding of the world, that description through communication is an essential part of understanding . . . each person's ability to make sense, and to organize an understanding of the world, depends upon the ability to communicate about that understanding. 'Reality' is only maintained by its communication, and such communication is particularly urgent at times of stress. (England, 1986: 110–12)

To recap: our brains are programmed to make experience meaningful. The language and cognitive structures that our brains use in the process of making sense are formed in the interactions which we have with other people. Thus, the sense we are driven to make is not simply the application of some innate personal programming but is the product of the social rules and outlooks that become established in our own cognitive make-up.

If we are to gain new understandings of the meaning of our own experiences, we have to use the medium in which we originally learned to understand the meaning of those experiences. Hence, describing our experiences requires us to use language as the medium which provides them with shape and meaning. In making such descriptions, the meanings we give to experience become available for public as well as self-scrutiny.

13 Narrative

The next step on from simple description is to tell a story. Events are told in the form of a narrative; experiences are structured around a story. Most of the 'talking cures' have an interest in biography, and it seems that unravelling one's past is very therapeutic. The therapist is as much audience as fellow actor, as much prompter as critic.

The recognition that the story plays a central part in human affairs has received considerable attention over the last decade. As a metaphor for understanding people and their behaviour, it offers a richer, more dense fabric than the traditional metaphors of science – the machine and the organism. Whereas science looks for explanations and causes, the story is intent on finding a *meaningful account*.

The machine as a metaphor dominates our view, not just of the sciences, but of the social sciences too. In the world of the machine, things are caused, rules can be found, predictions can be made. Formal connections exist between one set of events and another. It is a consistent world and a regular place. It is located within a logical universe whose principles of operation can be determined. Underlying all actions and reactions are a set of rules that constitute a *text* for the way all things behave and can be read. There is thus a general concern with finding the 'truth of things' and a need to know how things 'really are'.

The objective sciences have had a powerful impact on the way we approach people and things. The scientist is interested in generating universal rules that apply to particular instances. For all situations of a particular kind there are held to be common mechanisms determining their performance. This is in contrast to those who feel that a specific event can only be understood in its particular *context*. The interest focuses on what things *mean* to people and it is to meaning that the enquirer turns as she seeks to understand.

Contained in the metaphor of 'context' is the belief that there is no underlying consistency or universal logic in human affairs. The running together of certain ideas at particular times, the contingent association of people and perspectives, the situationally constructed panoply of thoughts and feelings all produce an event which is densely textured. 'Contained in the metaphor,' explains Sarbin (1986: 6), 'is the idea of constant change in the structure of situations and in positions occupied by actors.' The individual's understanding of the situation in which she finds herself affects her actions. The things that people say and do have no meaning outside the context in which they are said and done.

In contrast to the scientist, who wishes to produce universal formulae which are independent of context, the artist explores the meaning of experience as it arises *in* context. We need to know the particulars of a situation – what the various participants know, believe, think and feel – before we can understand what is going on. A vehicle that handles context particularly well is the story, the narrative. In contrast to the images of the machine and the play of physical forces, the narrative metaphor turns to drama and story-telling.

Much of traditional psychology attempts to free itself of context, striving to identify the mechanisms that drive behaviour. 'It is as if there is a moral imperative to reduce the drama of humanity to the play of impersonal forces' (Sarbin, 1986: 10). And in even more severe tones, Sarbin reprimands psychology for ignoring the common-sense wisdom to be found in fables and mythic tales. He quotes John Dewey (1922), who believed that

> The novelist and the dramatist are so much more illuminating as well as more interesting commentators on conduct than the schematizing psychologist. The artist makes perceptible individual responses and thus displays a new phase of human nature evoked in new situations. In putting the case visibly and dramatically he reveals vital actualities. The scientific systematizer treats each act as merely another sample of some old principle, or as a mechanical combination of elements drawn from a ready-made inventory. (1922: 145–6)

The narrative is taken as a fruitful metaphor for understanding human action. People and the things they say and do are accounted for in credible stories, narratives that 'ring true'. So, rather than look for some fundamental truth in situations, the artist is interested in how experience is endowed with meaning: a 'narrative truth'. This relative notion of truth means that many aspects of a particular situation or case cannot generalize to other situations or cases. 'Our discoveries,' concludes Spence (1982: 295), 'may be highly situational and need to be understood in their immediate context; it would be a mistake to reduce them to some general law because, by so doing, we might lose the very ingredient that made them effective in the specific case.' Indeed, many things only make sense 'in context'. One of the arguments against testing children on specific, isolated items is that most of us only begin to understand and remember bits of information or the purposes of a procedure as they relate to the overall situation – the context.

The narrative is built on concern for the human condition. What we know, think and feel about a situation affects our actions. The introduction of one piece of information and the meaning which it has for us can profoundly influence our experience of an event. 'It is the difference,' says Bruner (1986: 14), 'between Oedipus sharing Jocasta's bed before and after he learns from the messenger that she is his mother.' Stories are understood in terms of what the actors think and believe; the reality of the situation is defined by feelings and desires. So, whereas a good scientific theory is *testable*, a good story is *believable* (Bruner, 1986: 14). The two positions are neatly summarized by Bruner in these words:

> the 'reality' of most of us is constituted roughly into two spheres: that of nature and that of human affairs, the former more likely to be structured in the paradigmatic mode of logic and science, the latter in the mode of story and narrative. The latter is centered around the drama of human intentions and their vicissitudes; the first around the equally compelling, equally natural idea of causation. (1986: 88)

Putting the Mind Back into Psychology

In talking about meaning and intentions, in recognizing beliefs and desires, we are putting the mind back into psychology. The mind, once again, is seen as an instrument of construction. Picasso and Blake, Wittgenstein and Kafka did not find the worlds they produced. They invented them (Bruner, 1986: 97).

Laboratory psychology seemed largely irrelevant to 'human experience as it is really experienced' (Wyatt, 1986: 207). There was a need to return *meaning* to the centre stage of human affairs. Gradually, there was a move away from seeing people as mere 'processors of information', to recognizing them as 'constructors of meaning'. And wherever we discover meaning, we find interpreters.

We have no direct access to the way people construct the meaning of a particular experience. Interpretation becomes a powerful dimension in human affairs. The complex interplay between the psychological development of the individual and other people produces minds that seek understanding, people who impose meaning, and actors who make interpretations. If psychology is an interpretative discipline, we need to seek out the rules that human beings bring to bear in creating meanings in cultural contexts. Bruner continues: 'These contexts are always *contexts of practice*: it is always necessary to ask what people are *doing* or *trying* to do in that context' (1990: 188, emphasis in original). Perhaps psychologists can learn as much from the humanities as they can from the sciences.

One way of proceeding is not to rely solely on what people *do* but also to value what they *say*. In the past, little worth was given to what people said themselves about their actions. Only observable behaviour was seen as valid.

> There is a curious twist to the charge that 'what people say is not necessarily what they do.' It implies that what people *do* is more important, more 'real' than what they *say*, or that the latter is important only for what it can reveal about the former. It is as if the psychologist wanted to wash his hands altogether of mental states and their organization, as if to assert that 'saying', after all, is *only* about what one thinks, feels, believes, experiences. How curious that there are so few studies that go in the other direction: how does what one *does* reveal what one thinks or feels or believes? (Bruner, 1990: 17)

The 'cognitive revolution', beginning in the 1950s, began the process of bringing the mind back into psychology. Psychologists began to be interested in what people knew, believed and wanted. 'The emphasis shifted from performance (what people *did*), to competence (what they *knew*)' (Bruner, 1986: 94). The mind was the thing that organized knowledge and stored experience. What people said became of paramount interest. Once again, the mental state of the individual had to be considered.

Narrative and the Organization of Experience

Stories seem to be one of the ways in which we naturally organize experience. They help create understandable order in human affairs as well as explain everyday experience. As we reflect on experience, so we construct stories. It seems that the brain is inclined to organize its understanding of the world in the style of a narrative. Events, people and objects are most easily understood and remembered if there is a story-like connection between them: this happened and *then* this happened. Most stories involve a setting in which various characters appear.

Carrithers (1991) believes that we attempt to understand people in terms of *characters* and *plots*. People's characters are shaped by the plots in which we see them, and the plots develop in terms of the characters that populate them. 'Narrativity . . . consists not merely in telling stories, but of understanding complex nets of deeds and attitudes . . . as part of an unfolding story' (Carrithers, 1991: 310). I evaluate the actions of others in the context of the story. Given the character of the individual and the plot (as they see it and as I see it), I imagine what people are thinking and feeling, and I anticipate what they will do. The reader and the read, the observer and the observed exist in a complex interplay of attempts at mutual mind-reading.

Bruner (1990: 50) mentions the work of Kenneth Burke, who proposed that well-formed stories are composed of an Actor, an Action, a Goal, a Scene and an Instrument – plus Trouble. The story seeks to follow the way that Trouble is handled, and possibly resolved. In the words of Sarbin (1986: 3), a story is a symbolized account of actions of human beings which 'is held together by recognizable patterns of events called plots. Central to the plot structure are human predicaments and attempted resolutions.' In short, human beings appear to impose structure and sequence on the flow of experience. If we did not impose some kind of framework on the constant buzz of experience, we should make little sense of the world about us.

The narrative is recognized as a particularly effective way in which we organize experience. Indeed, it appears that what is not structured narratively does not get remembered. It is within such structures and sequences that the actions of ourselves and others are recognized and understood. It is interesting to note that we always assume that what other people say and do must be making some sense. Mancuso (1986: 99–100) observes that those who emphasize the epistemological significance of context and the construction of understanding assert that experience has no meaning outside the individual's existing knowledge system.

Living in social groups, we need to make sense of the actions of others, and the narrative form offers a potent cognitive strategy in which both our perceptions and our conceptions of other people can be organized. Robinson and Hawpe (1986: 112–13) note the several strengths of the narrative as a way of organizing experience: it is an economic cognitive device; it can be applied to almost any aspect of social life; it is selective in so far as it retains only the key features of the experience; it uses familiar structures in which experiences are ordered and categorized.

Bruner (1990: 43–4) describes further properties of the narrative. It is inherently sequential. People and events only have meaning in the context of the plot. They generally find themselves in situations which change and to which they have to react. Thought and action, feeling and belief are required. The situation and the responses to it reveal the character of the actors. Furthermore, it is the plausibility of the account that renders the narrative 'truthful' and not the causally proven relationship between one action and another.

It seems, then, that there is a general desire not just to achieve logical coherence but also to 'get the story right'. We dislike ambiguity. Mental schemata are assembled which allow us to handle new information and fresh experiences. One of the fundamental postulates of Kelly's (1955) personal construct theory is our need to achieve coherence in the organization of our psychological experiences. And it seems that the narrative form is a particularly effective way of bring structure and sequence to our thoughts and feelings. 'The need to make our life coherent,' believes Fuller, 'to make a story out of it, is probably so basic that we are unaware of its importance' (quoted in Mancuso, 1986: 101). A coherent story is a powerful device in which unrelated facts can be woven together to the satisfaction of both narrator and audience.

Our Need to Impose Meaning on Experience

Many psychologists believe that our desire to find our experiences meaningful is inborn. Indeed, it is not simply a search for meaning, as if somehow 'meaning' is out there and has to be found. Rather, faced with the busy hum of experience, we *impose* meaning and wilfully make sense.

Present two or three pictures to someone and that person will connect them in some way to make a story. A number of intriguing experiments reveal how deeply ingrained is our need to impose meaning on experience. Sarbin (1986: 12) reports some early work in which an apparatus set in motion two or more coloured rectangles. Although the movements of the rectangles were meaningless, people asked to observe their motion saw purpose and cause in their toing and froing. 'For example, if rectangle A stopped after moving towards B, and if then rectangle B began to move, the observers would say that B "got out of the way" of A' (Sarbin, 1986: 12). In the write-up, the experimenters note the amusing descriptions given by some of the observers: 'It is as if A's approach frightened B and B ran away'; 'It is as if A, in touching B, induced an electric current which set B going.' The meaningless movements of the rectangles were assigned meaning. Moreover, the preferred idiom of understanding was that of the narrative: this happened and then that happened.

Bruner (1986: 47) describes a similar experiment. First, he notes that surprise is an extremely useful phenomenon to those interested in the mind and its workings. It reveals what we take for granted in the world. Our central nervous system appears to store models of the world into which we attempt to place new experiences. Past experiences, if met sufficiently often, allow the brain to build models and neurological structures into which new experiences can be accommodated. As the infant develops, more and more of the world around him or her can be processed quickly and efficiently within the neuronal structures and pathways previously established. Indeed, the brain begins to 'expect' to see and understand things in terms of its ingrained structures. And such expectations give meaning to many current experiences. We attend to what we *expect* to see, even when things are not as they appear. We see the shapes of animals in the clouds, pictures in ink blots, faces in dots and squiggles arranged randomly. The maturing brain increasingly looks for meaning and sense in new situations based on established models. These models arise out of the neuronal structures which the brain has patterned as it has been repeatedly exposed to experiences of which it needed to make sense if the infant was to cope with the world in a sensible and effective manner.

Familiar sights and sounds can easily be accommodated into our existing models. But new sensations demand greater attention. Some may enter an expected pattern. Others may modify that expectation. And yet others may jar so much that they force us to develop new models of how the world is working in this particular aspect. In general, though, we perceive the world in terms of the conceptual models already established in our brains.

The experiment described by Bruner involved a person recognizing a playing-card. The observer was given only milliseconds of exposure to each displayed card. The display consisted of both normal playing-cards and ones in which the colour and suit were reversed – a red six of clubs, for example. Not only did the reversed cards take longer to be 'recognized', 'But more interestingly, our subjects went to extra-ordinary lengths to "regularize" the reversed cards to make them conform to their canonical pattern. I recall one reporting that our red six of clubs was indeed a six of clubs, but that the illumination inside the tachistoscope was rather pinkish!' (Bruner, 1986: 47).

Constructing and Reconstructing Stories

The narrative form emerges as a particularly powerful way of organizing experience. It is built into our day-to-day dealings with each other;
it is recognized in the conversations between mother and children; it
appears every time we are faced with having to make sense of diverse
events. We link together all manner of disparate experiences. Events
are reconstructed in order make sense. The need to make sense seems
to be an overwhelming urge.

Biologically, it helps us negotiate the world in a generally effective
and efficient manner, and no doubt evolution has ensured that our
brains are programmed to seek order, structure and sense in those
aspects of the world that matter. But the meaning we give to our
experience may not always be helpful, and it is this side of the drive
to make sense that has been addressed by therapists and counsellors.
Furthermore, it also seems that some people find it hard to make
sense of their experiences; they cannot tell a coherent story that
accounts for their condition:

> Narrative truth can be defined as the criterion we use to decide when a
> certain experience has been captured to our satisfaction; it depends on
> continuity and closure and the extent to which the fit of the pieces takes
> on an aesthetic finality. Narrative truth is what we have in mind when we
> say that such and such is a good story, that a given explanation carries
> conviction, that *one* solution to a mystery must be true. Once a given
> construction has acquired a narrative truth, it becomes just as real as any
> other kind of truth; this new reality becomes a significant part of the
> psychoanalytic cure. (Spence, 1982: 31)

What emerges from this line of thinking is the idea that the past is
not a fixed thing, lying somewhere deep in the memory banks of the
brain simply to be recovered by some archaeologist of the mind.
People rework their past experiences as they tell their tale. In this
model, the individual *reconstructs* her past rather than *recovers* it.
There is a shift from discovery to creation (Spence, 1982: 177). The
implications for treatment techniques such as psychoanalysis are
profound. The past can no longer be viewed as something which is
buried or preserved or repressed, available for recovery given the right
techniques of clinical excavation. In bringing the past into the
present, experiences are *reconstructed* to make sense in the context of
the individual's *current* frameworks of understanding.

Wyatt goes so far as to say that 'With the premise that reconstruction replaces recovery, the entire theory of psychoanalytic treatment
must be re-thought. We cannot speak of the healing effect of the

recovery of the repressed, when what seems to matter more is mean-ingful coherence' (Wyatt, 1986: 196). This is why Spence (1982: 29) is sceptical of the patient's ability to free-associate. In free association the patient is expected to supply the contents of the past without context. But in practice, as the patient recalls the past she usually describes it in a relatively structured fashion; a story begins to form. Narrative accounts supply both content and context.

Stories Which Hold Together and Are Complete

Rather in the manner of Raymond Williams, as we attempt to tell our story, we redescribe the world. Our experiences are re-examined; they receive a new meaning and become better understood. Gaps or confu-sions in our story are a cause of unease and discomfort. Unhappiness results if we cannot make a connected, coherent story out of it. 'Of course, I cannot fail to have a past, but I can let it be forgotten, or I can actively suppress it, or I can be so intent on my future project that I let my roots in the past grow weak. In either case I lose my identity' (Crites, 1986: 171).

However, some people just have bits of their story missing. Selves and identities remain incomplete. For example, women who have suffered the trauma of sexual abuse as young girls often cannot remember large chunks of their childhood; they have gaps and blanks in their autobiographies. Adopted people are not only often curious about their origins, but they also appear to have a developmental need to make the story complete. Considerable time and energy might be spent on tracing the details of one's past, and many adopted people are not content until they make contact with their biological mother, not necessarily to establish a permanent relationship with her, but simply to round off their own biography. The search is less for a sense of identity and more a desire to ask about one's story and place oneself in a narrative that accounts for one's experiences and actions from birth until death.

Haimes and Timms (1985) asked adopted people about their experiences of searching for a birth parent. They recognized the power of creating a narrative self in the need to search, and offer a number of revealing quotes to make the point. For example, one adopted person summed up her dilemma with these words:

I've thought about [tracing my natural parents] as the only method of finding out. I mean it's a very difficult or very hard decision to make about that but I suppose as I get older I realize more and more life is such an extraordinary thing in what happens to one, it's terrible not having a part of one's story, it's very hard to account for the way one is. (Haimes and Timms, 1985: 64)

Polkinghorne (1988: 150) suggests that we achieve our personal identities and self-concept through narrative:

it makes our existence into a whole by understanding it as an expression of a single unfolding and developing story. We are in the middle of our own stories and cannot be sure how they will end; we are constantly having to revise the plot as new events are added to our lives. Self, then, is not a static thing.

We continually reconstruct the way we understand ourselves. This is what clients seek to do in therapy, hence the need to talk and tell one's story.

14 Dialogue

Dialogue is the third of the 'talking' methods we use to help recognize and rethink the meaning we give to personal experience. In this method, the counsellor is a much more active participant in the search for meaning. What the client says (and does not say) is subject to joint reflection and speculation, analysis and criticism. Vigorous dialogue and debate between counsellor and client lead to new understandings and better ways of coping. Dialogue works well because (1) it uses a social relationship as the 'natural' way to explore meaning, (2) it encourages the client to try to make sense of past and present experience, (3) it challenges the client to make better sense of future experience and (4) it enables the client to recover control of the meaning of his or her own experience.

The Formation of the Self in Dialogue

We learn to cope with the world by modelling it and constantly striving to make sense of experience. But both the models we hold and the sense which we make arise out of our relationships with other people and their cultural practices. Thus, the character of the experience influences the way the brain structures itself in order to deal precisely with that kind of experience. Social life is full of 'meaning', and in order to become socially competent, the child must learn to understand these meanings. The reflexive quality of social relationships and personal development informs all social life and has to be grasped by the child if any sense is to be made of people.

In earlier chapters we established that evolutionary advantages were gained from co-operative behaviour and that the ability to co-operate was possible because we could imagine what other people might be thinking, feeling and planning; we possess a 'theory of other minds'. It is also the case that as we interact with other minds we begin to understand them. The medium in which most of this takes place is language. Through talk and other forms of communication, we begin to make sense of what our own actions mean and what other people's actions mean. From the outset, children want to know why people say the things they say and do the things they do. They posit that other minds have mental states; they provoke reactions in those around them and monitor the effects of their own behaviour. It is as if they are programmed to explore social relationships and the psychological make-up of other people. Understanding others is inherently satisfying, socially critical and biologically necessary.

Most of this understanding takes place as people communicate with the child and use language. It is through conversation that we become self-conscious and aware of others and their psychological condition. We use language to construct our understanding of things and other people. It comes as no surprise, then, to recognize that when, as adults, we want to make sense and understand the meaning of experience, we do this by wanting to talk. Talking in social relationships was the way we first learned to make sense of ourselves as well as of others, and it is by talking in social relationships that we continue to try to make sense of ourselves and others.

So, whereas description and narrative highlight the value of talk as a way of constructing experience, dialogue emphasizes the critical importance of relationships and the two-way nature of therapeutic conversations. Dialogue echoes the characteristics that have been identified in the developmental processes in which we first learned to make sense of ourselves and other people. Although there is much truth in the proverb 'a trouble shared is a trouble halved', the more basic value of dialogue is its ability to return the client to a social relationship in which the meaning of experience can be identified, examined, understood and changed.

In order to cope, the growing child needs to make sense of the sense that other people make. Thus, the sense that the child learns to make will, in broad cultural terms, be the kind of sense that people make in her social world. In this way, the social is 'interiorized'.

The developmental dialogue between the child and the world of others produces an individual who is socially competent, socially cognizant and socially constructed. In the counselling relationship we re-enter the medium in which meanings are created and defined. Meanings arise in the communication of experience. Therefore meaning can only be examined in relationships which offer clients and counsellors the opportunity to understand the meaning of experience and the chance to communicate that understanding (England, 1986: 21). If meaning is to be understood and sense is to be made, the troubled individual has little choice but to re-enter social relationships, for that is where he or she will find the kind of experiences that the brain understands and knows how to use in its struggles to make a better sense.

The distressed client can be compared to an iron tool forged by a blacksmith that has lost its sharpness and shape. The implement was formed in heat and by the heavy hammer blows of the blacksmith. In the furnace the iron once more becomes malleable and amenable to being reshaped by the efforts and intentions of the craftsperson. It would be no good hitting the iron when cold. Considerable effort would produce little effect. Bending or cutting would not work. Nor would heating alone bring about the desired end. For the tool to be re-formed, it has to be returned to the environment that gave the iron its original shape: blasting heat and purposeful blows.

Personal Constructs

George Kelly wrote *The Psychology of Personal Constructs* in 1955, a book in which he presented the challenging notion that men and women are in business to understand their own nature and the way the world, including other people, works. This understanding is constantly tested in terms of how useful or effective it is in anticipating events and producing worthwhile actions. In this sense, men and women behave rather like 'scientists'. They have views or theories about the way things work which produce expectations or hypotheses. Our actions are a continual experiment with life, the results of which (if we are good scientists) feed back into our theories and understandings. Thus, 'Behaviour is seen not as a reaction but as a proposition, not as the answer but as the question . . . a person's behaviour will make little ultimate sense to us unless we understand the questions which they were asking' (Bannister and Fransella, 1986: 31). But clearly, we cannot erect a new theory for every experience, and so we develop a number of constructs that are designed to help us anticipate, interpret, lock into and handle particular types of experience.

Some constructs are more serviceable than others. The meaning that each person gives to his or her experience explains why some people cope and others do not in ostensibly similar situations. And if a particular type of experience continues to fail to match up to an established construct, the successful individual will be able to revise the construct, while the frustrated person will continue to use the old construct even though he or she finds the experience increasingly difficult to handle.

In the face of demanding and unfamiliar situations, those who employ constructs which are poor at assimilating new experiences cope either by avoiding them or by trying to make them fit existing systems, however inappropriate. Constructs are *hypotheses* and not *rules* (Bannister and Fransella, 1986: 19). If our construct is rigid and constrains the way we view, understand and interpret a person or a situation, we use our construct in a rule-like manner: for example, we might believe that women make poor mechanics, or that all accountants are dull. In these examples, we would see no exceptions to this rule, so that upon meeting a qualified female car mechanic or a joke-telling accountant, no matter what evidence existed to the contrary, we should still not see them as anything other than impractical or dull. A less constricting construct would allow exceptions and variations to exist and would free the observer to make sense of people in a more flexible and versatile fashion. There is more than one way to view an accountant. His behaviour is not forever fixed or final. We might recognize that, although accountants are inclined to be dull, a particular accountant might be a live-wire or charismatic or exciting. 'When we use constructs propositionally our world becomes potentially richer and we are less likely to be trapped into conflict by the rigidity of our stance' (Bannister and Fransella, 1986: 19).

People who are able to construe people and situations in a variety of ways might be described as 'cognitively complex' (see Bieri, cited in Bannister and Fransella, 1986: 106; Adams-Webber, 1969). This skill is particularly important if people are to handle social situations. The more cognitively complex person generally shows more skill in inferring the personal constructs of other people in a social situation. In brief, socially skilled people are good at accurately construing the construction processes of others. They recognize not only that the other person is making some kind of sense of the situation but also that the behaviour of the other will be based on that understanding. They are less inclined to stereotype people and so can respond to individuals more accurately, appropriately and sensitively. Treatment of those who use cognitively simple constructs involves helping them generate more versatile constructs which allow their users to recognize a greater range of human character and behaviour, and so behave more effectively in social situations.

The main interest of the psychologist should be to understand how people experience the world – what does an individual's behaviour mean; what is she trying to achieve and based on what understanding; what sense is he making of this situation and these people? Psychology should be concerned with defining individual experience and action. 'Perhaps our signal failure as psychologists to measure psychological aspects of the person,' reflect Bannister and Fransella (1986: 61), 'derives from our habit of asking them to answer *our* questions rather than noting the nature of the questions which *they* are asking.' If we make this switch, not just as psychologists but also as counsellors, we become interested in the way people interpret the world and the meaning they give to their experience. We want to understand the way they see things and make sense.

Constructing and Deconstructing Texts

Counselling and therapy offer two types of dialogue, though in practice they often overlap. One involves the helper encouraging the client to talk and be clear, to express and reflect. Although much active listening takes place, the counsellor is also very much involved in the dialogue, seeking clarification and understanding. The second type of dialogue finds the counsellor acting as both listener and critic. She attempts to help the client understand the meaning of his experience, develop new meanings and find more effective understandings. In this second type of dialogue, the counsellor is more demanding and challenging as she and the client struggle to make sense of his experience.

Under these more vigorous relationship regimes, descriptions and stories are not under the sole authorship of the client. What is said and how it is said are jointly produced by counsellor and client. In the way the counsellor reacts and by what excites her interest she helps shape the story, she colours the description. There is a constant interaction between the client and counsellor, the teller and the told.

In this sense, the relationship between counsellor and client is hermeneutic. There is no fixed truth to be found when a counsellor hears a client describe her experience. Whatever meanings emerge are a product of the encounter between the client and the counsellor. Just as a book or text written by an author several centuries ago was a product of its time and place, and so cannot be understood by a present-day reader in quite the same way as it was understood by the author or the original readers, so the client's tale or text can only be interpreted in the context and meaning frameworks of the present. The meaning of a text is constituted by the reader as she interprets the meaning of that text within the terms of her own current position.

In the case of the client, there are two readers of the client's text:

the client and the counsellor. The interpretations that both make of the 'text' produce a jointly sponsored understanding of the meaning of the described experience. The experience becomes structured and integrated into the client's current understanding of the self. 'At base,' writes Steele (1986: 259), 'hermeneutics is dialogue; the engagement between text and reader, client and therapist, other and self in coming to mutual understanding or in clarifying disagreement. Grounded as they are in conversations between analyst and analysand, psycho-analytic psychologies share with hermeneutics a fundamental commit-ment to making sense of human communication.'

All of us, including clients in counselling, extend our understanding of ourselves by gauging the way others react to what we have said and done. The sharing and examination of meaning connect us with the experiences of others in our community. This can be reassuring. It provides us with a benchmark for assessing our own experience as well as helping us to generate more versatile constructs with which to understand ourselves and others.

If she is to help people understand their experience, the counsellor or therapist, as interpreter, must become thoroughly immersed in and familiar with the text with which she is engaged if understanding is to be achieved. The counsellor must cultivate the text. Spence (1982: 191) believes that listening is both subjective and constructive; 'we are always shaping material in order to understand it', and it is incum-bent on counsellors, therapists and analysts to understand how their needs and experiences affect their interpretation of the client as text. At root, the counsellor should be helping the client understand the meaning of his own text, his own experiences.

Thus, past experiences allow us to plan for and cope with the future. Our analysis and evaluation of actions carried out in the past affect what we do in the future, particularly when we meet new or unexpected situations. 'We live,' says Eccles (1989: 229), 'in a time paradigm of past–present–future. When humans are consciously aware of the time NOW, this experience contains not only the memory of past events, but also anticipated future events.' *But*, as we have seen, the past is not a fixed matter – it can be reworked, reinter-preted and redefined. In this way, by altering our understanding of past experiences, we can change future actions and future experiences.

The Counsellor as Critic

The client's account, seen as a 'text', and the meanings given to that text have to be critically examined by the counsellor. England (1986) develops the notion of the counsellor as both artist and critic with considerable eloquence. We have already heard that each of us is constantly constructing an understanding of the world, and that in attempting to communicate that understanding we find meaning in our experience. The counsellor, as artist, is intent on understanding the meaning of the client's experience. Her ability to explore such understanding is helped by the understanding she has of the nature and origins of her own thoughts and feelings, beliefs and desires. Creativity is the ability to describe and share an understanding. The artist is someone who can explore an experience from the inside and understand that experience. But more important for the artist is the ability to express and *communicate* that experience in ways which allow others to understand it too.

The creative artist discovers and organizes new descriptions of experience. These can be expressed in a variety of media – words, sights and sounds, poems, paintings and music. If the artist is good, her work will communicate an understanding of the meaning of the experience to others. The work of art will help other people achieve a new understanding; the world will look different as a result of the communicated experience. We are moved by the emotional insights offered by a violin concerto; we are excited, even disturbed, by the intensity of a colourfully charged painting. The artist is someone skilled in helping others experience new meanings. In this sense, the counsellor is an artist.

To paraphrase England (1986: 116), the task of the counsellor is to understand the meaning of experience in the other and to communicate that understanding. It is necessary to know how the client interprets his or her world, how things are being seen and understood, what meaning is being given to a particular experience. In communicating her understanding of the other's experience, the counsellor will feed new ideas into the dialogue which help the client rethink and restructure the meaning of his or her own experience.

But the counsellor is also a critic. While always accepting and respecting the client and striving to be reliable, attentive and sympathetically responsive, and while always encouraging the client to take the initiative, the counsellor is in no sense passive. 'For example,' says Bowlby (1988: 152), when a patient wastes time talking about everything and anything except his thoughts and feelings about people, it will be necessary to draw his attention to his avoidance of this area ... With another patient, who perhaps is very willing to explore memories of childhood, there will be many occasions when a therapist can usefully ask for more detail or raise questions.

It is the purpose of artistic criticism, and art, to realize subjectivity, not to deny it. This process is not to abandon judgement but rather to judge, strenuously and detachedly, the nature of our own diverse experience. We see, then, that the counsellor and the client, the critic and the subject, pass through a number of distinct stages (England, 1986: 121).

First, the 'experience' has to be explored and identified. Second, the experience has to be expressed and given shape and form. And finally, there is the stage of 'analysis' in which the picture, which is an expression of the experience, is judged in terms of its coherence, its narrative truth, its ability to capture and convey a mental condition, an emotional perspective. The counsellor actively explores with the client the basis on which he is perceiving his world. In pushing for clarity and coherence, the counsellor is struggling with the client to establish an understanding of the meaning of an experience that makes sense, that can handle the emotions, the people and the situations with which the client has to cope. Inconsistencies and absurdities in the story are challenged. In Kelly's language, the counsellor is helping the client reconstruct the meaning that he or she gives to experience.

The psychotherapist helps the client test the validity and usefulness of the constructs he or she is in the habit of using in the problem situation. In partnership, the therapist and client examine the difficulties together. The therapist does not have an answer in advance of the enquiry. The client needs to grasp the nature of his or her governing models, trace their history and try to understand what has led to the world being seen in this particular way (Bowlby, 1988: 139). The relationship between therapist and client is based on co-operation:

> each must try to understand what the other is proposing and each must do what he can to help the other understand what he himself is ready to try to do next. They formulate their hypotheses jointly ... Often a beginning therapist finds it helpful to close his cerebral dictionary and listen primarily to the subcortical sounds and themes that run through his client's talk. Stop wondering what the words literally mean. Try to recall, instead, what it is they sound like. Disregard content for the moment; attend to theme ... But at other times the therapist will bend every effort to help the client find a word, the precise word, for a newly emerged idea.

Such an exact labeling of elusive thoughts is, at the proper time, crucial to making further inquiries and to the experimental testing of hypotheses. (Kelly, 1969: 228–30)

Making Better Sense

Exploration is a shared enterprise in which the psychotherapist helps the client develop more elaborate constructs out of which flow more versatile responses. The helper, in making her observations and offering her comments, feeds new information, fresh interpretations and outlooks into the client's mental schemata. The new information introduced by the counsellor is of a particular kind which the client may not easily fit into his or her existing psychological constructs. The fresh inputs may contain ideas that suggest new ways of patterning experience and alternative frameworks in which to make sense. To this extent, the counsellor challenges and disturbs old understandings and meaning structures. Once 'the patient has grasped how and why he is responding as he is, he will be in a position to reappraise his responses and, should he wish, to undertake their radical restructuring' (Bowlby, 1988: 118).

Given our present state of ignorance about how change occurs in the minds of others, the introduction of new understandings might set off a train of cognitive restructuring, the end result of which might be entirely unpredictable. Chaos theory suggests that small changes in initial conditions produce a snowball effect which may have large, unforeseen consequences. Many systems, such as the circulation of gases, are extremely sensitive to minute changes in initial conditions. The final state of the system cannot be calculated from a knowledge of initial inputs. This is a phenomenon known as the 'butterfly effect':

> This extreme sensitivity on the initial data implies that the circulatory patterns of the atmosphere might be ultimately decided by the most minute disturbance. It is a phenomenon sometimes called the butterfly effect, because the future pattern of weather might be decided by the mere flap of a butterfly's wing. (Davies, 1987: 52)

Given that the brain and its relationship with the environment are a highly complex and elaborate system, it should not surprise us that small changes in initial conditions (a thoughtful observation made by the counsellor) sometimes produce significant changes in the client's cognitive schema. The new information has the effect of knocking old arrangements of thought into new patterns. Conversely, intended effects planned by the technically purposeful therapist may have totally unintended consequences once they enter the complex neuro-physiological system of the client. Bringing about change in the mental perspective of the other is not really possible unless the therapist appeals to the interpretative character of the client rather than her presumed susceptibility to psychological manipulation. Psychotherapists should therefore experiment *with* people instead of *on* people (Bannister and Fransella, 1986: 161). Robust dialogue encourages old meanings to be challenged and new ones to be forged.

PART IV: THE FORMATION AND RE-FORMATION OF THE SELF IN SOCIAL RELATIONSHIPS

15 The Formation of the Self in Social Relationships

When clients speak of their experiences of counselling and therapy, they reveal not only what works but why it works. The views of the consumer lead us to consider the significance of social relationships in the formation of the self and the implications this has for therapy. There is a developmental requirement to make sense of other people. This is achieved by understanding the self and using this self-awareness to make sense of others by analogy. However, it also has to be appreciated that the self is formed as the infant and the maturing brain relate to and operate in a social environment.

Being of the World

Nature does not require the brain to enter the world with a set of predetermined models of how things work or how they must be read. Instead, the brain is simply programmed to try to make sense whenever and wherever possible in ways which are appropriate and useful. Different parts of the brain continue to mature and develop throughout early childhood. This allows different neurological structures to form in relation to the experiences of which they have to make sense. Therefore, the characteristics of the phenomenon being experienced influence the formation of the neuronal structures, and the neuronal structures are the things which we have to make sense of the phenomenon. This is an extremely neat trick performed by the brain:

> human beings cannot obtain an objective view of the universe. Everything we experience is mediated by our brains. Even our vivid impression that the world is 'out there' is a wonderful trick. The nerve cells in our brains

create a simplified copy of reality inside our head, and then persuade us
that we are inside it, rather than the other way round ... What better
way to build simplified models of the world than to exploit simplicities that
are actually there? Brain puns that get too far from reality are not useful
for survival. (Stewart, 1992: 28)

Assuming a fully functioning brain and good-enough environmental
experiences, the brain becomes precisely tuned to those bits of the
environment of which it has to make sense if the individual is to function, cope and survive. In effect, the brain develops and relates to the
world in such a way that the 'outside' gets established on the 'inside',
and this is why the 'outside' can make sense. The brain is saying that
'On receipt of external sensations, I shall simplify so as to give me a
useful and working sense of experience.' Having established mental
structures to model experience in the light of that experience, future
experiences of that kind will be made sense of in terms of the models
held. This becomes my reality, a reality constructed from experience,
but then inverted to make sense of subsequent experience using the
simplified models. What is in my head is the result of the 'outside'
getting on the 'inside', but once on the 'inside' it then makes sense
of the 'outside' in terms of the brain's internal models.

This is why we can say that the mind is not something that just
appears *in* the world; mind is a consequence of the brain's processing
structures being *of* the world. In particular, being *of* the social world
means that our selves are formed in relationship with other selves.
Moreover, as other people and their relationships constitute the social
world, which is also a world of meaning, our minds form within
meaningful social relations. In this way we are able to understand the
meaningfulness of social life.

Without being in relationship, individual minds would not arise.
The individual would not become human. This phenomenon is not
peculiar to the social world. Zohar (1991) is keen to make comparisons
with the quantum world (in fact, she goes further and sees mind and
self as features of this quantum world) and reminds us that subatomic
particles such as the electron only come into being in relationship
with other electrons in the elusive world of wave/particle duality.
More familiar analogies are to be found in the social world. Not until
the baby is born is the woman a mother or the child a daughter. The
experience of *being* a mother or *being* a daughter requires the existence
of a relationship with the other. Without that relationship neither the
mother nor the daughter exist as such. Furthermore, this relationship,
once it exists, is influenced by other people who have views about
relationships of that kind.

Therefore, in matters of personal meaning and social understanding, we can never be on the outside looking in. There is no such position, even if one party claims to be occupying the alleged site. Personal meaning and social understanding only make sense within whatever goes on between people, including counsellors and clients. Although psychotherapeutic practices may advise procedures which require the therapist to be an external observer, in practice it is impossible for the client to experience the professional encounter in this way. Indeed, all that clients say about the psychotherapeutic experience bears this out. The personal attributes of the therapist *matter*; the qualities of the relationship *matter*; the personal understandings achieved *matter*. What does *not* matter is the technical orientation of the therapist and the procedures associated with that school of therapy, except in so far as they affect the quality of the relationship.

What clients say about counselling and therapy throws considerable light on key aspects of human experience. Their views encourage us to make a paradigmatic shift in our understanding of psychological development. And we need to make this shift if we are to understand why clients say what they do about counselling and therapy. In turn, this should help us to understand the things which work and the things which do not work in the psychotherapeutic encounter.

The paradigm which houses our understanding of psychological and social development combines the traditional split between 'nature' and 'nurture', between inheritance and culture. There are weak and strong versions of the combination, both of which we shall consider.

But first we need to contrast it with the more perspectively static outlines drawn in the traditional 'nature' and 'nurture' accounts of human growth. In these accounts of the development of human behaviour, explanations are dichotomized – behaviour is seen as either innate *or* learned, biological *or* cultural. The biological version sees behaviour as genetically determined. As the child matures, her behaviour proceeds along biologically prescribed lines. The cultural version pays much greater attention to experience. The child learns how to behave as she responds to the demands of the environment.

Nature

In accounts based on genetic determinism, the way an individual develops and the kind of individual into which he or she develops are laid down in the genetic blueprint of that individual. This is a form of rationalism in which the entity in question contains within its make-up the rules for its own progress. When these are worked out, the end product is a logical deduction from the initial premises. Knowledge, talents, skills and abilities of one kind or another are a priori; they are acquired without being derived from experience. Experience has no significant bearing on the outcome and it is generally played down in discussions about behaviour:

> the individual is born with the principles of his subsequent intellectual development already built in. Hence there is a sense in which, according to this view, there is no new development. What we may *call* that is in fact prefigured in the structure with which the individual is equipped when born. (Hamlyn, 1978: 8)

In the case of the brain and the personality, structures in the brain determine how the individual will experience the world. There is an *unfolding* of the inherent properties of the individual as he or she develops. Experience, if it is mentioned at all, acts merely as a trigger for the release and unfurling of various behaviours and potentialities. Experience is little more than a catalyst. It helps the individual work out what is already implicit in the innate structures (Hamlyn, 1978: 28). In this sense, behaviour and knowledge come *with* experience but not *from* experience. 'Experience may be the occasion for our coming to know something without its being the case that we get the knowledge from experience' (Hamlyn, 1978: 29).

Chomsky's work on language and its development is located within this school of thought. He is not convinced that a child's mere exposure to language is sufficient for her to gain an extensive vocabulary as well as to abstract the complex grammatical rules that inform language use. Empirical experience is not enough. Therefore there must be innate knowledge 'wired' into the structures of the brain which allows the child to compose the rules of grammar. There is a 'deep structure' to all languages which reflects the innate ability of human beings to be linguistically competent. In other words, although a particular language is not present in the young infant's brain, she does have the innate capacity to absorb linguistic experience into mental systems that are pre-programmed to handle language. The child's innate knowledge of the deep and universal structural properties of language helps her organize particular language experiences according to the principles built into the neurological structures of the brain.

Experience, on this model of human development, is accommodated within the cognitive schemata generated by the individual mind. The world is interpreted by the individual according to whatever cognitive systems he or she has for making sense of the world. The subject defines the experience rather than the experience defining the subject. This is not quite an idealist position. The argument still maintains that, although the world is being defined by the individual, it is being defined along broadly programmed lines that biology and evolution have found to be effective for the survival and functioning of human beings.

The idealist would not anchor the interpretativist abilities of the individual in the material structures of the brain. It would simply be the case that human beings are organisms which do not respond to the world in a mechanical way. They have the capacity to create mental representations of their experience which help find meaning and purpose in the events of the world. If outcomes can be predicted, people can develop active control over their environment. For example, in George Kelly's view:

> people are constantly interpreting and reinterpreting their environment, building mental pictures or maps (known as cognitive structures or templates) which are used to get a grip on the world. Humans are therefore constantly making and remaking the reality in which they live, as well as their own selves, for individuals work with the meaning of events rather than just by responding to them. (Burkitt, 1991: 22)

The individual is at the centre of experience and makes sense of the world using structures and capacities that are the property of the individual and not of the world being experienced. In working with clients, the counsellor holding these views encourages people to recognize that it is they who are responsible for the way their world is constructed and understood. Personal construct theorists do not believe that there is a reality independent of our construction of it.

Nurture

In contrast to the idea of a genetic blueprint, other theories emphasize the part which *experience* plays in shaping the development of the individual. There are no genetically inherited principles that guide development; rather it is the contingent accumulation of experiences that build up the behavioural capacities of the individual. The organism's relationship with the world is entirely empirical. Experience, entering the brain through the senses, builds up our knowledge of the world and creates the characteristics peculiar to each individual. Whatever sense we make of people and things comes about through experience. The organizing principles that inform how we understand the world are inherent in the properties of the world and are not initially present in our own cognitive structures.

Behaviourists represent an extreme version of this model of human development. We can only change people's behaviour and understanding by changing their experience. If we manipulate the way the world reacts and responds to what the client does, his or her behaviour can be reshaped. If other people become more rewarding in their responses, the shy client might gain in confidence and become more outward-going and sociable. On the other hand, if a mother stops paying attention to her toddler every time he has a temper tantrum, the child might calm down, especially if his parent learns to respond more positively when he is being good rather than when he is being bad.

Nature with Nurture – Weak Version: Genes and the Environment

There are two positions that seek to *combine* the properties of the nature and nurture models of human development. The first is less ambitious and retains many of the characteristics that you would expect if you wanted the best of both worlds. The second is altogether more novel. It suggests a dialectical relationship between biology and experience that offers a more fluid model of the development of self in human beings. It is this second position that begins to suggest ways in which we might understand the counselling experiences of clients. Nevertheless, the more dialectical but less hermeneutical version of 'nature with nurture' still has a great deal of relevance to the current analysis, and it is to this version that we turn first.

The individual has an in-built set of principles which lay down the broad pattern of his or her development, but experience of the actual world plays a critical part in the way this programme is worked out. Cognitive development is seen as involving the individual actively developing his or her *potentialities* in relation to his or her experience of the world. The properties of the environment are discovered as the individual acts upon it, by way of either accommodation or assimilation. Piaget comes close to this position, suggesting that the development of the understanding in relationship to experience still has to conform to the neurological structures that guide overall development. Human understanding supplies the concepts to which experiences are assimilated. The bias is still towards crediting the individual with an innate ability to organize experience, but there is a greater recognition that experience itself modifies the mental schema used to make sense of the world.

There is a nice circular process between biology and experience. The sheer range of experience has to be regularized so that the individual can manage and survive in the world. The brain is structured in such a way as to make sense of experience, but the experiences met modify the composition and workings of the neurological structures so that the brain is increasingly predisposed to 'read' experiences of those kinds in that way. In our infant struggles to comprehend what is happening around us, the brain creates models to help it interpret experience. These models inevitably simplify the dense complexity of the world but they offer a basis for making some kind of working sense. The brain is constantly looking for patterns and relationships.

Models of how the world might be viewed are then built up. These models help us understand the world more easily and more quickly, but they also prefigure how subsequent experiences which are broadly of that kind will be interpreted. With experience, the brain becomes good at making sense of the things which are important to the child's survival. This includes the social as well as the physical environment. In the general run of things, an individual fares better in the world by being able to regularize and systematize experience, allowing him or her to achieve greater anticipation and control of the environment. Although modelling the world simplifies the full complexity of experience, the alternative would be a world of buzzing and confusing sensation in which the individual would not be able to cope or survive.

However, there is a price to be paid. Occasionally, either a particular model will be weak at helping an individual cope with an aspect of experience (through poor, confused or inconsistent early experiences in the relevant area), or subsequent experiences become so changed that old models can no longer make useful sense of what is going on. For example, infants who have had confusing and inconsistent social experiences at the hands of their caretakers may not cope too well with the demands of interpersonal life.

Hinde offers some useful illustrations from animal and human ethology. For example, smiling, laughing and crying appear naturally in deaf- and blind-born babies, suggesting that their development does not require imitation or learning from others. 'However, there are marked cultural differences in the situations that elicit these movements, in the extent to which they are enhanced or concealed, and in the responses they elicit, indicating that their subsequent use is much affected by experience' (Hinde, 1987: 58). In another example, Hinde discusses the way in which biological and experiential factors interact in development. Environments which individuals select for themselves, and environments which parents provide for their off-spring, are genetically influenced:

> Thus heredity and environment are not fully independent. In fact genotype–environment correlations may arise in several ways. First, children actively select and create their own environments from that which is provided, and how they do so will be affected by their genetic constitution. This has been termed 'active' genotype–environment correlation. Second, parents may not only pass on genes conducive to a particular characteristic, but also be themselves predisposed genetically to give their children an environment that augments the characteristic in question: for instance parents who are shy might not only pass on genes predisposing towards shyness but also provide an environment in which children saw fewer strangers and thus never got used to them (passive correlation). Third, parents may react differently to children of different genotypes (reactive correlation). (Hinde, 1987: 60)

According to this version, then, individual development is chan-nelled rather than entirely predetermined. We have three factors determining the development of an individual:

1 The basic genetic programme that instructs the individual to make sense of the world, handle it and use it but without saying precisely how this will be done.
2 Dispositions, characters and temperaments which, though often inherited, are in themselves peculiar to the individual as far as interacting with the environment is concerned.
3 Experience of a material and social environment, the quality of which is unique for each individual.

Hinde (1987: 63) believes that we must reject on the one hand genetic determinism, and on the other the *tabula rasa* view that human development is totally determined by experience as conveyed to the brain by the senses. The combination of genetic programming, temperament and experience produces an infinite number of possible developmental paths such that for any one individual the road taken will be unique to him or her.

Even so, this highly productive interactional model of human development still recognizes a distinct individual subject who inhabits an objective external world. And though there is increasing recogni-tion that the most important element in the external world is the child's experience of other people, nevertheless we still have a picture in which the individual and society act one upon the other as separate and divided realms. But it is possible to take one more step beyond this position and witness the breakdown of the boundary between the individual self and society. Here we find a world peopled by social selves rather than self-contained individuals who experience the world as an external and objective phenomenon.

Nature with Nurture – Strong Version: the Formation of Social Selves

For much of its history, psychology has regarded the social environment as a source of contamination in the study of the individual. 'The true object of psychology was the individual considered in abstraction from culture: the social was something which had to be stripped away to reveal this object' (Ingleby, 1986: 299). However, there has been a gradual appreciation that the part played by the social environment is not only interesting, but fundamental to the formation of the self.

The adventurous mood into which this way of thinking propels us is nicely captured by Burkitt (1991: 1) in the opening paragraph of his excellent book on the social formation of personality:

> The view of human beings as self-contained unitary individuals who carry their uniqueness deep inside themselves, like pearls hidden in their shells, is one that is ingrained in the Western tradition of thought. It is a vision of the person captured in the idea of the person as a monad – that is, a solitary individual divided from other human beings by deep walls and barriers: a self-contained being whose social bonds are not primary in its existence, but only of secondary importance. This understanding of people as monads creates one of the central problems of the social sciences, a problem that has become known as the division between society and the individual. What, it is often asked, is the relationship between society and the individual? The question assumes from the very outset that these concepts represent two opposing entities which are fundamentally divided. The problem then becomes one of creating theories which can conceptualize the 'links' between the social and individual worlds, an enterprise doomed to failure because of the dichotomous way that the problem is conceptualized in the first place.

In most models the individual, as a monad, is separated from the outside world by a boundary which marks the end of the self and the beginning of the other. Influences, running both ways, may cross the boundary just as the gravity of the Moon affects the Earth and the gravity of the Earth affects the Moon. From the Renaissance onwards, people began to define themselves and experience themselves as separate, autonomous 'egos' – 'epistemic subjects', scientific investigators interrogating the outside world, trying to make sense of the reality beyond the self (Ingleby, 1986: 303). As the psychological monad, 'The isolated individual therefore becomes not a historical and social product but a biologically given entity whose individuality is contained inside itself from birth' (Burkitt, 1991: 17).

In contrast, there are those who see the individual as a social construction entirely formed within the prevailing discourse – the self as a product of the ideas, practices, knowledge and understandings of a particular time and place. There is no discrete self that enters the world independent of social discourse. There is no dialectic between identity and social action. 'Thus,' writes Burkitt (1991: 100), 'the practical production of language by humans is ignored and instead concentration is focused on the discursive production of individuals by language.'

Language is the medium in which our thoughts, actions and interactions gain their meaning. Just as there is a social a priori, language too is prior to us and it creates the possibility of subjective consciousness. We exist and become social beings *inside* language. We cannot step outside language; there is no such point. We would not be, nor would we know what to think or how to think, outside language. By using language we are exploring what our experiences mean; it is in our use of language that we try to make sense of experience. Furthermore, our experiences and perceptions are not received as raw data and bare facts which are *then* interpreted. Rather, my subjective outlook, created within the brain–experience dynamic and designed to help me make sense of my experiences, influences both what I see and what it means. We see purpose and meaning, even in the inherently meaningless.

The language we use acts as a pervasive medium which shapes what we know and how we know it.

> It is not just that language has its own rules that we happen to be unable to opt out of; the point is rather that we are constituted within the rules, and exist only in this framework, so that there is no sense in the notion of opting out. Language goes through our heads from ear to ear. (Cupitt, 1990: 36)

Our language-generated world means that our experiences of reality are in constant debate. We are always immersed in an evolving discourse in which our ideas and thoughts, beliefs and understandings are formed. The world is represented as the expression of our own various interpretations and understandings.

So it is that in 'determination by discourse' we witness the 'death of man' as the subjective centre of sense and understanding. Within this debate, we observe a number of wholesale reversals: culture is placed before nature, public before private, superstructure before base, the social before the individual, structure before behaviour, meaning before being (Cupitt, 1990: 52).

In order to escape the limitations of such dichotomous thinking, the challenge is to describe the development of the self in terms which capture both the dynamics and the dialectics of relationships between individuals and other people. The constant interaction between the properties and characteristics of the individual and the qualities of the social environment produces a fast-evolving dynamic.

A hermeneutical dialogue forms. Human beings are capable of self-interpretation, a capacity which involves an understanding of the self which in turn is partly constituted by this very understanding. The natural sciences, which seek causal relations between objects, cannot cope with this view.

No longer is the individual seen as a solitary soul, destined to face the world alone. One of life's major problems for human beings is the problem of understanding other human beings; but the social relationships into which we enter as infants constitute a medium which allows us to recognize others as well as become self-conscious. The self arises in relationship to others.

The brain has to be pictured as a very special mass of biological material which has the capacity to form structures that can process and make sense of experience when exposed to those experiences. As sensations are received and flow as experiences through the brain, the brain begins to develop neurological circuits that begin to make *a* sense of the experiences and thereby render them *meaningful*.

However, particularly with social experiences, the meaningfulness is not a personally defined thing. The meaningfulness of other people and social life is already present in the world of language and human interaction. The infant is programmed to establish meaning (in order to cope with the world), and programmed to develop neurological structures at times of developmental sensitivity that are attuned to the particular properties of the experiences met at that time. Among the many experiences to which the child will be exposed will be those which are already socially meaningful. In other words, meaningfulness is a feature of both the self and society.

It has to be emphasized that the brain is *not* programmed to make a particular sense, it is simply programmed to try to make some sense. It is the subtlety of the brain's hermeneutic relationship with its environment that enables it to make the appropriate kind of sense in that social situation, given the right conditions. The 'sense' which is made or the 'social meaningfulness' of the situation is what is inherent in the situation itself.

In this view, there are no longer two worlds, no 'centres' of truth lodged in either subject or object. Human beings are part of the fabric of the interpersonal world; they are inextricably embedded in social interaction. Their minds do not subjectively structure experience. Instead, the biological need to cope with the environment requires the individual to structure his or her own thinking to solve the material and social problems of living. The personal and cognitive make-up of the individual forms as he or she learns to cope with and make sense of experience. And as a significant part of the world is other people, the patterns of meaning that inform the social world are part of the experience which has to be understood. As the individual interacts with others, the social meanings which inform that interaction have to be understood. In this way, established social meanings enter the internal cognitive make-up of the individual which he or she then uses to understand and interpret relationships and other people. Individuality is therefore socially based (Burkitt, 1991: 2).

Summary

We might sum up this picture of the formation of the self in social relationships under the following five points:

First, the infant enters the world with a brain programmed to be interested in things and people, but in the main it is given few clues about how to make sense of this world. Indeed, the prime instruction is simply that, if you want to survive, then you have to make sense.

Secondly, one of the key characteristics of other people, both individually and collectively, is that they view their own actions as meaningful. Any behaviour indicates purpose and intention, desire and belief. The world 'out there' is a field of interaction in which people are busy relating one to another, seeking to understand and to be understood.

Thirdly, in order to make sense of other people and how they act, the infant has to generate models and ideas about what might be going on. A vital piece of human behaviour is the ability to interpret other people's actions and interactions and decide what they mean. Needing to understand other people makes us social and this makes us human. Our experience of social relationships is both the problem and the solution. By modelling what appears to be going on, we begin to develop a working sense of what is happening *in terms of the characteristics of the social situation of which we need to make sense.* The young, maturing brain, particularly at times of critical sensitivity, is able to modify its own structures in the light of its own experiences.

Fourthly, the social world thus enters the head of the individual, and the self that arises to deal with the environment of other people is formed as the brain finds itself immersed in language and social relationships. It is this immersion in the social world that produces neurological structures that are able to make sense of that social world. The brain's mental processes are shaped in the light of experience in such a way that they are then precisely able to interpret that experience. In this way, the properties of the environment, be they material or social, define the personal and processing properties of the brain, which when self-conscious becomes the individual self. Thus, there is no boundary between the social environment and the individual self.

Therefore, if you and I are raised in the same culture and same language environment, what runs through your head also runs through mine. 'Our like-mindedness and capacity for mutual understanding are therefore secured by the public character of linguistic meaning' (Cupitt, 1990: 161).

Language is what we use when we communicate with others, and we communicate with others to promote understanding, make sense of actions and relationships. We need language to be the kind of social creatures that we are. Language, therefore, carries meaning, and meaning is the corollary of social interaction. What we do holds and conveys meaning to other people. The meaning of my actions has to be interpreted by you in order for you to understand me and for me to feel understood (as I would wish to be understood – or misunderstood, depending on my purposes). Our social nature is embedded in the language we use. Language carries the ideas, expectations, understandings and beliefs that comprise a culture, a social group.

Talking activates the language field in which the self originally formed, so that we might wonder whether it is the act of talking itself (rather than talk acting as a vehicle for carrying out the actions and content of a particular therapeutic technique) that is potentially helpful. If this is the case, then to this extent at least it is talking that cures and not behavioural or psychodynamic or person-centred counselling as such.

If language and its utterance are the medium in which and through which the individual self is formed, a client who wishes to re-form the self needs to immerse herself in talk. Therapists and counsellors all too often mistake the packaging for the content. It is less the specific procedures and techniques and more the opportunity to engage in an active conversation about oneself that brings about understanding – dialogue rather than definition. Hence, when clients are asked about their experiences of counselling, the answers come back in the language of relationships. They value the experience of talking in a social relationship and not the merits of a particular therapeutic technique. Talk returns the individual to the matrix of social relations out of which we all emerge as self-conscious, reflexive beings. Our understandings of self and others are formed as we endeavour to communicate in a field of social meaning and relationships. We therefore have to return to that field if we are to reflect on and change those understandings. Particular counselling procedures are therefore simply a framework for holding dialogue.

The key points to grasp, then, are that developmentally the self is formed in the hermeneutic relationship between biology and culture, between the maturing brain and social experience; that culture is carried in language; that language carried into the brain is the basis on which we learn to recognize and understand ourselves and others; and that attempts to revise the mental models which we use in order to understand the world require us to employ practices which helped to form the models in the first place, namely communicating within the context of social relationships.

Fifthly, this line of enquiry reverses the traditional order of investigation in psychology. Burkitt (1991: 118) quotes Seve, who writes:

> Until now psychology has sought above all to understand man by way of the animal, the adult by way of the child, the normal individual by way of the sick, the total system of the personality by way of its isolated functions, and the content of this personality by way of certain forms of activity. We think the time has come to supplement this rather unfruitful effort by a real effort in the opposite direction.

The client's view is one such 'effort in the opposite direction'.

16 The Nature of the Counselling Relationship

Whatever the counselling style or psychotherapeutic orientation, most practices involve two people who meet, talk and form a relationship structured around a system of ideas purporting to explain human behaviour. The argument has been that it is not the particular set of ideas which forms the basis of success, simply the fact that an intellectual structure is created which houses the talk and the relationship.

Most psychologies and their application in schools of therapy and counselling explain the individual as an isolated self who emits behaviours that can be examined and understood by an objective observer. Theories are developed which seek to explain why individuals do what they do using universal principles that are true for all people in situations of that kind. The individual self can be examined in isolation, a self-contained entity whose behaviour can be influenced either by internal states or by external influences, but who nevertheless remains distinct and fundamentally separate from the social world around.

The heavy strain of individualism present in modern thought stems from the philosophy of Descartes. The self remains an essentially isolated entity. We meet on the 'outside' as individuals who, at best, have only contingent external relationships with each other. Cartesian isolation was complemented by Newton's physics. Matter, like Descartes's minds, consisted of so many discrete, separate and indivisible atoms:

> The notion of a relationship as a set of *external* influences enacted between strangers became the paradigm for all relationship . . . Billiard balls don't 'meet', they don't get inside each other and alter each other's internal qualities. They've no means to do so because each is always and only itself and wholly impenetrable to any outside influences. Like Descartes' minds, they relate to each other only indirectly, by way of external forces which cause them to attract or repel one another or to bump against one another from time to time. During collision they suffer an impact and may undergo a change of position and momentum, but they remain the same in themselves before, during and after the collision. (Zohar, 1991: 111)

Many therapists and counsellors understand and explain the individual client using the universal principles sponsored by their preferred theory. The practitioner, with her theory, assumes that she remains on the outside, feeding in corrective procedures which are guided by her theoretical orientation.

Centring and Decentring the Locus of Truth

There is a problem when you try to combine strategies designed to *explain* people with philosophies intended to *understand* them. Like oil and water, they do not mix. They occupy different epistemological domains. One is 'modern' and scientific, the other is subjective and humanistic. Part of the problem when client and counsellor meet is that, while one is trying to explain and treat, the other wants to be understood and helped.

With the Nietzschean death of God and the rise of 'man', the belief has grown that all things can be explained and manipulated, managed and controlled, including men and women. In the modern vision the world is constructed like a machine which operates according to laws and formulae which in principle are knowable and usable. In this sense, people are no different to objects. Human beings can be investigated and the principles on which they work can be identified and used to diagnose and treat. With sufficient effort the world and all therein can be explained and ultimately be controlled by people.

The practitioner and the professional possess bodies of knowledge which account for the individual and his or her behaviour. These bodies of knowledge rationalize, systematize and codify what is known about the subject. In this ordered form, bodies of knowledge can be passed on from one generation of professionals to another during courses of training and preparation. The practitioner has the 'Word' – an authoritative text – which defines the other's experience. Only those who have been properly trained have received the 'Word' and only they know what the 'Word' means and how it should be interpreted. The 'truth' is revealed only to the priests of the 'Word', whatever their particular Word or therapeutic text happens to be. Counsellors seek to explain the client's experience in terms of the favoured text, the preferred theory.

Explanations are imposed on the other's experience by the professional. The concepts and measures that are used to make sense of the client lie outside his or her own experience. The client is explained in terms of the counsellor's framework of understanding which sets out to capture the distressing experience and so render it intelligible.

There is no debate; the client remains passive before the gaze of the counsellor, and the experience is made to fit the external frame, which it is said is built out of objective truths.

Counsellors determine the nature of the occasion. They set the tone, ask the questions and make their observations through particular theoretical spectacles. It is the therapist's definition which determines the kind of things that should happen on occasions of this kind. Those who hold power can decide what knowledge is to count as relevant, what ideas are to be used and how situations are to be defined. Davis (1986: 70) shows how a client's initial version of her 'troubles' is transformed during the course of a 45-minute therapy session into a problem suitable for psychotherapeutic work. 'The problem,' she concludes, 'becomes viewable as a construction, requiring considerable work on the part of the therapist. His main activity, in fact, resides in persuading the client to accept the problem, as defined by him.'

In therapy, there is a 'construct' in which all transactions and understandings take place including what clients say. All utterances are understood and accounted for within the logic of the particular counselling construct. It is not possible to speak outside the construct, for once inside the therapeutic relationship, all that is said is said within the conceptual boundaries of that psychotherapeutic perspective. The only escape for the client is not to return. The client is not free to develop an alternative construct. A client who wishes to talk a different language will find that what she says will be either ignored or forbidden, recast or simply not understood.

However, even when we recognize that many therapies are not scientific, nevertheless in most counselling relationships, the power to define the client's experience still appears to lie with one party or the other. There is a 'centre', an individual subject who has privileged access to the truth, who holds the key which alone can unlock the contents of the client's experience. This 'centre' of truth is usually located in the counsellor or in her school of practice, but a few techniques shift the responsibility of explanation towards the client, particularly the person-centred approaches. Depending on which side of this epistemological divide the therapy lies, the alleged locus of 'truth' lies either with the counsellor or with the client.

It is consistent, therefore, for practices which centre the truth in either the therapist or the client to judge the effectiveness of counselling and therapy by measuring the behaviour and actions of the individual client before and after treatment, or even to ask the client how satisfied he or she was with the experience of counselling.

Answers will be obtained. However, they only measure the things which are generated by the preferred theoretical orientation. They see what they want to see; they hear what they want to hear. But if the understanding is wrong, it will take the argument so far but no further. If the practice and observations remain obdurately stuck, it may be the theory which has to change and not the skills of the technician.

If there is no dialogue in which new understandings are created, the outcome of the therapeutic encounter is rather like trying to capture the essence of running water in a bucket. No matter what you do, the bucket will always contain roughly the same amount of water. The shape and size of the container determine what is held; the rest is lost. This is what the traditional human sciences and their applications are doing. They believe their theories can contain the essential character of human beings. When the theory meets a subject, it will certainly capture a good many qualities, so the theoretician and the practitioner never go away empty handed. But they mistake having something for explaining everything. The bucket contains water but it tells you little about the nature and character of running streams. The experience makes no sense once it is extracted from its moving context. That is why hydrologists and poets look at, stand in and boat on streams in order to understand them as they are. And for similar reasons, that is why counsellors and therapists should promote, enter and explore dialogue.

There are no truths or absolutes, only contingencies, relativities and interpretations (Cupitt, 1990: 16). Dialogue itself can contain these cross-currents of difference and inconsistency; yet in grappling with them, a provisional, working sense can be forged. The client is left with some control over his or her own experience and what it might mean. And if there is no outside authority who claims to know the 'Word' of the true text, then the client is free, she is able to examine meanings, and she is offered the chance to explore her own truths.

Psychology's Phlogiston Theories

The situation with counselling and therapy is reminiscent of the seventeenth-century debates about the nature of chemical reactions. What explains the burning of wood or the corrosion of metals? The late-seventeenth- and early-eighteenth-century answer was *phlogiston*, which spawned phlogiston theory. In this view, burning was caused by the liberation of something known as 'phlogiston'. After a material had burned, it left behind a 'dephlogisted' substance or ash. Becher, in 1669, said that all substances were made of three kinds of 'earth': the vitrifiable, the mercurial and the combustible. When a substance burns, combustible earth or phlogiston (from the Greek meaning 'burned'), as Stahl was later to call it, is released. Similarly, when a metal corrodes, it was said to be losing phlogiston.

However, observations became increasingly difficult to explain using phlogiston theory. Some substances appeared to *gain* weight when they burnt or corroded. The theoreticians, as they are wont to do before they finally abandon an old theory, devised increasingly exotic explanations and made several last-ditch attempts to save phlogiston theory. One imaginative way to explain weight gains was to suggest that in some cases phlogiston had a negative weight; lose phlogiston through burning or corrosion and the original substance will therefore show an increase in weight! And when hydrogen was discovered with its very light weight and extreme flammability, it was said to be pure phlogiston. But the theory became untenable and was eventually overthrown by the French chemist Lavoisier between 1770 and 1790. He showed that the newly discovered element oxygen was always involved, particularly when a metal was burnt or suffered corrosion. The new theory of 'oxidation' explained far more chemical reactions in which burning was taking place. The original substance combines with oxygen from the air to form a new compound, which sometimes might be a gas (carbon dioxide in the case of wood), in which case what remains loses weight, or sometimes it might be a solid (magnesium oxide in the case of magnesium), in which case what remains shows a gain in weight.

'Modern' ideas see the individual self as a self-contained phenomenon, explainable within the boundaries of its own discrete existence. However, like phlogiston theory, they explain some things but not others. The clients' experiences of counselling and therapy reveal a deeper structure that underlies many of the 'surface' theories. Each surface theory recognizes an aspect of human behaviour and develops an explanation of that behaviour or characteristic. Within that limited field, the theory works well; but when we meet yet another manifestation of human behaviour, we exhaust the explanatory power of that particular theory. We need a new one to help explain the new behavioural outcrop.

The Surface Expressions of a Deeper Structure

Each manifestation of an applied psychological theory is like one of the several tips of an iceberg. The topography of each ice pinnacle is unique, but beneath the water they are linked to a common source. Or, like magnetism and electricity, we might study them separately and say all kinds of interesting things about each one, not suspecting that they are intimately related, and at a deeper level of investigation are found to be different manifestations of the same force. Not until the brilliant work of James Clerk Maxwell in the second half of the nineteenth century were these phenomena unified in his theory of electromagnetism, which was described by a set of simple, elegant equations. We now know how to make electricity in a magnetic field and conversely how to produce magnetic fields out of electrical currents.

But matters have not rested there. There are now serious attempts to unify the four fundamental forces of nature (electromagnetism, gravity, the strong nuclear force and the weak nuclear force). The hope is to link these four forces at some deep level of explanation. In other words, each force is a particular expression at a certain level of some deeper, more fundamental force and the equations which describe it. There are already promising signs that electromagnetism and the weak force are really two aspects of a unified electroweak force (Davies and Brown, 1988).

Returning to the clients' experiences of counselling, if the psychotherapeutic practices appear different but the messages of consumers remain the same, maybe the messages are pointing to a different type and a deeper level of explanation. A particular theory and its application are really no more than a vehicle for carrying the important content of the encounter: talking and relating. What was previously thought of as the carrier is now in fact the carried. And what before was seen as a variety of theoretical packages sent by a common medium (talk and relationships) can now be understood as a single package capable of being transmitted by a variety of media (the various methods of psychotherapy). But it must be added that, although talking and relating are the level at which we wish to explore what is going on when counsellor and client meet, some carriers (the techniques and procedures associated with particular theoretical schools) are better at handling the contents than others. Indeed, some carriers severely damage the contents – the talk and the relationship find it difficult to become established.

Talk and relationships provide clients with experiences which are expressed in a form which the brain can both use and understand in its search for meaning and in its constant attempts to make sense. Those in counselling extract certain experiences from their dealings with the counsellor. These experiences are not arbitrarily extracted, but neither do they follow the theoretical logic of the counsellor's own psychotherapeutic school of thought. Rather, they arise as a result of the brain's early experiences of relationships and language. The brain structures itself in terms of these experiences. This being the case, the self and its structures are able to make sense of social experience in the same terms in which the social experiences shaped the brain and its ability to make sense of the social world in the first place.

This explains the uncanny consistency of clients' experiences of counselling and therapy. Clients are able to extract some useful elements from most, though not all, psychotherapeutic encounters, whatever their theoretical orientation. The extracted elements can be handled within the mental schemata that have evolved in the social formation of the self, schemata which are designed to make sense of relationships and language. But what is extracted is filtered through an entirely different conceptual matrix to the one sponsored by the counsellor and her psychotherapeutic orientation. Many counsellors make the mistake of assuming that the perceived benefits experienced by the client are sponsored by the same framework of understanding that is being used by the practitioner. In fact what the client is doing is simply removing those bits of the encounter which fit her way of doing things and which suit her purposes.

The fact that bits are being removed may be nothing to do with the accuracy of the explanation or the efficacy of the treatment. Human beings get what they can out of situations, no matter how thin the material. My long conversation with the real-estate agent in which I dutifully listen to the many merits of the property which he is attempting to sell is endured because I need to know the price of the house which my neighbour is selling. I am not sufficiently honest to admit this fact, and so I let the agent feed me vast amounts of information which is of no use. Learning the value of my neighbour's property tells me the price for which I might be able to sell my own house, which will determine whether or not I change my job and move to a new town.

In a similar case, understanding the behaviour of young teenagers in a small town might be worth a second look. The boys and girls attend separate schools. The level of attendance at church Sunday school, the library and the wildlife film club is high, which pleases parents, and yet disappointingly there is only a modest improvement in the children's religious knowledge, reading habits and understanding of animal behaviour. Some of the educational inputs stick, but in most cases the amounts are small, and in the case of some children there are no gains in knowledge whatsoever. On closer study it seems that most children attend the church, the library and the film club primarily to meet the opposite sex. These three events provide the only opportunity to meet students from the other school. The majority of the adolescents extract as much as they can of talking to the opposite sex during each of the occasions. Something is extracted from all three situations, although the darkened hall of the film club offers the most prized experience, while the library is felt to be the least rewarding.

What all clients bring to the counselling encounter is a socially formed self which arises within the relationship between biology and social experience. The neurological structures which form within this relationship develop along similar lines within the same culture and this allows human society and social beings to arise. It is the method of self-formation and the relationship between inheritance and social experience which explain why different people undergoing different types of counselling extract and report the *same* kind of experiences, whatever the type of psychotherapy. Clients are not responding to the technical components of the particular counselling school but simply to whatever incidental scraps of talk, dialogue and relationship happen to be present in the therapeutic encounter. We should therefore not be surprised to learn that most clients get something out of therapy and that what they get is reported in broadly the same terms.

The Brain's Quest to Make Sense

However, even this analysis of the therapeutic relationship is incomplete. We have built up an argument which says that a secure relationship encourages people to explore their feelings. Exploring feelings requires the client to talk. Talk uses language, and language helps us to define experience. The client's ultimate need is to make sense and to cope. Talking, which helps define experience, generates material which the brain knows how to use in its search to make sense.

However, because the need to make sense is the brain's constant quest, it is not only the identification and clarification of experience achieved during talk which help the client begin to make sense; it is also the ideas that emerge in dialogue with the therapist that feed into this process. Because many therapeutic techniques offer the client a way of making sense of his or her experience, the explanations sponsored by the technique will be inherently attractive to some clients. The 'sense' being offered by the therapist and his or her psychotherapeutic outlook becomes part of the dialogue. It helps define the context and the character of the social relationship in which the client has become immersed. Immersing ourselves in social relationships is the way most of us create the conditions which produce the experiences which help us to make sense. Whatever the therapist says by way of explanation becomes part of the relationship. The explanation may help clients account for their feelings, the behaviour of others, and the quality of their interpersonal life. If the proffered explanation does not help the client make sense, it is ignored.

It is 'the making sense' which is important, no matter what it looks like or from where it comes. Making some sense is generally better than making no sense. Thus, although no psychotherapeutic school possesses *the* 'truth' (for no such 'truth' exists), nevertheless each psychotherapeutic explanation might become functionally 'true' in the context of that psychotherapeutic relationship, to the extent that it helps a particular client make sense of his or her experience. The injection of particular ways of making sense into the therapeutic dialogue then becomes part of the linguistic material that the client may or may not be able to use in his or her search for meaning and understanding.

Again, this may provide us with a clue about why different therapies have similar levels of success and failure. It is not that they are all equally true or equally false, or that some are more true than others, but each one offers a way of making sense in its own particular way which will be attractive to some but not to all clients.

So, the odd conclusion is that, along with the usual 'non-specific' factors found in all psychotherapeutic encounters, including the quality of the relationship and the opportunity to talk, clients value experiences which help them make sense. This increases the amount of personal control a client has over the meaning given to his or her own experience which boosts confidence and self-esteem. I say odd, because particular ways of making sense are usually *peculiar* to each school of therapy. They are therefore normally viewed as factors which are 'specific' to that technique. But as I have laboured to show, it is the 'making sense' which is the critical element, no matter what that 'sense' might be, and therefore 'making sense' can be viewed as a non-specific factor. A particular kind of 'sense' associated with a specific school of therapy is, at best, merely an instance of the general 'non-specific' of making sense.

Psychotherapy as Ontogeny

Based on an analysis and interpretation of clients' experiences of counselling and therapy, the idea has been put forward that the psychological and social development of the child explains both how and why psychotherapy with adults succeeds in some cases and fails in others. The social formation of the self in infancy determines the basis on which individual selves can be re-formed in adulthood. Hence, psychotherapy replicates ontogeny.

As other people are one of the most important things of which to make sense, much of 'other people' experience, particularly in the early years, takes place within the attachment relationship itself. If the relationship is 'good enough', four things can happen: (1) In relationship with others and using the medium of language, the child begins to form a sense of self and comes to know his or her *own* mind. (2) The experience of relating to others helps the child begin to understand *other* minds. (3) The relationship 'holds' the inchoate mind while it develops a fully integrated sense of self and continues to explore and make sense of the environment beyond the immediate relationship. (4) The net result of these opportunities to make sense of the self, of other people and of the environment is an increased ability to cope with the world and to survive physically, practically and socially.

Secure relationships, talk and the search for meaning are also the stuff of psychotherapy. Clients use language to explore, define and understand the meaning of experience. The descriptions which clients give of their experiences of counselling and therapy allow us to identify the following psychotherapeutic sequence, a sequence which necessarily mimics the developmental phases of early childhood in which the self originally formed:

Therapeutic Alliance

↓

Talk and Dialogue

↓

Making Sense

↓

Controlling the Meaning of Experience

↓

Coping Better with Life

We are all embedded in a world of language and social relations from the day we are born. So, because we are *of* the world and not just simply *in* the world, any changes in the way we understand ourselves and other people tend to take place within the world of language and relationships. Therapies that seek, at least in epistemological terms, to locate either the therapist or the client or both outside the world of relationships and dialogue will not succeed; or, if they do, the success will be accidental – there are no actual experiential points that lie outside the relationship or language.

Meaning lies in the relationship between things and in the contexts which things in relation create. Therefore, meanings can only be understood in context. A word wrenched out of a line of poetry can be recognized and examined, but outside of its context it is not fully understood or appreciated. The context (the poem) creates the word, and the word helps form the context. Thus, understanding is the outcome of interactions between interpreters and texts. Understanding is a 'constructive performance' (Klemm, 1986: 37). Human beings constantly interpret the situations in which they find themselves even though there are others who attempt to pre-define the situations through rules, habits, clinical frameworks and technical procedures.

The relationship becomes a new context in which things can be understood. Thus, within the dialogue, new words are spoken and new contexts created. This new speech and fresh arrangement of language offers the possibility of new thoughts being thought. It is possible to contemplate alternative meanings and to construct more serviceable understandings. 'In this view, texts are no longer repositories of objective meaning so much as they are potentialities for recontextualizing meaning. Understanding is no longer a mode of knowing, but a dialogical activity' (Klemm, 1986: 38). There are no objective, fundamental truths in human relationships, only working truths. These decentred, contingent truths help people make sense of and control the meaning of their own experience. This is how we learn to cope.

Controlling the Meaning of Experience

Clients feel a strength and a satisfaction in being able to understand for themselves why they and the people with whom they relate act and feel as they do. However, being able to make sense of one's experience is a prior stage to being in control of the meaning of one's own experience. Being in control raises self-esteem. It empowers.

The client-perspective studies reveal two areas in which clients seek to control the meaning of their own experience. The first involves clients making sense of their own mental state and emotional condition. Those who are besieged by feelings of anxiety, or who are overwhelmed by strong emotional tides, feel that they are not in control of the meaning of their own experience.

If a person understands the origin and nature of his or her feelings, the next step is to try to regain some control. If the individual knows why she repeatedly finds herself in hopeless relationships with needy people, why he avoids challenging but potentially rewarding situations, or why she feels so inadequate, there is a sudden release from the prison of not knowing why things are like they are. Making sense has a liberating quality and encourages people to take control of what is happening, what things shall mean in future and what actions to take.

For example, women who had been sexually abused as girls and who had received counselling were able to recognize the origin of many of their feelings of guilt, worthlessness and low self-esteem. Talking about the past helped many women recognize the impact that the trauma of sexual abuse was having on their present lives. With support and counselling the women were increasingly able and confident to put the blame where it properly lay – on their fathers and stepfathers, uncles and unknown assailants and not on themselves (Smith, 1992). This was the first step in gaining control over the meaning of their own experience.

The second area over which clients seek control is the content and meaning given to interpersonal encounters, including the psychotherapeutic relationship itself. If the relationship does not make sense, then it becomes a source of concern and anxiety. Clients either stay in the relationship and struggle to understand what is going on or they terminate contact. If they do make sense of what is going on, it might not be the sense intended by the therapist. The client, feeling more settled now that she has a working understanding of what is taking place and consequently feeling more in control of things, may blithely remain in the relationship even though there is no communication taking place between client and therapist that addresses the problem which brought the client to therapy. The condition that brought her to therapy remains unchanged, but the uncertainty and problem of the therapeutic relationship itself have been resolved, at least for the moment (see Rennie, 1992, for a thorough examination of this phenomenon).

If one distils and distils the messages that are contained in the accounts given by clients of their experiences of counselling and therapy – the need for acceptance and regard, and the search for understanding and meaning – it might be possible to claim that one is left with one very condensed but none the less quintessential observation: *clients seek to control the meaning of their own experience and the meanings that others give to that experience.* Control helps clients to cope, and it empowers. It boosts self-esteem and personal confidence, and ultimately it encourages people to believe that they are valued and worthwhile human beings.

BIBLIOGRAPHY

Adams-Webber, J.R. (1969) 'Cognitive complexity and sociality', *British Journal of Social and Clinical Psychology*. 8: 211–16.

Ainsworth, Mary D. Salter (1967) *Infancy in Uganda: Infant Care and the Growth of Attachment*. Baltimore: Johns Hopkins University Press.

Ainsworth, Mary D. Salter (1973) 'The development of infant–mother attachment', in B.M. Caldwell and H.N. Ricciuti (eds), *Review of Child Development Volume 3*. Chicago: University of Chicago Press.

Ainsworth, Mary D. Salter (1982) 'Attachment: retrospect and prospect', in Parkes and Stevenson-Hinde, op. cit. pp. 3–30.

Alexander, Leslie B. and Luborsky, Lester (1986) 'The Penn Helping Alliance Scales', in Greenberg and Pinsof, op. cit.

Allen, Laura (1990) 'A client's experience of failure', in Mearns and Dryden, op. cit. pp. 20–7.

Anastasiow, Nicholas (1990) 'Implications of the neurobiological model for early intervention', in J. Meisels and Jack P. Shonkoff (eds), *Handbook of Early Intervention*. Cambridge: Cambridge University Press. pp. 196–216.

Astington, Janet W., Harris, Paul L. and Olson, David R. (eds) (1988) *Developing Theories of Mind*. Cambridge: Cambridge University Press.

Bannister, Don and Fransella, Fay (1986) *Inquiring Man: The Psychology of Personal Constructs* (3rd edn). London: Croom Helm.

Baron-Cohen, Simon (1991) 'Precursors to a theory of mind: understanding attention on other', in Whiten, op. cit. pp. 233–52.

Baron-Cohen, Simon, Leslie, A.M. and Frith, U. (1986) 'Mechanical behaviour and intentional understanding of picture stories in autistic children', *British Journal of Developmental Psychology*, 4: 113–25.

Barrett-Lennard, Geoffrey T. (1986) 'The relationship inventory now: issues and advances in theory, method and use', in Greenberg and Pinsof, op. cit. pp. 439–55.

Berger, Peter L. and Berger, Brigitte (1981) *Sociology: A Biographical Approach*. London: Penguin.

Bergin, Allen E. (1971) 'The evaluation of therapeutic outcomes', in Bergin and Garfield, op. cit. pp. 217–70.

Bergin, Allen E. and Garfield, Sol L. (eds) (1971) *Handbook of Psychotherapy and Behavior Change: An Empirical Analysis*. New York: Wiley.

Blakemore, Colin (1988) *The Mind Machine*. London: BBC Books.

Board, Francis A. (1959) 'Patients' and physicians' judgements of outcome of psychotherapy in an outpatient clinic', *A.M.A. Archives of General Psychiatry*. 1: 185–96.

Bowlby, John (1969) *Attachment and Loss, Volume I: Attachment*. London: Hogarth Press.

Bowlby, John (1979) *The Making and Breaking of Affectional Bonds*. London: Tavistock.

Bowlby, John (1988) *A Secure Base: Clinical Applications of Attachment Theory*. London: Routledge.

Bruner, Jerome (1986) *Actual Minds, Possible Worlds*. Cambridge, MA: Harvard University Press.

Bruner, Jerome (1990) *Acts of Meaning*. London: Harvard University Press.

Buber, Martin (1953) 'Distance and relation', *Psychiatry*, 16: 104.

Burkitt, Ian (1991) *Social Selves: Theories of the Formation of Personality*. London: Sage.

Cantley, Caroline (1987) *Coventry Mental Health Crisis Intervention Team: The Views of Clients and Their Families*. Birmingham: Social Administration Dept, University of Birmingham.

Carey, S. (1985) *Conceptual Change in Childhood*. Cambridge, MA: MIT Press.

Carrithers, Michael (1991) 'Narrativity: mindreading and making societies', in Whiten, op. cit. pp. 305–18.

Cashmore, Ellis E. and Mullen, Bob (1983) *Approaching Sociological Theory*. London: Heinemann.

Chomsky, Noam (1972) *Language and Mind*. New York: Harcourt Brace Jovanovich.

Crites, Stephen (1986) 'Storytime: recollecting the past and projecting the future', in Sarbin, op. cit.

Cupitt, Don (1990) *Creation Out of Nothing*. London: SCM Press.

Danish, S.J. and Kagan, N. (1971) 'Measurement of affective sensitivity: toward a valid measure of interpersonal perception', *Journal of Counseling Psychology*, 18: 51–4.

Davies, Paul (1987) *The Cosmic Blueprint*. London: Unwin Hyman.

Davies, P.C.W. and Brown, J. (1988) *Superstrings: A Theory of Everything?* Cambridge: Cambridge University Press.

Davis, Ann, Newton, Steve and Smith, Dave (1985) 'Coventry crisis intervention team: the consumer's view', *Social Services Research*, 14 (1): 7–32.

Davis, Kathy (1986) 'The process of problem (re)formulation in psychotherapy', *Sociology of Health and Illness*, 8 (1 March): 44–74.

Deutsch, F. and Madle, R.A. (1975) 'Empathy: historic and current conceptualizations, measurement, and a cognitive theoretical perspective', *Human Development*, 18: 267–87.

Dewey, John (1922) *Human Nature and Conduct*. New York: Holt.

Dinnage, Rosemary (1989) *One to One: Experiences of Psychotherapy*. London: Penguin.

Dunn, Judy (1986) 'Growing up in a family world: issues in the study of social development in young children', in Richards and Light, op. cit. pp. 98–115.

Dunn, Judy (1988) *The Beginnings of Social Understanding*. Oxford: Blackwell.

Dunn, Judy (1991) 'Understanding others: evidence from naturalistic studies of children', in Whiten, op. cit. pp. 51–62.

Eccles, John C. (1989) *Evolution of the Brain: Creation of the Self*. London: Routledge.

Edmunds, Mary (1992) 'Co-dependency and counselling'. Unpublished MSW interview transcripts, University of East Anglia, Norwich.

England, Hugh (1986) *Social Work as Art: Making Sense for Good Practice*. London: Allen & Unwin.

Erikson, E.H. (1950) *Childhood and Society*. New York: Norton.

Eysenck, H.J. (1952) 'The effects of psychotherapy: an evaluation', *Journal of Consulting Psychology*, 16: 319–24.

Fairbairn, W.R.D. (1952) *Psychoanalytic Studies of the Personality*. London: Tavistock Publications.

Feifel, Herman and Eells, Janet (1963) 'Patients and therapists assess the same psychotherapy', *Journal of Consulting Psychology*, 27 (4): 310–18.

Fitts, William H. (1965) *The Experience of Psychotherapy: What It Is Like for Client and Therapist*. Princeton, NJ: Van Nostrand Reinhold.

Fodor, J.A. (1987) *Psychosemantics: The Problem of Meaning in the Philosophy of Mind*. Cambridge, MA: Bradford Books/MIT Press.

France, Ann (1988) *Consuming Psychotherapy*. London: Free Association Books.

Frank, J.D. (1961) *Persuasion and Healing*. Baltimore, MD: Johns Hopkins University Press.

Frith, Uta (1989) *Autism: Explaining the Enigma*. Oxford: Blackwell.

Frith, Uta (1991) *Autism and Asperger Syndrome*. Cambridge: Cambridge University Press.

Goldstein, Arnold P. and Michaels, Gerald Y. (1985) *Empathy: Development, Training and Consequences*. Hillsdale, NJ: Erlbaum.

Goldstein, Howard (1973) *Social Work Practice*. Columbia: University of South Carolina Press.

Greenberg, Leslie S. and Pinsof, William M. (eds) (1986) *The Psychotherapeutic Process: A Research Handbook*. New York: Guilford Press.

Greenough, W.T. and Juraska, J.M. (1986) *Developmental Neuropsychobiology*. Orlando, FL: Academic Press.

Grierson, Myra (1990) 'A client's experience of success', in Mearns and Dryden, op. cit. pp. 28–40.

Guardian (1991a) 'Speaking in tongues: a feminine angle on analysis', 29 January.

Guardian (1991b) 'Illness diagnosed in obsessive bores', 14 September.

Guntrip, H. (1969) *Schizoid Phenomena, Object Relations and the Self*. New York: International University Press.

Haimes, Erica and Timms, Noel (1985) *Adoption, Identity and Social Policy*. Aldershot: Gower.

Halmos, Paul (1965) *The Faith of the Counsellors*. London: Constable.

Hamlyn, D.W. (1978) *Experience and the Growth of Understanding*. London: Routledge & Kegan Paul.

Hannon, Eleanor (1968) 'Shared experience', *Social Casework*, March: 156–9.

Harris, Paul (1989) *Children and Emotion: The Development of Psychological Understanding*. Oxford: Blackwell.

Harris, Paul (1991) 'The work of the imagination', in Whiten, op. cit. pp. 283–304.

Heckman, S.J. (1986) *Hermeneutics and the Sociology of Knowledge*. Oxford: Polity Press.

Heine, Ralph W. (1953) 'A comparison of patients' reports on psychotherapeutic experiences with psychoanalytic, nondirective and Adlerian therapists', *American Journal of Psychotherapy*, 7: 16–23.

Hinde, Robert A. (1982) 'Attachment: some conceptual and biological issues', in Parkes and Stevenson-Hinde, op. cit. pp. 60–76.

Hinde, Robert A. (1987) *Individuals, Relationships and Culture: Links between Ethology and the Social Sciences*. Cambridge: Cambridge University Press.

Hocken, Shiela (1977) *Emma and I*. London: Gollancz.

Hood, L. and Bloom, L. (1979) 'What, when and how about why: a longitudinal study of early expressions of causality'. *Monographs of the Society for the Study of Child Development*. 44: 6.

Howe, David (1989a) *The Consumers' View of Family Therapy*. Aldershot: Gower.

Howe, David (1989b) *Birth Mothers: The Post-Adoption Centre; First Three Years*. Research Report No. 4. Norwich: University of East Anglia.

Howe, David (1990) 'The consumers' view of the Post-Adoption Centre', *Adoption and Fostering*, 14 (2): 32–6.

Howe, David and Hinings, Diana (1989a) *Adopters and Their Families: The Post-Adoption Centre; First Three Years*. Research Report No. 2. Norwich: University of East Anglia.

Howe, David and Hinings, Diana (1989b) *Adopted People: The Post-Adoption Centre; First Three Years*. Research Report No. 3. Norwich: University of East Anglia.

Howe, David, Sawbridge, Phillida and Hinings, Diana (1992) *Half a Million Women: Mothers Who Lose Their Children by Adoption*. London: Penguin.

Humphrey, Nicholas (1986) *The Inner Eye*. London: Faber & Faber.

Ingleby, David (1986) 'Development in social context', in Richards and Light, op. cit. pp. 297–317.

Kagan, Jerome (1989) *Unstable Ideas: Temperament, Cognition, and Self*. London: Harvard University Press.

Kaschkak, Ellyn (1978) 'Therapist and client: two views of the process and outcome of psychotherapy', *Professional Psychologist*, 9 (May): 271–7.

Katz, R.L. (1963) *Empathy: Its Nature and Uses*. New York: Free Press.

Keefe, T. (1976) 'Empathy: the critical skill', *Social Work*, 21: 10–14.

Keefe, T. (1979) 'The development of empathic skill', *Journal of Education for Social Work*, 15: 30–7.

Kelly, George (1955) *The Psychology of Personal Constructs*. New York: Norton.

Kelly, George (1969) 'Personal construct theory and the psychotherapeutic interview', in B.A. Maher (ed.), *Clinical Psychology and Personality: Selected Papers of George Kelly*. London: Wiley.

Klein, Josephine (1987) *Our Need for Others and Its Roots in Infancy*. London: Tavistock.

Klemm, D.E. (1986) *Hermeneutical Enquiry, Volume I: The Interpretation of Texts*. Atlanta, GA: Scholars Press.

Kline, F., Adrian, A. and Spevak, M. (1974) 'Patients evaluate therapists', *Archives of General Psychiatry*, 31 (1): 113–16.

Leslie, A.M. (1987) 'Pretense and representation: the origins of "theory of mind"', *Psychological Review*, 94: 412–26.

Leslie, Alan M. (1988) 'Some implications of pretense for mechanisms underlying the child's theory of mind', in Astington et al., op. cit. pp. 19–46.

Leslie, Alan M. (1991) 'The theory of mind impairment in autism', in Whiten, op. cit. pp. 63–78.

Lide, Pauline (1966) 'Dynamic Mental Representation: an analysis of the empathic process', *Social Casework*, March: 146–51.

Light, Paul (1986) 'Context, conservation and conversation', in Richards and Light, op. cit. pp. 170–90.

Lipkin, Stanley (1948) 'The client evaluates nondirective psychotherapy', *Journal of Consulting Psychology*, 12: 137–46.

Llewelyn, S.P. and Hume, W.I. (1979) 'The patient's view of therapy', *British Journal of Medical Psychology*, 52: 29–35.

Lomas, Peter (1973) *True and False Experience*. London: Allen Lane.

Lomas, Peter (1981) *The Case for a Personal Psychotherapy*. Oxford: Oxford University Press.

Luborsky, L., McLellan, T., Woody, G., O'Brien, C. and Auerbach, A. (1985) 'Therapist success and its determinants', *Archives of General Psychiatry*, 37: 471–81.

Macarov, D. (1978) 'Empathy: the charismatic chimera', *Journal of Education for Social Work*, 14: 86–92.

McLeod, John (1990) 'The client's experience of counselling and psychotherapy: a review of the research literature', in Mearns and Dryden, op. cit. pp. 66–79.

Maluccio, Anthony N. (1979) *Learning from Clients*. New York: Free Press.

Mancuso, James C. (1986) 'The acquisition and use of narrative grammar structure', in Sarbin, op. cit. pp. 91–110.

Marmar, Charles R., Horowitz, Mardi J., Weiss, Daniel S. and Marziali, Elsa (1986) 'The development of the therapeutic alliance rating system', in Greenberg and Pinsof, op. cit.

Marvin, R.S. (1977) 'An ethological-cognitive model for the attenuation of mother-child attachment behavior', in T.M. Alloway, L. Krames and P. Pliner (eds), *Advances in the Study of Communication and Affect, Volume 3: The Development of Social Attachments*. New York: Plenum Press.

Matt, George E. (1989) 'Decision rules for selecting effect sizes in meta-analysis: a review and reanalysis of psychotherapy outcome studies', *Psychological Bulletin*, 105 (1): 106–15.

Mayer, John and Timms, Noel (1970) *The Client Speaks: Working-Class Impressions of Casework*. London: Routledge & Kegan Paul.

Mead, George Herbert (1910) 'Social consciousness and the consciousness of meaning', in Andrew J. Reck (ed.) (1964), *Selected Writings: George Herbert Mead*. Chicago: University of Chicago Press.

Mead, George Herbert (1934) *Mind, Self and Society*. Chicago: University of Chicago Press.

Mearns, Dave and Dryden, Windy (eds) (1990) *Experiences of Counselling in Action*. London: Sage.

Mearns, Dave and Thorne, Brian (1988) *Person-Centred Counselling in Action*. London: Sage.

Merrington, Diana and Corden, John (1981) 'Families' impressions of family therapy', *Journal of Family Therapy*, 3: 243–61.

Midgely, Mary (1979) *Beast and Man: The Roots of Human Nature*. London: Methuen.

Morris, Charles W. (1934) 'Introduction', in Mead, op. cit. pp. ix–xxxv.

Oldfield, Susan (1983) *The Counselling Relationship: A Study of the Client's Experience*. London: Routledge & Kegan Paul.

Olson, David R., Astington, Janet W. and Harris, Paul L. (1988) 'Introduction', in Astington, Harris and Olson, op. cit. pp. 1–15.

Orlinsky, David E. and Howard, Kenneth I. (1986) 'The psychological interior of psychotherapy: explorations with the therapy session reports', in Greenberg and Pinsof, op. cit. pp. 477–501.

Parkes, Colin Murray and Stevenson-Hinde, Joan (eds) (1982) *The Place of Attachment in Human Behaviour*. London: Tavistock.

Phillimore, Peter (1981) *Families Speaking: A Study of Fifty-One Families' Views of Social Work*. London: Family Service Unit.

Polkinghorne, Donald (1988) *Narrative Knowing and the Human Sciences*. Albany, NY: SUNY Press.

Rees, Stewart (1978) *Social Work Face to Face*. London: Edward Arnold.

Rees, Stewart and Wallace, Alison (1982) *Verdicts on Social Work*. London: Edward Arnold.

Reik, Theodor (1964) *Listening with the Third Ear*. New York: Pyramid Books.

Rennie, David (1985) 'An early return from interviews with clients about their therapy interviews: the functions of the narrative'. Paper presented at the 34th Annual Meeting of the Ontario Psychological Association, Ottawa, 15 February.

Rennie, David (1990) 'Toward a representation of the client's experience of the psychotherapeutic hour', in E. Lietaer, J. Rombauts and R. van Balen (eds), *Client-Centred Experiential Psychotherapy in the Nineties*. Leuven: Leuven University Press. pp. 155–72.

Rennie, David (1992) 'Qualitative analysis of the client's experience of psychotherapy: the unfolding reflexivity', in S. Toukmanian and D. Rennie (eds), *Psychotherapy Process Research*. Newbury Park, CA: Sage.

Richards, Martin P.M. (1974) *The Integration of a Child into a Social World*, Cambridge: Cambridge University Press.

Richards, Martin and Light, Paul (eds) (1986) *Children of Social Worlds: Development in a Social Context*. Cambridge: Polity Press.

Rieber, W. (1983) *Dialogues on the Psychology of Language and Thought*. New York: Plenum Press.

Robinson, John A. and Hawpe, Linda (1986) 'Narrative thinking as a heuristic process', in Sarbin, op. cit. pp. 111–25.

Robinson, Leslie A., Berman, Jeffrey S. and Neimeyer, Robert A. (1990) 'Psychotherapy for the treatment of depression: a comprehensive review of controlled outcome research', *Psychological Bulletin*, 108 (1): 30–49.

Rutter, Michael (1980) 'Attachment and the development of social relations', in Michael Rutter (ed.), *Developmental Psychiatry*. Washington, DC: American Psychiatric Press.

Sainsbury, Eric (1975) *Social Work with Families: Perceptions of Social Casework among Clients of a Family Service Unit*. London: Routledge & Kegan Paul.

Sainsbury, Eric, Nixon, Stephen and Phillips, David (1982) *Social Work in Focus: Clients' and Social Workers' Perceptions in Long-Term Social Work*. London: Routledge & Kegan Paul.

Sarbin, Theodore R. (ed.) (1986) *Narrative Psychology: The Storied Nature of Human Conduct*. New York: Praeger.

Scarr, Sandra and McCartney, Kathleen (1983) 'How people make their own environments: a theory of genotype–environment effects', *Child Development*, 54: 424–35.

Scheler, Max (1954) *The Nature of Sympathy* (1913, trans. P. Heath). London: Routledge & Kegan Paul.

Schutz, Alfred (1972) *The Phenomenology of the Social World*. London: Heinemann.

Shapiro, David A. and Shapiro, Diana (1982) 'Meta-analysis of comparative outcome studies: a replication and a refinement', *Psychological Bulletin*, 92 (3): 581–604.

Smith, David (1992) 'The long-term effects of child abuse on the mental health of adult women'. Unpublished MSW thesis, University of East Anglia, Norwich.

Smith, Mary Lee and Glass, Gene V. (1977) 'Meta-analysis of psychotherapy outcome studies', *American Psychologist*, Sept.: 752–60.

Spelke, E.S. and Cortelyou, A. (1981) 'Perceptual aspects of social knowing: looking and listening in infancy', in M.E. Lamb and L.R. Sherrod (eds), *Infant Social Cognition*. Hillsdale, NJ: Erlbaum.

Spence, Donald P. (1982) *Narrative Truth and Historical Truth: Meaning and Interpretation in Psychoanalysis*. New York: Norton.

Stark, Werner (1954) 'Editor's introduction', in Max Scheler, *The Nature of Sympathy*. London: Routledge & Kegan Paul.

Stebbins, G.L. (1982) *Darwin to DNA, Molecules to Humanity.* New York: Freeman.

Steele, Robert S. (1986) 'Deconstructing histories: toward a systematic criticism of psychological narratives', in Sarbin, op. cit. pp. 256–75.

Stewart, Ian (1992) 'In the beginning was the number', *Guardian*, 19 June: 28.

Storr, Anthony (1979) *The Art of Psychotherapy.* London: Butterworth/Heinemann.

Strupp, Hans, Fox, Ronald and Lessler, Ken (1969) *Patients View Their Psychotherapy.* Baltimore, MD: Johns Hopkins University Press.

Suh, Chong S., Strupp, Hans H. and O'Malley, Stephanie Samples (1986) 'The Vanderbilt process measures: the Psychotherapy Process Scale (VPSS) and the Negative Indicators Scale (VNIS)', in Greenberg and Pinsof, op. cit.

Swingewood, Alan (1984) *A Short History of Sociological Thought.* London: Macmillan.

Taylor, Charles (1985) *Human Agency and Language.* Cambridge: Cambridge University Press.

Trevarthen, C. (1983) 'Interpersonal ability of infants as generators for transmission of language and culture', in A. Oliverio and M. Zappallin (eds), *The Behavior of Infants.* New York: Plenum Press.

Truax, C.B. and Carkhuff, R.B. (1967) *Towards Effective Counselling and Psychotherapy.* Chicago: Aldine.

Truax, Charles B. and Mitchel, Kevin M. (1971) 'Research on certain therapist skills in relation to process and outcome', in Bergin and Garfield, op. cit. pp. 299–344.

Walker, Moira (1990) *Women in Therapy and Counselling.* Milton Keynes: Open University Press.

Whiten, Andrew (ed.) (1991) *Natural Theories of the Mind: Evolution, Development and Simulation of Everyday Mindreading.* Oxford: Blackwell.

Whiten, Andrew and Perner, Josef (1991) 'Fundamental issues in the multidisciplinary study of mindreading', in Whiten, op. cit. pp. 1–18.

Williams, Raymond (1965) *The Long Revolution.* London: Penguin.

Winnicott, D.W. (1958) *Collected Papers: Through Paediatrics to Psychoanalysis.* London: Tavistock.

Winnicott, D.W. (1965) *The Maturational Processes and the Facilitating Environment.* New York: International Universities Press.

Woodward, Joan (1988) *Understanding Ourselves: The Uses of Therapy.* London: Macmillan Press.

Wyatt, Frederick (1986) 'The narrative in psychoanalysis', in Sarbin, op. cit. pp. 193–210.

Zohar, Danah (1991) *The Quantum Self.* London: Flamingo.

NAME INDEX

SUBJECT INDEX